THE MASTERCHEF COLLECTION

THE MASTERCHEF COLLECTION

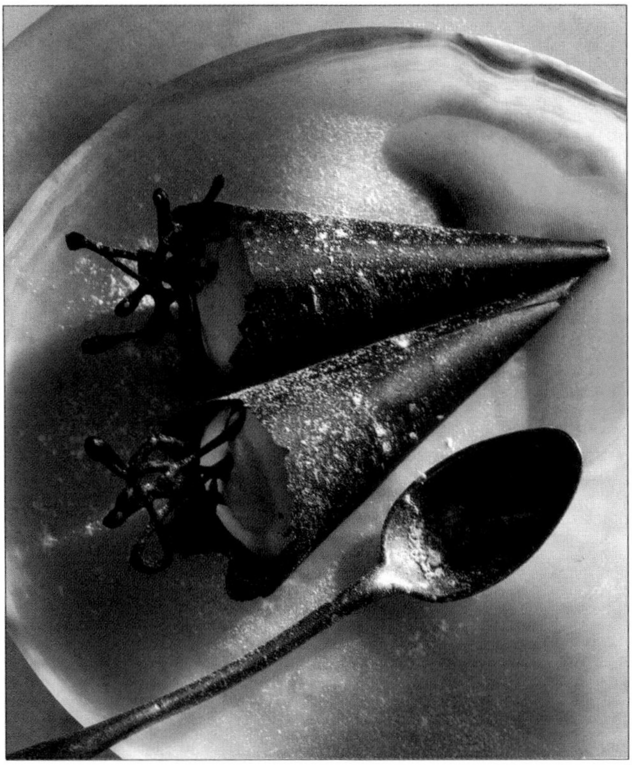

TED SMART

This book is dedicated with gratitude to all of the MasterChef Contestants.

First published in 1995

1 3 5 7 9 10 8 6 4 2

A TED SMART publication 1995

First published in the United Kingdom in 1995 by
Ebury Press
Random House, 20 Vauxhall Bridge Road, London SW1V 2SA

Random House Australia (Pty) Limited
20 Alfred Street, Milsons Point, Sydney,
New South Wales 2061, Australia

Random House New Zealand Limited
18 Poland Road, Glenfield
Auckland 10, New Zealand

Random House South Africa (Pty) Limited PO BOX 337, Bergvlei, South Africa

Random House UK Limited Reg. No. 954009

A CIP catalogue record for this book is available from the British Library

MasterChef
A Union Pictures Production for BBC TV
Series devised by Franc Roddam
Executive Producers: Bradley Adams and Richard Kalms
Producer and Director: Richard Bryan

Editor: Janet Illsley
Design: Clive Dorman
Special Photography: Gus Filgate
Food Stylist: Louise Pickford
Photographic Stylist: Penny Markham

ISBN 0 09 181073 6
Typeset by Clive Dorman & Co.
Colour separations by Colorlito, Milan, Italy
Printed and bound in Spain

Contents

• **Notes** •

Quantities are given in metric and imperial measures. Follow one set of measurements only, not a combination, because they are not interchangeable.

All spoon measures are level.

Fresh herbs are used unless otherwise stated.

Ovens must be preheated to the temperature specified in the recipe.

All recipes serve 4.

SOUPS & STARTERS

Marrow and Cumin Soup

2 medium potatoes, about 225 g (8 oz) total weight
salt and freshly ground black pepper
1 small marrow, or 450 g (1 lb) courgettes
10 ml (2 tsp) cumin seeds
150 ml (¼ pint) soured cream
chopped parsley, for sprinkling

Peel the potatoes, place in a saucepan and cover with plenty of salted water.

Peel and core the marrow or courgettes, cut into pieces and put into a steamer. Tie the cumin seeds in a square of muslin and add to the marrow.

Place the steamer on top of the saucepan of potatoes. Bring to the boil and simmer for about 20 minutes until the potatoes are tender and the marrow is softened. Discard the cumin.

Put the marrow or courgettes and potatoes in a blender or food processor with 600 ml (1 pint) of the cooking water. Work until smooth, then return to the pan. Reheat gently. Divide between warmed soup bowls and top each serving with a generous swirl of soured cream and a sprinkling of chopped parsley. Serve at once.

Ann Neale

Light Crab Bisque

1 cooked crab, weighing about 700 g (1½ lb)
60 ml (4 tbsp) olive oil
1 stick celery, sliced
1 small onion, chopped
1 leek, diced
1 carrot, diced
60 ml (4 tbsp) sherry
450 g (1 lb) tomatoes, chopped
½ bottle medium white wine
300 ml (½ pint) water
pinch of saffron strands
salt and freshly ground white pepper
50 g (2 oz) plain flour
50 g (2 oz) butter, softened
parsley or chervil sprigs, to garnish

Scrub the crab thoroughly under cold water to rid it of any remaining grit. Discard the inedible dead man's fingers and stomach sac from the crab (if not already done). Break off the claws and extract all of the white meat. Using a teaspoon, scoop out into separate bowls the white and dark meat from the shell. Break the shell into pieces and reserve.

Heat the olive oil in a large pan, add the celery, onion, leek and carrot and sauté until softened. Add the pieces of crab shell and sauté for 2 minutes. Add the sherry and allow it to evaporate. Add the tomatoes, wine, water, brown crabmeat and saffron and bring to the boil. Reduce the heat and simmer for 45 minutes.

Strain through a fine sieve into a clean saucepan, pressing hard to extract all of the juices. Bring back to the boil and season with salt and pepper to taste. Blend the flour into the softened butter to make a beurre manie and gradually whisk into the bisque, a piece at a time, until slightly thickened.

To serve, divide the white crabmeat between warmed soup plates, then pour on the bisque. Garnish with sprigs of parsley or chervil.

Elaine Bates

Light Crab Bisque

CONSOMMÉ OF SHIITAKE MUSHROOMS

125 g (4 oz) shiitake mushrooms
125 g (4 oz) cultivated button mushrooms
1.2 litres (2 pints) light chicken stock
3 egg whites
salt and freshly ground black pepper
4 flat-leaf parsley sprigs, to garnish

"That consommé was peerless."

Diana Rigg

Set aside 4 good shiitake mushrooms for the garnish. Finely chop the rest, along with the button mushrooms.

Bring the chicken stock to a simmer in a saucepan. Add the chopped mushrooms, cover and simmer for 12 -15 minutes. Strain the flavoured stock and discard the cooked mushroom pulp. Allow the stock to cool briefly.

Beat the egg whites in a bowl until beginning to foam, then whisk into the cooled stock. Continue whisking until a good foamy 'head' appears on the surface.

Return the stock to a gentle heat and slowly bring to a simmer, stirring continuously. Let the consommé simmer gently for 30 minutes. As the egg whites cook they rise to the surface, drawing up any impurities. At the end of cooking, a solid crust will have formed on the surface, leaving the stock below sparkling and clear. Make a hole in the crust with a ladle, remove from the heat and leave to rest for a few minutes. Pour the clear stock through a jelly bag or a muslin-lined fine sieve.

Remove the stalks from the remaining shiitake mushrooms and finely slice the caps. Place in a small saucepan, moisten with a little of the consommé and cook over a low heat for no more than 30 seconds. Divide the mushroom slices between 4 warmed soup bowls.

Reheat the consommé thoroughly, but do not boil. Check the seasoning, then pour into the soup bowls, allowing the sliced mushrooms to float in the consommé. Serve immediately, garnished with parsley.

Roger Hemming

SWEET AND SOUR TOMATO SOUP

4 large beefsteak tomatoes
15 ml (1 tbsp) olive oil
2 cloves garlic, chopped
425 g (15 oz) can chopped tomatoes, sieved
15 ml (1 tbsp) sugar
30-45 ml (2-3 tbsp) balsamic vinegar
45 ml (3 tbsp) chopped basil
salt and freshly ground black pepper
30 ml (2 tbsp) basil oil

COOK'S NOTE

To make your own basil oil, half-fill a bottle or jar with basil leaves then fill with olive oil. Leave to infuse for 1-2 weeks before using.

Cut a thin slice off the top of each tomato and scoop out the flesh, leaving a 5 mm (¼ inch) thick shell. Deseed and finely chop the tomato flesh.

Heat the olive oil in a pan and sauté the garlic until softened. Add the chopped tomato flesh, together with the sieved canned tomatoes. Bring to the boil, lower the heat and simmer gently for about 3 minutes. Add the sugar and balsamic vinegar to taste. Simmer for 1-2 minutes, stirring to dissolve the sugar. Add the chopped basil and simmer for 5-10 minutes. Season with salt and pepper to taste.

Meanwhile, stand the tomato shells in a baking tin and trickle the basil oil over them. Bake in a preheated oven at 190°C (375°F) mark 5 for 5 minutes to heat through.

To serve, stand each tomato shell on a warmed serving plate and fill with the tomato soup. Garnish with basil leaves and serve at once, with crusty bread if desired.

Gillian Humphrey

> *"It was light and had a wonderful flavour, sweet and sour, and slightly crunchy."*
>
> Sue MacGregor

Spicy Butternut Squash and Apple Soup

40 g (1½ oz) butter
1 onion, finely chopped
1 large clove garlic, crushed
700 g (1½ lb) butternut squash, peeled, seeded and cut into chunks
3 Granny Smith apples, peeled, cored and cut into chunks
750 ml (1¼ pints) chicken stock
5-10 ml (1-2 tsp) ground cumin
salt and freshly ground black pepper
60 ml (4 tbsp) crème fraîche

To Garnish:
1 red apple, quartered, cored and sliced

Cook's Note

Butternut squash is shaped like a large peanut and has a tan-coloured hard skin which must be peeled off before cooking.

Melt the butter in a heavy-based saucepan, add the onion and sauté until soft. Add the garlic and sauté for a further 2 minutes. Add the squash, apple and chicken stock. Simmer for about 15 minutes, until the squash is tender. Stir in the cumin and salt and pepper to taste.

> *"Fabulous. The soup was wonderful."*
>
> Nick Nairn

Using a blender or food processor, purée the soup in batches until smooth, transforming the puréed soup to a clean saucepan. Heat through, then divide between warmed soup bowls. Add a spoonful of crème fraîche to each portion and garnish with the apple slices.

Holly Schade

Creamy Lemon Grass and Basil Soup

with Seafood

24 large raw prawns
16 green-lipped mussels (thawed if frozen)
40 g (1½ oz) butter
75 g (3 oz) shallot, finely chopped
1 clove garlic, crushed
300 ml (½ pint) dry white wine
3 lemon grass stalks, bruised
1 kaffir lime leaf
15-30 ml (1-2 tbsp) lemon juice, to taste
300 ml (½ pint) single cream
30 ml (2 tbsp) shredded basil leaves
2 rashers sweet-cured back bacon, derinded and chopped
2 egg yolks
salt and freshly ground black pepper

Garlic Croûtes:
50 g (2 oz) butter
1 clove garlic, crushed
4-6 slices French bread
30 ml (2 tbsp) finely chopped basil

Shell and de-vein the prawns, reserving the shells.

To make the stock, melt 25 g (1 oz) of the butter in a saucepan, add the prawn shells and fry until pink. Add half of the chopped shallot with the garlic and cook until translucent. Add 300 ml (½ pint) water, the wine, lemon grass and kaffir lime leaf. Bring to the boil, reduce the heat and simmer for 30 minutes. Strain the stock and adjust the flavour with lemon juice.

"*I thought the soup worked very well indeed. I liked the delicacy of the lemon grass.*"

Stephen Bull

Meanwhile prepare the garlic croûtes. Melt the butter in a pan, add the garlic and cook until softened. Add the bread slices and fry until golden on both sides; drain on kitchen paper. Toss in the chopped basil and keep warm.

Bring the stock to the boil in a large pan. Add the prawns and cook until just pink, about 2-3 minutes. Remove with a slotted spoon and set aside. Add the mussels to the stock, heat through, then remove and set aside. Add the cream and shredded basil and simmer for 2-3 minutes. Meanwhile, cook the remaining shallot and the bacon in the rest of the butter until tender.

To serve, add the onion and bacon to the soup, with the prawns and mussels. Heat through, then transfer the seafood to warmed soup plates. Off the heat, work the egg yolks into the soup. Season with salt and pepper to taste and ladle over the seafood. Serve immediately, with the garlic croûtes.

Gillian Humphrey

Creamy Lemon Grass and Basil Soup

Parsnip and Coriander Soup

45 ml (3 tbsp) olive oil
1 medium onion, finely chopped
2 cloves garlic, finely chopped
700 g (1½ lb) parsnips, peeled and diced
5 ml (1 tsp) turmeric
5 ml (1 tsp) ground cinnamon
30 ml (2 tbsp) chopped fresh coriander leaves
5 ml (1 tsp) ground coriander
1.2 litres (2 pints) vegetable stock
salt and freshly ground black pepper
120 ml (4 fl oz) creamed coconut

To Finish:
desiccated coconut for sprinkling
40 ml (8 tsp) natural yogurt
coriander leaves

Heat the oil in a large saucepan and fry the onion and garlic for a few minutes until tender. Add the parsnips, turmeric, cinnamon, chopped coriander leaves and ground coriander. Cook for 2 minutes, stirring all the time to ensure that the parsnips are thoroughly coated in all the flavourings.

Add the vegetable stock and bring to the boil. Cover and simmer for about 10-15 minutes until the parsnips are tender.

Remove from the heat and purée in a blender or food processor until smooth. Season well. Return the soup to the pan and stir in the creamed coconut over a low heat.

Serve in individual bowls, sprinkled with desiccated coconut. Swirl 10 ml (2 tsp) natural yogurt on to each portion and sprinkle with coriander leaves to serve.

Nicholas Pound

Leek and Mussel Soup

1.4 kg (3 lb) mussels
6 leeks
25 g (1 oz) butter
15 ml (1 tbsp) diced carrot
15 ml (1 tbsp) diced onion
15 ml (1 tbsp) diced celery
½ small potato, peeled and chopped
600 ml (1 pint) fish stock
1 shallot, chopped
1 thyme sprig
1 parsley sprig
¼ bay leaf
150 ml (¼ pint) white wine
salt and freshly ground black pepper

To Garnish:
chopped chives

"*The soup has a nice cool taste and colour.*"

Loyd

Scrub the mussels thoroughly in cold water and remove their beards.

Chop 5 leeks. Heat the butter in a pan, add the chopped leeks, carrot, onion and celery and sweat them gently for 5 minutes. Add the potato and fish stock and cook, uncovered, for about 25 minutes until the leeks are completely soft. Purée in a blender or food processor and pass the mixture through a sieve.

Put the shallot, herbs, mussels and white wine in a large saucepan. Cover tightly and cook over a high heat for 5 minutes, shaking the pan from time to time. Remove from the heat and discard any mussels that have not opened. Strain the liquor through a muslin-lined sieve to remove any grit. Remove the mussels from their shells. Add the strained liquor and mussels to the leek purée. Reheat, then season with salt and pepper to taste.

Shred the remaining leek and steam briefly for 2-3 minutes until tender. Divide the leek between warmed soup bowls, then pour in the soup. Garnish with chopped chives to serve.

Suzanne Wynn

TIMBALE OF CRAB

WITH HERBS IN A DILL-SCENTED SAUCE

Timbales:

125 g (4 oz) firm white fish fillet (eg brill or turbot), skinned
salt and freshly ground white pepper
1 egg white
60 ml (2 fl oz) double cream
15 ml (1 tbsp) dry sherry
freshly grated nutmeg, to taste
few chervil leaves
few tiny dill sprigs
225 g (8 oz) crabmeat
8-12 fine asparagus spears

Sauce:

300 ml (½ pint) fish stock
90 ml (3 fl oz) dry sherry
90 ml (3 fl oz) double cream
15 ml (1 tbsp) chopped chervil
15 ml (1 tbsp) chopped dill
125 g (4 oz) unsalted butter, chilled and diced

To prepare the fish mousse, trim the fish, cut into chunks and work in a blender or food processor until smooth. With the machine running, add a pinch of salt and the egg white through the feeder tube; process briefly until the mixture stiffens. Transfer to a bowl and gradually beat in two thirds of the cream. Stir in the 15 ml (1 tbsp) sherry and season with salt, pepper and nutmeg to taste. Cover and chill in the refrigerator.

Butter 4 individual moulds and press a few chervil leaves and dill sprigs onto the base of each one.

For the sauce, combine the fish stock and sherry in a saucepan and boil until reduced by three quarters.

Season the crabmeat with salt and pepper to taste, then mix with the fish mousse. The mixture should be just firm enough to hold its shape; if too firm add more of the cream; if too soft, chill for longer. Divide the fish mixture between the moulds, packing it well down, and cover each one with buttered foil.

Stand the moulds on a sheet of greaseproof paper in a bain-marie or roasting tin containing enough boiling water to come halfway up the sides of the moulds. Bake in a preheated oven at 200°C (400°F) mark 6 for 15 minutes.

Meanwhile, trim and peel the asparagus, then steam or cook in boiling salted water for 2 minutes. Drain.

To finish the sauce, stir in the cream, then gradually add the butter a piece at a time, whisking constantly on and off the heat. Stir in the chervil and dill.

To serve, turn each mousse out onto a warmed serving plate. Surround with the dill sauce and asparagus. Serve at once.

Fiona Phelps

COOK'S NOTE

For optimum flavour, use freshly prepared white crabmeat for the timbales. If you are unsure of preparing the crab yourself then ask your fishmonger to do so for you, or at least to separate the body from its shell and pull off the legs and claws. Remember to discard the stomach sac and inedible feathery gills or 'dead mans fingers.'

Gingered Crab Cakes

with Sweet Pepper Sauce

125 g (4 oz) waxy potato (eg Romano)
225 g (8 oz) very fresh crab meat (mixed white and brown meat)
30 ml (2 tbsp) chopped parsley
5 ml (1 tsp) grated fresh root ginger
2.5 ml (½ tsp) freshly ground nutmeg
pinch of cayenne
salt and freshly ground black pepper
30-45 ml (2-3 tbsp) seasoned flour
groundnut oil for shallow-frying

Sweet Pepper Sauce:
15 ml (1 tbsp) olive oil
2 cloves garlic, crushed
1 shallot, finely chopped
2 medium red peppers, seeded and chopped
¼ large red chilli, finely chopped (optional)
4-5 basil leaves
salt and freshly ground black pepper
300 ml (½ pint) light fish stock
60 ml (2 fl oz) double cream

To Serve:
flat-leaved parsley or basil leaves
Roasted Pepper Salad (see right)

Cook's Note

The chilli gives the sauce a slight kick, but you can omit it if preferred.

Cook the potato in boiling water for 10 minutes. Drain and allow to cool a little, then grate coarsely and place in a bowl. Add the crab meat, parsley, ginger, nutmeg, cayenne and seasoning; mix together using a fork, taking care not to damage the potatoes or crab meat.

Carefully shape into 8 flat cakes, squashing the mixture together with your hands. Dip the crab cakes in seasoned flour to coat. Place on a tray and chill in the refrigerator for at least 10 minutes, or until ready to cook.

> *"The crab cakes were particularly good."*
>
> Stewart Cameron

To make the sweet pepper sauce, heat the olive oil in a pan, add the garlic and shallot and sweat until softened. Add the red peppers, chilli if using, basil, seasoning and stock. Bring to the boil, lower the heat and simmer for 20 minutes. Transfer to a food processor or blender and process until smooth. Pass through a sieve into a small pan and add the cream. Set aside. Reheat gently before serving.

To cook the crab cakes, heat the groundnut oil in a heavy-based frying pan. Add the crab cakes and fry for about 2-3 minutes each side until crisp and golden brown. Drain on kitchen paper. Garnish with parsley or basil and serve with the red pepper sauce and salad.

Clare Askaroff

Roasted Pepper Salad

• To serve with the Gingered Crab Cakes •

1 red pepper
1 yellow pepper
1 orange pepper
extra-virgin olive oil
salt and freshly ground black pepper

Halve the peppers and remove the seeds. Place cut-side down in a roasting tin and drizzle with olive oil. Place under a preheated hot grill for about 10 minutes until the skins are blackened and blistered. Immediately place in a bowl, cover tightly and leave to stand for about 15 minutes; the steam created will help to lift the skins.

Peel the peppers and finely shred the flesh. Place in a bowl with 15 ml (1 tbsp) olive oil, season liberally with salt and pepper, and toss to mix. Leave until ready to serve; do not refrigerate.

Clare Askaroff

Gingered Crab Cakes with a Sweet Pepper Sauce

GINGERY CRAB

SERVED ON A BED OF SWEET PEARS

1 dressed crab, weighing about
1.1 kg (2½ lb), shells reserved
50 ml (2 fl oz) olive oil
25 g (1 oz) fennel leaves
4 cardamom seeds
1 clove garlic, crushed
1 thyme sprig
1 large Provençal tomato, chopped
150 ml (¼ pint) medium white wine
15 g (½ oz) fresh root ginger, finely chopped
4 ripe pears
15 g (½ oz) butter
15 ml (1 tbsp) light brown sugar
150 ml (¼ pint) whipping cream
50 g (2 oz) Parmesan cheese, freshly grated
salt and freshly ground pepper
snipped chives, to garnish

"A lovely surprise... the crab with the pears, and very delicate."

Cherie Lunghi

Heat the oil in a large saucepan, add the crab shells and cook on a high heat for 3-4 minutes. Lower the heat and add the fennel, cardamom, garlic, thyme and tomato. Cook gently for a few minutes, then add the wine and 300 ml (½ pint) water. Simmer for 30 minutes.

Meanwhile, heat about 150 ml (¼ pint) water in a small pan. Add the ginger and cook for about 20 minutes, until tender. Drain and reserve.

Strain the stock and return to a clean pan. Boil steadily to reduce to approximately 90 ml (3 fl oz). Set aside.

Carefully peel and core the pears, then cut each one lengthwise into 4 pieces. Place in a casserole dish with the butter, brown sugar and 150 ml (¼ pint) water. Cover and poach gently in a preheated oven at 190°C (375°F) mark 5 for about 1 hour until tender. Keep warm.

Place the prepared crab meat in a saucepan and heat through gently over a low heat. Keep warm.

Pour the concentrated stock into another pan. Add the reserved ginger, the cream and the cooking juice from the pears. Heat the sauce through over a low heat, stirring.

Preheat the grill to high. Arrange 4 pear segments on each of 4 flameproof serving plates. Spoon the crab meat into the middle. Place a spoonful of sauce over the crab and spread the rest around the sides. Sprinkle the Parmesan over the crab. Place under a hot grill until lightly browned. Season with salt and pepper, garnish with chives and serve immediately.

Jill O'Brien

MUSSELS AU GRATIN

24-30 mussels
1 onion, chopped
few parsley sprigs
1 thyme sprig
50 g (2 oz) butter
5 ml (1 tsp) lemon juice
1 clove garlic, crushed
30 ml (2 tbsp) chopped parsley
25 g (1 oz) white breadcrumbs
25 g (1 oz) freshly grated Parmesan cheese

Scrub the mussels clean under running cold water and discard any with open or cracked shells. Put the onion, parsley and thyme in a saucepan with 300 ml (½ pint) water and bring to the boil. Simmer, covered, for 5 minutes. Add the mussels and cook quickly, shaking the pan constantly until the shells open. Remove from the heat and discard any mussels which have not opened. Leave to cool slightly.

Discard the empty half shells and arrange the mussels in individual gratin dishes. Melt the butter and stir in the lemon juice and garlic. Spoon the flavoured butter over the mussels and scatter over the parsley. Mix the breadcrumbs and Parmesan together and sprinkle over the top. Cook under a preheated grill for about 3 minutes until golden. Serve immediately.

Sarah Giles

Note: Allow 6 mussels per person, but cook a few extra ones to allow for any which do not open up on cooking.

Mussels and Scallops in a Saffron Sauce

with Fresh Tagliatelle and Tomatoes

175-225 g (6-8 oz) mussels, cleaned
6-8 scallops, cleaned
2 plum tomatoes
25 g (1 oz) unsalted butter

Pasta Dough:
250 g (9 oz) plain flour
pinch of salt
2.5 ml (½ tsp) olive oil
2 eggs (size 2)
3 egg yolks (size 2)

Sauce:
10 ml (2 tsp) olive oil
½ small onion, finely chopped
1 clove garlic, finely chopped
200 ml (7 fl oz) white wine
1.25 ml (¼ tsp) saffron threads, crushed
75 ml (2½ fl oz) double cream

To Serve:
finely chopped basil

To make the pasta dough, put the flour, salt and olive oil into a food processor (fitted with a dough hook if you have one). Process for a few seconds, then add the eggs and egg yolks. Process until the dough comes together and forms a smooth ball. Wrap in cling film and leave to rest in the refrigerator for at least 30 minutes.

Slice off about a quarter of the dough; keep the rest wrapped so it does not dry out. Put the dough through a pasta machine on its thickest setting a few times, dusting with a little flour if it is too sticky. Proceed through the machine settings, gradually narrowing the setting each time until you reach No. 6. Fit the tagliatelle cutters and pass the pasta through. Hang the tagliatelle to dry. Repeat with the rest of the dough. (You will only need to use about half of this pasta; the rest can be frozen for future use.)

For the sauce, heat 10 ml (2 tsp) olive oil in a pan, add the onion and garlic and cook until softened. Add the white wine, bring to the boil, then add the saffron. Take off the heat and set aside for 20-30 minutes to allow the saffron to 'infuse'.

Put the tomatoes in a bowl, pour on boiling water and leave for 30 seconds. Remove with a slotted spoon and peel away the skins. Halve, deseed and chop the flesh into small pieces; set aside.

Reheat the wine, then add the mussels, cover with a tight-fitting lid and cook for 3-4 minutes until the shells have opened; take care to avoid overcooking them. Remove the mussels with a slotted spoon and set aside, discarding any that remain open. Strain the wine sauce through a muslin-lined sieve into a clean pan.

Slice each scallop horizontally into two or three rounds, depending on size. Heat the butter in a heavy-based pan, add the scallops and sear over a high heat for 30 seconds each side. Meanwhile add the cream to the wine sauce and simmer to reduce a little. Add the mussels and scallops and keep warm over a low heat.

Add the tagliatelle to a large pan of boiling water. Cook for 1-2 minutes only, until al dente (tender but firm to the bite). Drain and add to the mussels and scallops. Toss lightly to mix, adding the chopped tomato. Serve at once, sprinkled with finely chopped basil.

Joanna Crossley

> *"I thought that was delicious, excellent."*
>
> Ginny Elliot

Stir-Fried Tiger Prawns

with White Cabbage, Coconut and Shrimp Paste

16-20 raw tiger prawns
75 ml (5 tbsp) sunflower oil
1 large shallot, finely chopped
1 clove garlic, finely chopped
5-10 ml (1-2 tsp) shrimp paste
5-10 ml (1-2 tsp) laos
350 g (12 oz) white cabbage, cored and shredded
250 ml (8 fl oz) coconut milk
sea salt and freshly ground black pepper

To Garnish:
2 spring onions, shredded
cayenne or paprika, for sprinkling

Remove the heads from the prawns. Heat 15 ml (1 tbsp) of the oil in a pan, add the shallot and garlic and cook over a low heat for 2 minutes without browning. Add the shrimp paste and laos and cook for a further 1 minute. Bring to the boil, then add the cabbage. Cover and cook for 10 minutes. Remove the lid and allow most of the liquid to evaporate, stirring to prevent sticking. Adjust the seasoning and keep warm.

Heat the remaining 60 ml (4 tbsp) sunflower oil in a sauté pan until smoking. Add the prawns and stir-fry for about 3 minutes until bright pink. Drain on kitchen paper.

Make shallow mounds of cabbage on 4 warmed serving plates. Arrange the prawns on the cabbage and scatter the spring onion over the plate. Sprinkle lightly with cayenne or paprika. Serve at once.

Derek Morris

Mussels with Rouille

24-32 mussels in shells
600 ml (1 pint) dry white wine (approximately)
30 ml (2 tbsp) finely chopped shallots

Rouille:
5 cm (2 inch) piece of French loaf
pinch of saffron threads
4 cloves garlic, crushed
1 egg yolk
90 ml (6 tbsp) olive oil
5 ml (1 tsp) paprika
large pinch of cayenne pepper
salt and freshly ground black pepper

To Serve:
selection of salad leaves (eg frisée, lamb's lettuce, oakleaf lettuce)
herb sprigs (eg coriander, parsley, snipped chives)
a little extra-virgin olive oil

Soak the mussels in a large bowl of cold salted water with a tablespoonful of flour or oatmeal added for about 2 hours to help rid them of grit. Scrub the shells clean and pull off each beard. Discard any mussels which remain open on being sharply tapped against a hard surface.

Place the mussels in a large pan and pour in enough wine to cover. Add the shallots, cover and bring to the boil. Cook over a high heat for about 5 minutes, just until the shells open. Remove from the heat and discard any mussels which remain closed; drain. Strain and reserve 90 ml (6 tbsp) cooking liquor. Allow the mussels to cool, then cover and chill in the refrigerator.

To make the rouille, cut the bread into small cubes and place in a bowl with the saffron threads. Pour on the reserved mussel cooking liquor and leave to soak for 10 minutes. Meanwhile, put the crushed garlic into a blender or food processor with the egg yolk. With the machine running, add the oil, drop by drop, as if you were making mayonnaise. When the mixture thickens, pour onto the soaked bread and mix well. Season with the paprika, cayenne and salt and pepper to taste.

To serve, toss the salad leaves and herbs in a little olive oil until glossy, then arrange on individual serving plates. Serve the mussels on the bed of salad leaves topped with a spoonful of the rouille.

Peter Anderson

Mussels with Rouille

Warm Salad of Fragrant Mussels

1-1.4 kg (2-3 lb) mussels
2 shallots, chopped
125 ml (4 fl oz) white wine
freshly ground pepper
lemon juice to taste
2 carrots, cut into matchsticks

Sauce:
pinch of saffron
pinch of curry powder (your own blend, or bought)
90 ml (3 fl oz) double cream
40 g (1½ oz) butter, in pieces

To Finish:
1 small curly endive
45 ml (3 tbsp) finely snipped chives
pinch of garam masala (your own blend, or bought)

Scrub the mussels thoroughly under running cold water and remove their beards. Put the mussels on a rack in a large roasting tin. Sprinkle with the shallots and white wine and cover tightly with foil. Bake in a preheated oven at 240°C (475°F) mark 9 for 8-10 minutes, depending on size, until they open.

Meanwhile, blanch the carrots in boiling water for 30 seconds. Drain, rinse in cold water and drain.

Remove the mussels from their shells, catching the juices in the roasting tin and discarding any that have not opened. Put the mussels in a bowl, sprinkle with pepper and a little lemon juice and keep warm.

To make the sauce, carefully strain the mussel cooking liquid through a very fine sieve or a couple of thicknesses of muslin into a pan. Add the saffron and curry powder and reduce by half; strain again. Mix in the cream and simmer until the sauce is thick enough to just coat the back of a spoon. Swirl in the butter to thicken.

Roll up the curly endive and cut into fine strips. Add to the sauce with the mussels, carrots, and most of the chives. Check the seasoning and add lemon juice if wished. Keep warm but do not boil. Arrange decoratively on warmed plates, finishing with a few chives and a dusting of garam masala.

Orlando Murrin

Garlic Prawns

on a Bed of Leeks

1 large leek
12 raw king or tiger prawns
30 ml (2 tbsp) olive oil
1 clove garlic, crushed
15 ml (1 tbsp) Thai fish sauce (nam pla)
5 ml (1 tsp) brown sugar
5 ml (1 tsp) lightly crushed black peppercorns

To Garnish:
chopped coriander leaves

Cut the leek into fine strips, about 3 cm (1¼ inches) long. Add to a pan of boiling salted water and cook briefly until just tender; drain well.

Shell the prawns, removing the heads but leaving the tails intact. Cut centrally along the back of each prawn and remove the dark intestinal vein. Flatten the prawns out slightly.

Heat the oil in a wok, add the prawns and garlic, and stir-fry for 2 minutes. Add the fish sauce, sugar and peppercorns and stir-fry until the prawns are pink and just tender.

Arrange the leek julienne to form a nest on each warmed serving plate. Place 3 prawns in each nest, pour over the cooking juices and sprinkle with chopped coriander leaves to serve.

Jenny Rees

King Prawn and Papaya Salad

12 raw king prawns, shelled, de-veined and rinsed
45 ml (3 tbsp) olive oil
225 g (8 oz) raspberries
1 papaya
125 g (4 oz) smoked back bacon, derinded

To Serve:
300 g (10 oz) mixed salad leaves (eg rocket, watercress and frisée)

Put the prawns in a bowl, pour on the olive oil and set aside until ready to cook.

Purée the raspberries in a food processor, then pass through a fine sieve to remove the pips.

Cut the papaya into quarters, scoop out the seeds and remove the skin. Slice each quarter lengthwise, leaving the tip intact to form a fan.

Remove the fat from the bacon, then grill until crispy. Chop into small pieces.

Cook the prawns under a pre-heated grill, for about 2-3 minutes, turning occasionally, until pink.

To serve, arrange a portion of salad leaves in the middle of each serving plate. Place a papaya fan to one side. Sprinkle some of the crispy bacon over the salad and top with the prawns. Pour on a little of the raspberry purée and serve immediately.

Kevin Sumner

Squid Ink Risotto

with Monkfish and Prawns

30 ml (2 tbsp) olive oil
1 small onion, finely chopped
2 cloves garlic, finely chopped
225 g (8 oz) fennel, cored and finely chopped
225 g (8 oz) Arborio rice
750 ml (1¼ pints) fish stock
2 sachets of squid ink
225 g (8 oz) monkfish fillet, skinned and cubed
125 g (4 oz) Parmesan cheese, freshly grated
freshly ground black pepper
25 g (1 oz) butter
12 large prawns, or 4 medium langoustines

To Garnish:
parsley or chives

Cook's Note

Use the special Italian risotto rice – Arborio – for this starter. It readily absorbs plenty of liquid, resulting in a wonderful creamy texture.

Heat the olive oil in a heavy-based pan, add the onion and sweat gently until softened. Add the garlic and fennel and cook, stirring occasionally, for 3 minutes. Add the rice and cook, stirring constantly, for 2 minutes.

> *"...a stunning dish... it was just really out of this world."*
>
> Willi Elsener

Meanwhile, heat the stock in another saucepan. Add about 250 ml (8 fl oz) of the hot stock to the rice and cook, stirring, until absorbed. Add the squid ink and monkfish. Continue adding the stock a ladleful at a time, as each addition is absorbed. Continue until the rice is plump and tender yet still has some bite. (You may not need to add all of the stock.) Stir in the Parmesan, pepper and butter.

Meanwhile cook the prawns or langoustines in a large pan of boiling water for 4 minutes, or until pink.

To serve, divide the risotto between individual serving bowls and garnish with the prawns or langoustines and parsley or chives.

Holly Schade

Skewered Oysters and Scallops

with a Sweet Pepper Sauce

8 oysters
8 scallops (4 with corals), cleaned
6 rashers of thin-cut back bacon, preferably Ayrshire
2 red peppers
1 yellow pepper
1 orange pepper
10 small shallots, blanched for 2 minutes and peeled
5 ml (1 tsp) sugar
75 ml (5 tbsp) Muscadet or other dry white wine
8 cloves garlic, peeled
15-30 ml (1-2 tbsp) olive oil
1 onion, thinly sliced
1 thyme sprig, leaves only

To Garnish:
thyme sprigs

Remove the oysters from their shells and carefully roll a piece of bacon round each one. Thread the oysters and scallops alternately onto 4 kebab skewers, allowing 2 oysters and 2 scallops per skewer. Finish each skewer with a scallop coral. Set aside in a cool place until required.

"I thought the scallops were beautifully cooked, exactly the right texture."

William Waldegrave

Halve, core and deseed the peppers, then cut each one into 1 cm (½ inch) strips. Cut 8 diamond shapes from the yellow pepper, 8 from the orange pepper, and 16 from the red ones. Set aside.

To make the sauce, chop the remaining red pepper flesh and two of the shallots. Place in a saucepan with 2.5 ml (½ tsp) sugar and the wine. Cook for 10-15 minutes until tender, then work in a food processor or blender until smooth, and pass through a sieve.

Chop the remaining rashers of bacon and fry in a non-stick pan without additional fat until crisp. Remove with a slotted spoon and set aside. Sauté the garlic and the whole shallots in the bacon fat remaining in the pan until golden, adding a little olive oil if needed.

Heat 15 ml (1 tbsp) olive oil in another frying pan, add the sliced onion with the thyme and remaining 2.5 ml (½ tsp) sugar; cook until soft. Add the pepper diamonds and cook until softened. Add the bacon strips and keep warm.

Cook the kebabs under a preheated hot grill for 5-6 minutes, turning once or twice. Meanwhile, reheat the pepper sauce.

To serve, spread a pool of red pepper sauce on each warmed plate. Spoon the onions and pepper diamonds to one side, garnishing with the shallots and garlic. Mark a criss-cross pattern on each scallop with a hot metal skewer and place the kebabs on the sauce. Garnish with thyme and serve at once.

Marion MacFarlane

Skewered Oysters and Scallops with a Sweet Pepper Sauce

Oysters and Scallops in Cream Sauce

with Parmesan

12 oysters
6 scallops
150 ml (¼ pint) double cream
salt and freshly ground pepper
freshly grated Parmesan cheese for sprinkling

Prise open the oyster and scallop shells over a bowl to collect the liquid. Pass the liquid through a fine-meshed conical sieve to remove any grit and place in a saucepan. Bring to the boil and simmer until reduced by about two thirds.

Clean the scallops and halve the white meat, discarding the coral. Add to the pan with the oysters. As soon as the liquid begins to bubble, remove the oysters and scallops with a slotted spoon and wrap in a warm, damp towel.

Add the cream to the liquid. Bring to the boil and cook, stirring, until the sauce is thick enough to coat the back of the spoon. Check the seasoning.

Divide the oysters and scallop pieces between individual gratin dishes. Spoon over the sauce and sprinkle lightly with Parmesan. Place under a preheated hot grill until the topping is lightly browned. Serve immediately.

Gordon Irvine

Lightly Poached Oysters with Trompettes

1 cucumber
salt and freshly ground black pepper
24 oysters, scrubbed clean
150 g (5 oz) unsalted butter, chilled and diced
2 large shallots, finely chopped
15 ml (1 tbsp) dry white wine
5 ml (1 tsp) white wine vinegar
5 ml (1 tsp) single cream
squeeze of lime juice (optional)
15 ml (1 tbsp) oil
24 horn of plenty mushrooms (trompettes), cleaned
pinch of paprika (optional)

Cook's Note

If available, use Colchester rock oysters for this starter, as they have a very good flavour.

Peel the cucumber, reserving about 50 g (2 oz) of the peelings. Prepare a garnish of small lozenges, about 1 cm x 5 mm (¾ x ¼ inch), from the cucumber flesh. Sprinkle these with a little salt and freeze for 1 hour. Finely chop the cucumber peelings. Open the oysters and drain, reserving the juices; clean thoroughly.

Melt 5 ml (1 tsp) of the butter in a small saucepan, add the chopped cucumber peelings and shallots and sweat gently until softened. Add the wine and vinegar and allow to reduce until only 5 ml (1 tsp) of liquid remains. Reduce the heat to a minimum, then add the cream and 10 ml (2 tsp) of the reserved oyster juices.

Gradually whisk in the butter, a piece at a time, on and off the heat, until it is all incorporated. Purée in a blender or food processor until smooth, then pass through a fine sieve into a small jug. Season with salt and pepper, and add a squeeze of lime juice if desired. Keep warm by placing the jug in a bowl of warm water.

Rinse the cucumber garnish and warm gently in a bowl over a pan of hot water.

Heat the oil in a sauté pan, add the mushrooms and sauté gently until softened.

Heat the rest of the oyster juices in a shallow pan. When the juices are very hot, add the oysters and poach for 3 seconds only. Remove with a slotted spoon and drain.

To assemble, place a spoonful of the beurre blanc in the centre of each warmed serving plate and arrange 6 oysters on top. Interleave the oysters with trompettes and garnish with the cucumber lozenges and a pinch of paprika if desired.

Ross Burden

Grilled Red Mullet on Stir-fried Vegetables

with a Cream Sauce

4 red mullet, each 200-225 g (7-8 oz)

Stir Fry:
30 ml (2 tbsp) sesame oil
2 cloves garlic, finely chopped
25 g (1 oz) fresh root ginger, peeled and cut into julienne
50 g (2 oz) carrot, cut into julienne
50 g (2 oz) red pepper, cored, seeded and cut into julienne
50 g (2 oz) yellow pepper, cored, seeded and cut into julienne
50 g (2 oz) spring onions, sliced
50 g (2 oz) radish, sliced
50 g (2 oz) mooli, peeled and cut into julienne
50 g (2 oz) Chinese leaves or cabbage, shredded
125 g (4 oz) bean sprouts

Sauce:
150 ml (¼ pint) dry white wine
150 ml (¼ pint) fish stock
150 ml (¼ pint) double cream
25 g (1 oz) butter, diced
salt and freshly ground black pepper

Cut the head and fins off the red mullet, leaving on the tails. Using a knife, remove the scales working from the tail towards the head. Take the fillets off the bone leaving the skin on. Carefully remove any remaining bones from the centre of the fillets. Rinse the fish and set aside in a cool place.

To make the fish stock for the sauce, put the head and bones from the mullet into a pan and cover with 300 ml (½ pint) water. Bring to the boil and skim the surface. Simmer gently for 15-20 minutes, skimming as necessary, until reduced to approximately 150 ml (¼ pint). Strain the stock through a fine sieve and set aside.

"The red mullet was delicious"

Loyd

Preheat the grill to high. Meanwhile, heat the sesame oil in a wok or large pan until hot. Add the garlic and ginger and stir for a few seconds, then add the remaining vegetables and stir-fry for 2-3 minutes. Remove from the wok and keep warm.

To make the sauce, add the wine to the wok and reduce by two thirds, then add the fish stock and boil until reduced by half. Add the double cream, bring to the boil then simmer for 2 minutes.

Meanwhile, grill the mullet skin-side up for 2-3 minutes until the skins begin to turn golden; this is sufficient to cook the fillets through without turning them.

To finish the sauce, remove from the heat and add the butter a little at a time, swirling it into the sauce until it is incorporated and the sauce is shiny. Check the seasoning.

To serve, pile the stir-fried vegetables in the centre of warmed serving plates. Arrange the mullet skin-side up and slightly overlapping on top. Surround with the sauce and serve at once.

Michael Deacon

Warm Salad of Scallops

in a Herb Butter Sauce

8 large shelled scallops with corals

Herb Butter Sauce:

125 g (4 oz) unsalted butter
1 egg yolk
1 small bunch each of fresh tarragon, parsley, chervil and chives, chopped
4 basil leaves, chopped
juice of ½ lemon
salt and freshly ground black pepper

To Serve:

4 handfuls of mixed salad leaves, (eg, frisée, lamb's lettuce, radicchio, rocket, watercress)

Clean and trim the whole scallops, then cut in half horizontally, retaining the coral. Place on a piece of kitchen paper in the refrigerator to firm up.

For the sauce, put the butter, egg yolk, herbs, lemon juice and a little seasoning in a food processor and process until the mixture becomes light in texture and colour.

Place the scallops in a single layer in a shallow ovenproof dish. Season with salt and pepper, then cover with the buttery herb mixture. Cook under a preheated grill for about 5 minutes until the sauce is bubbling and browned – by which time the scallops will be cooked. Check the seasoning.

Arrange 4 scallop halves in a circular pattern on each warmed serving plate with some of the sauce. Place a mound of mixed leaves in the centre of each plate. Drizzle a little more of the sauce over the top and serve at once.

Gill Tunkle

Salad of Grilled Scallops and Celery Leaves

with Sesame Croûtons

6 large scallops in shells, cleaned (corals reserved)
150 ml (¼ pint) milk
duck fat for deep-frying
30 celery leaves
salt and freshly ground white pepper

Croûtons:

2 slices day-old white bread
30 ml (2 tbsp) sunflower oil
10 ml (2 tsp) sesame oil
15 ml (1 tbsp) sesame seeds

Salad:

4 handfuls of lamb's lettuce
small handful of rocket leaves
few red chicory leaves (optional)
7.5 ml (½ tbsp) walnut oil
45 ml (3 tbsp) sunflower oil
15 ml (1 tbsp) white wine vinegar

First prepare the croûtons. Cut the bread into 1 cm (½ inch) dice. Mix the sunflower and sesame oils together and brush all over the bread cubes. Sprinkle evenly with the sesame seeds. Bake in a preheated oven at 180°C (350°F) mark 4 for 20-30 minutes until golden and crunchy.

For the salad, wash and thoroughly dry the salad leaves; set aside. For the dressing combine the walnut oil, sunflower oil, wine vinegar and seasoning in a screw-topped jar and shake well to combine.

To prepare the scallops, remove the corals from the scallops and pierce each one with a knife. Poach gently in the milk for 30 seconds, then drain and cut into smaller pieces.

Heat the duck fat in a suitable pan and deep-fry the celery leaves for a few seconds until golden; drain on absorbent paper.

Slice each scallop horizontally to make thin discs. Preheat a cast-iron griddle or heavybased pan until very hot, add the scallop discs and cook briefly until seared and golden.

To serve, toss the salad leaves with the dressing and divide between 4 serving plates. Arrange the scallop slices on top and sprinkle with the hot croûtons and scallop corals. Serve at once.

Sophie Buchmann

Salad of Grilled Scallops and Celery Leaves with Sesame Croûtons

WARM SALAD OF GRIDDLED SCALLOPS

WITH A SAFFRON DRESSING

16 small scallops, cleaned
2 heads of chicory
1 head of radicchio
2 red peppers
2 yellow peppers
2 large courgettes
1 large carrot (optional)
knob of butter
4 rashers smoked streaky bacon, derinded and diced
60 ml (4 tbsp) olive oil
2 cloves garlic, crushed

Dressing:
2 pinches of saffron strands
150 ml (¼ pint) white wine
375 ml (13 fl oz) fish stock
juice of 1 lemon
pinch of cayenne pepper
120 ml (4 fl oz) apple juice
2 shallots, chopped

To Garnish:
salad leaves

COOK'S NOTE

Served with fresh crusty bread or ciabatta, this makes a good, light lunch.

To make the dressing, put all of the ingredients in a saucepan and bring to the boil. Cook over a moderate heat for 15-20 minutes until the liquid has reduced by about half.

Meanwhile, slice the scallops into rounds. Chop the chicory and radicchio into bite-sized pieces. Halve, core and deseed the peppers, then cut into thin strips.

Using a swivel vegetable peeler, pare the courgette lengthwise into long ribbons. Do the same with the carrot, if using.

> *"I did like the starter. It looks very pleasant... and not too heavy."*
>
> Rosemary Leach

Heat a knob of butter in a frying pan, add the bacon and fry until cooked and crisp; keep warm.

Heat the oil in a large frying pan, add the garlic and all of the vegetables and fry, stirring, for 3-4 minutes, until just tender.

Preheat a griddle, or the grill to high. Add the scallops and cook using a high heat, for 2-3 minutes, or until slightly tinged brown.

Pile the vegetables onto warmed serving plates, lay the scallops on top and sprinkle with the crispy bacon. Pour on the hot dressing and garnish with salad leaves. Serve at once.

Jenni Guy

BROCHETTES OF MONKFISH

WITH FLORENCE FENNEL AND STAR ANISE

350 g (12 oz) monkfish fillet
30 ml (2 tbsp) Greek yogurt
2.5 ml (½ tsp) ground star anise
350 g (12 oz) Florence fennel
15 ml (1 tbsp) sunflower oil
sea salt
freshly ground black pepper

To Serve:
1 small red pepper, halved, cored, deseeded and thinly sliced
a little oil
roasted sesame seeds, for sprinkling
fennel or parsley leaves, to garnish

COOK'S NOTE

To prevent scorching, pre-soak the kebab skewers in water.

Remove the skin from the fish, then cut into 2 cm (¾ inch) cubes and place in a bowl. Add the yogurt and star anise powder and stir to coat each piece of fish with the mixture. Cover and leave to marinate for 1 hour.

Meanwhile trim the fennel bulbs, quarter, then cut crosswise into thin slices about 5 mm (¼ inch) thick. Heat the oil in a sauté pan. Add the fennel with about 30 ml (2 tbsp) water and a sprinkling of sea salt. Cover and cook over a medium heat for 5 minutes, then remove the lid, increase the heat and sauté until the fennel is browned. Remove from the pan and keep warm.

Thread the pieces of monkfish onto 8 wooden skewers, reserving the marinade. Cook under a preheated high grill for about 2 minutes each side until browned. Meanwhile, add the remaining marinade to the fennel with 15 ml (1 tbsp) water and heat through gently. Season with pepper.

Sauté the red pepper slices in a little oil until soft. To serve, divide the fennel between warmed serving plates and sprinkle with roasted sesame seeds. Place two brochettes on top of each mound of fennel and garnish with the red pepper slices and fennel or parsley leaves.

Derek Morris

Seafood Parcels with a Chive and Lemon Sauce

50 g (2 oz) bean sprouts
50 g (2 oz) shelled queen scallops
50 g (2 oz) cooked peeled prawns
5 ml (1 tsp) grated fresh root ginger
30 ml (2 tbsp) chopped coriander leaves
salt and freshly ground black pepper
8 sheets filo pastry (maximum – less if very large)
about 50 g (2 oz) butter, melted

Chive and Lemon Sauce:
50 g (2 oz) butter
15 ml (1 tbsp) lemon juice
15 ml (1 tbsp) chopped chives

"*That's terrifically good.*"

Loyd

Blanch the bean sprouts for 30 seconds in boiling water; drain. Blanch the scallops in boiling water for 30 seconds; drain.

In a bowl, combine the prawns, scallops, bean sprouts, grated ginger and chopped coriander leaves. Season with salt and pepper to taste.

To make the parcels, take one sheet of filo pastry and brush it with melted butter. Top with a second sheet of filo and brush again with melted butter. Cut out a 15 x 10 cm (6 x 4 inch) 'double' rectangle. With the long side towards you, place an eighth of the filling in a sausage shape across the centre. Fold in the short sides over the filling, brushing them with a little melted butter, then roll up the parcel to completely enclose the filling. Repeat with the remaining filo and filling to make 8 parcels in total.

Place the parcels seam-side down on a greased baking sheet and brush with melted butter. Bake in a preheated oven at 230°C (450°F) mark 8 for 8-10 minutes, or until golden brown and crisp.

To make the sauce, melt the butter, then whisk in the lemon juice and chives. Drizzle the sauce over the parcels to serve.

Alison Fiander

Scallop Mousseline

inlaid with Crab

50-75 g (2-3 oz) white crabmeat (including small pieces of coral roe – if available)
210 g (7½ oz) cleaned scallops with corals (see cook's note)
5 ml (1 tsp) salt
freshly ground white pepper
1 egg (size 3)
150 ml (¼ pint) double cream
90 ml (3 fl oz) soured cream

To Serve:
Tartlets of Artichoke Purée (see right)
crab claw tips (optional)
red lumpfish roe (optional)
herb sprigs, to garnish

Cook's Note

If you prepare the scallops yourself, reserve the frills to make a stock for the tartlet filling. Alternatively you could use a light fish stock made by using fish bones (eg plaice or sole).

Put the scallops into a food processor, add the salt and pepper and work until smooth. Add the egg and process for 1 minute. Transfer to a bowl, cover and chill for at least 30 minutes. Gradually fold in the cream and soured cream.

Butter 4 dariole moulds or ramekins and divide half of the scallop mousseline between them. Spoon the white crab meat in a layer on top, placing a small piece of coral in the centre (if available). Top with the rest of the scallop mousseline. Settle the mixture by bumping the moulds gently on the work surface. Cover each with a circle of greaseproof paper. Put a folded newspaper in the bottom of a roasting tin and stand the moulds on top. Add enough hot water to come halfway up the sides of the moulds. Bake in a preheated oven at 180°C (350°F) mark 4 for 25 minutes.

To serve, allow the mousselines to stand for a few minutes. Carefully unmould onto one side of the plate and decorate with the small tips of crab claw. Arrange the warm artichoke tartlet on the other side and decorate the plate with small pieces of crab coral or fish roe and herbs.

Marion MacFarlane

Tartlets of Artichoke Purée

• To serve with Scallop Mousseline •

Pastry:
50 g (2 oz) plain flour
pinch of salt
25 g (1 oz) butter
10 ml (2 tsp) water (approximately)

Artichoke Purée:
225 g (8 oz) Jerusalem artichokes, peeled
reserved scallop frills (see cook's note)
salt and freshly ground black pepper
dash of lemon juice

To make the pastry, sift the flour and salt into a bowl. Rub in the butter until the mixture resembles fine breadcrumbs. Add sufficient water to bind the dough. Wrap in cling film and place in refrigerator for 30 minutes.

For the filling, simmer the scallop frills in about 150 ml (¼ pint) water for about 20 minutes to make a stock; strain into a clean pan. Add the Jerusalem artichokes and simmer for about 15 minutes. Drain the artichokes and place in a blender or food processor with a little of the stock. Work to a smooth purée. Add seasoning and lemon juice to taste.

Roll out the pastry thinly and use to line barquettes or other small decorative moulds. Prick the bases with a fork. Line with baking beans and bake blind in a preheated oven at 190°C (375°F) mark 5 for 10 minutes. Remove the beans.

Just before serving, spoon in the warm artichoke purée. Serve at once.

Marion MacFarlane

Scallop Mousseline inlaid with Crab, served with Tartlets of Artichoke Purée

Mousseline of Lemon Sole and Asparagus

with 'Fish Toasties'

8 thin asparagus spears
175 g (6 oz) skinned and filleted lemon sole
1 egg white (size 2)
salt
75 ml (2½ fl oz) crème fraîche
450 ml (¾ pint) double cream
cayenne pepper, to taste
15 g (½ oz) butter, melted

To Serve:
4 slices of wholemeal bread
few blanched and sautéed asparagus tips, or salad leaves, to garnish

Cook's Note

Chill the two mixing bowls needed for this recipe in the refrigerator for half an hour before using them.

Blanch the asparagus spears in warm water for 1 minute. Drain and dry well with kitchen paper. Place the asparagus in a blender or food processor and purée for 30 seconds. Set aside.

Check the lemon sole is free of skin and bones; remove any fine bones with a tweezer. Purée the sole in a blender, then transfer to a bowl, set over a larger bowl filled with crushed ice. Add the egg white and a generous pinch of salt and beat thoroughly until the mixture becomes firm and tight. Gradually beat in the crème fraîche until evenly blended, then repeat with the double cream. Mix in the puréed asparagus. Season with cayenne pepper to taste.

Brush 4 ramekins with melted butter. Fill with the sole and asparagus mixture, leaving 5 mm (¼ inch) at the top to allow for some expansion during cooking. Cover with buttered foil. Place the ramekins in a steamer and steam lightly for 20 minutes.

Whilst the mousselines are steaming, prepare the fish toasties. Cut 4 fish shapes out of each slice of bread and toast until crisp and browned on both sides; keep warm.

Turn the mousselines out onto individual serving plates and garnish with asparagus or salad leaves. Serve at once, accompanied by the 'fish toasties'.

Connie Stevens

Cotswold Trout on a Compote of Roasted Tomatoes

with Red Onion, Black Olive and Pesto Sauce

4 trout fillets, each about 200 g (7 oz)
120 ml (4 fl oz) extra-virgin olive oil
1 clove garlic, chopped
100 g (3½ oz) red onion, chopped
juice of 1 lemon
30 ml (2 tbsp) white wine
50 g (2 oz) stoned black olives, chopped
6 plum tomatoes
sea salt and freshly ground black pepper
10 ml (2 tsp) oil
20 g (¾ oz) basil leaves, shredded
12 coriander seeds
pinch of sugar

Basil Sauce:
50 g (2 oz) basil leaves
150 ml (¼ pint) extra-virgin olive oil
1 clove garlic
25 g (1 oz) pine nuts
20 g (¾ oz) Parmesan cheese, freshly grated
sea salt and freshly ground black pepper

First make the basil sauce: put all of the ingredients in a blender or food processor and work until smooth; set aside.

Heat the olive oil in a pan, add the garlic and onion and fry gently for 3 minutes. Add the lemon juice, wine and olives and cook for 4 minutes. Dice two of the plum tomatoes and add to the pan. Season with salt and pepper to taste, remove from the heat and allow to cool.

Halve the other 4 tomatoes and remove their seeds. Place in a pan with the 10 ml (2 tsp) oil and cook on a high heat for 1-2 minutes until lightly coloured. Transfer to a shallow baking tin, sprinkle with the shredded basil, coriander seeds, salt, pepper and sugar.

Spoon about a third of the onion and olive mixture into another baking tin and place the trout on top. Season with salt and pepper and spoon on the rest of the onion and olive mixture.

Place the tomatoes and trout in a preheated oven at 230°C (450°F) mark 8 for 4 minutes. Arrange the tomatoes on warmed serving plates and place the trout on top. Add the pan juices from the tomatoes to the onion and olive mixture. Sprinkle this over and around the trout and drizzle with the basil sauce. Sprinkle with sea salt and pepper. Serve at once.

John Thornburn

Roulade of Sole, Salmon and Trout

50 g (2 oz) smoked salmon pieces
50 g (2 oz) cream cheese
25 g (1 oz) unsalted butter, softened
salt and freshly ground black pepper
2 large fillets lemon sole, skinned
125 g (4 oz) smoked trout slices
2 bunches of watercress, stalks removed
600 ml (1 pint) fish stock
300 ml (½ pint) double cream (approximately)

To Garnish:
15 ml (1 tbsp) pink peppercorns in brine, drained
few watercress leaves

"I thought it was spectacular."

Anne Willan

Put the smoked salmon pieces and cream cheese in a food processor or blender. Add the softened butter and work until smooth. Season with salt and pepper to taste.

Lay the sole, skinned-side up, on a clean surface. Cover each one with a layer of smoked trout, then spread with the smoked salmon pâté and top with a single layer of watercress leaves. Roll up carefully and tie with fine cotton string to secure. Chill thoroughly.

Pour the fish stock into a small saucepan and bring slowly to the boil. Add the fish and poach gently for approximately 10 minutes, then remove. Cover the fish and keep warm.

Boil the stock rapidly to reduce by half, then blend with the rest of the watercress in a food processor or blender. Return to a clean pan and add cream to taste. Adjust the seasoning if necessary.

To serve, cut the roulades into slices, allowing three per person. Pool the watercress sauce on warmed serving plates and arrange the roulade slices on top. Serve at once, garnished with pink peppercorns and watercress leaves.

Sarah Johns

Quails Baked in Red Peppers

4 small boned quail
a little basil oil, or extra-virgin olive oil, for marinating
30 ml (2 tbsp) pine nuts
salt and freshly ground black pepper
a little ground coriander
freshly ground nutmeg
handful of basil leaves
2 large cloves garlic
4 small red peppers
60 ml (4 tbsp) extra-virgin olive oil

To Serve:
herbs (chives, chervil, basil), to garnish
Corn Muffins (see right)

Rub the quail all over with basil oil and leave to marinate for a few hours, or overnight if possible.

Toast the pine nuts in a small frying pan over a moderate heat until lightly browned. Season the birds well with salt and pepper, a sprinkling of ground coriander and freshly ground nutmeg. Place 2-3 basil leaves and 6 pine nuts in each quail cavity. Crush one of the garlic cloves and divide between the 4 birds.

To prepare the peppers, cut off the tops, making an opening large enough to accept the quails; reserve the tops. Remove the core and seeds. Drizzle a little olive oil in each pepper and carefully place the quails inside. Cut the remaining garlic clove into 4 slices and add a sliver to each pepper. Replace the tops and stand the peppers in a shallow ovenproof dish. Drizzle the remaining olive oil over the peppers and cook in a preheated oven at 200°C (400°F) mark 6 for about 30-40 minutes, basting the peppers occasionally.

To serve, carefully lift the peppers on to warm serving plates, spoon over some of the juices and garnish with herbs and the remaining toasted pine nuts. Serve with the corn muffins to soak up all the delicious juices.

Marion MacFarlane

Cook's Note

Try to buy free-range quail if possible. Many specialist outlets are now selling boned quail which are ideal. If small quail are unobtainable, use 2 large ones, halved, instead. As an alternative, halve, core and de-seed 2 large red peppers and cook the quails in the pepper halves (illustrated opposite).

Little Corn Muffins

• To serve with the Quail •

60 g (2¼ oz) cornmeal (coarse-ground)
65 g (2½ oz) plain flour
5 ml (1 tsp) sugar
7.5 ml (1½ tsp) baking powder
1.25 ml (¼ tsp) salt
1 small egg (size 5)
120 ml (4 fl oz) milk
15 ml (1 tbsp) corn oil
25 g (1 oz) sun-dried tomatoes in oil, drained

Stir all the dry ingredients together in a bowl and make a well in the centre. Beat the egg with the milk and oil, add to the well and mix into the flour to yield a smooth batter. Dry the excess oil from the tomatoes using kitchen paper, then chop finely and stir into the batter.

Spoon the batter into oiled small or medium muffin tins to half-fill the tins. Bake in a preheated oven at 220°C (425°F) mark 7 for 10-12 minutes until golden brown. Leave in the tins for a few minutes, then carefully remove and serve warm.

Marion MacFarlane

> "The corn muffins were wonderful."
>
> Loyd

Quails Baked in Red Peppers, served with Little Corn Muffins

Chicken Mousse with Mango

and a Lemon Ginger Sabayon

Mousse:

2 chicken breasts, about 450 g (1 lb) total weight, filleted and skinned
salt and freshly ground white pepper
2 egg whites, beaten
120 ml (4 fl oz) double cream, chilled
120 ml (4 fl oz) milk
2.5 cm (1 inch) cube of fresh root ginger, peeled and finely grated
1-2 mangoes, peeled and thinly sliced

Lemon Ginger Sayabon:

2 egg yolks
125 g (4 oz) butter, clarified and melted
juice of ½ lemon
120 ml (4 fl oz) double cream
30 ml (2 tbsp) chicken stock
salt and freshly ground black pepper

To Garnish:

few chives

Put the chicken in a food processor, add salt and pepper, and process until smooth. Mix in the egg whites, cream, milk and ginger. Pass through a drum or tamis sieve, or a food mill; this is important and will result in a light-textured mousse when cooked.

Line 4 ramekins with a layer of mango slices and spoon in the chicken mousse. Stand the ramekins in a bain-marie or roasting tin containing enough boiling water to come two thirds of the way up the sides of the dishes. Cover the tin loosely with foil and cook in a preheated oven at 180°C (350°F) mark 4 for about 30 minutes until firm to the touch. Remove from the bain-marie to stop the cooking process.

Meanwhile make the lemon ginger sauce. Whisk the egg yolks with 45 ml (3 tbsp) water in a saucepan over a gentle heat until thickened and doubled in volume. Remove from the heat and slowly add the melted butter, whisking constantly. Continue whisking over the heat and add the lemon juice, cream and chicken stock. Season with salt and pepper to taste. Whisk until the sauce resembles a custard in consistency.

To serve, gently unmould each mousse into the centre of a large warmed serving plate and surround with the sauce. Place a couple of chives on each mousse and position 2 or 3 slices of mango to one side on the sauce. Serve immediately.

Gill Tunkle

"Sensational."

Willi Elsener

Cook's Note

A savoury sabayon is made by the same method as a hollandaise sauce. The egg yolks are whisked with a little liquid over heat until thick and mousse-like, then the tepid melted butter is gradually whisked in. The finished sauce should resemble a custard in consistancy.

Stuffed Breast of Pheasant

with Caramelised Calvados Apples

4 boneless, skinless pheasant breasts
600 ml (1 pint) game stock

Pâté:
1 Cox's apple
75 g (3 oz) unsalted butter
15 ml (1 tbsp) Calvados
1 slice smoked back bacon, cut into strips
25 g (1 oz) finely chopped onion
leaves from 3 thyme sprigs
125 g (4 oz) chicken livers, trimmed and roughly chopped
salt and freshly ground black pepper

Caramelised Apples:
2 Cox's apples
50 g (2 oz) butter
30-45 ml (2-3 tbsp) Calvados
salt and freshly ground black pepper
30-45 ml (2-3 tbsp) double cream

To Serve:
few chopped toasted hazelnuts (optional)
flat-leaved parsley sprigs

Cook's Note

If possible, obtain hen pheasants for this recipe. Use the carcasses to make the game stock. You will also need 4 muslin squares, each 30 x 23 cm (12 x 9 inches), for cooking the pheasant breasts.

First make the pâté. Peel, core and slice the apple. Melt 25 g (1 oz) of the butter in a pan, add the apple with the Calvados and cook until soft; set aside. Meanwhile melt the remaining butter in a frying pan, add the bacon and onion and cook gently until softened. Add the thyme and chicken livers and cook for 1-2 minutes; do not overcook.

Place the apples and liver mixture in a food processor and process briefly to make a coarse paté. Season liberally with salt and pepper. Allow to cool slightly.

"Wonderful flavours."

Brian Turner

Carefully make a deep horizontal slit in each pheasant breast to form a pocket. Stuff with the paté, then wrap each one tightly in muslin and tie with string. Heat the stock in a wide shallow pan and season with salt and pepper. Add the parcels and poach for 7 minutes until just cooked. Remove the parcels from the pan and leave to rest (still wrapped) in a warm place.

Meanwhile, prepare the caramelised apples. Peel, core and slice the apples. Heat the butter in a pan and add the apples and 15 ml (1 tbsp) Calvados. Cook until the apples are golden and brown at the edges. Season liberally with salt. Remove the apples with a slotted spoon and keep warm. Deglaze the pan with the rest of the Calvados, then whisk in the cream. Season with salt and pepper to taste.

To serve, open up the parcels and slice each pheasant breast very carefully into 5-6 slices. Arrange in a semi-circle to one side of each warmed serving plate. Place a spoonful of caramelised apples on the other side. Reheat the sauce if necessary and drizzle over the meat. Sprinkle a few chopped toasted hazelnuts onto the apple and garnish with flat-leaved parsley.

Clare Askaroff

Warm Salad of Puy Lentils

and Spring Onions with a Mustard Dressing

10 ml (2 tsp) black mustard seeds
10 ml (2 tsp) yellow mustard seeds
salt and freshly ground black pepper
5 ml (1 tsp) Dijon mustard
15 ml (1 tbsp) balsamic vinegar
150 ml (¼ pint) olive oil, plus 30 ml (2 tbsp)
2 bunches of spring onions
200 g (7 oz) Puy lentils, rinsed
3 slices of white bread
a little olive oil, for brushing

To Serve:
selection of salad leaves (eg rocket, lamb's lettuce, oakleaf lettuce)

Roughly crush the black mustard seeds with 5 ml (1 tsp) of the yellow mustard seeds, using a pestle and mortar. Add a pinch of salt, some pepper, the mustard, balsamic vinegar and 150 ml (¼ pint) olive oil. Slice the spring onions into thin rounds, then toss in the dressing.

Add the lentils to a pan of boiling salted water and simmer over a moderate heat for about 15 minutes until just tender. Drain, rinse with boiling water, then drain thoroughly and toss with the dressing.

Brush the slices of bread with olive oil and grill on both sides until golden. Cut each into 4 triangles.

To finish, heat the 30 ml (2 tbsp) olive oil in a pan, then add the remaining yellow mustard seeds. Cook over a gentle heat until they just start to pop. Tip in the lentils and their dressing and just warm through. Arrange the salad leaves and lentils on individual plates. Garnish with the toast and serve.

Elaine Bates

Roquefort and Spring Onion Tartlets

Tartlets:
350 g (12 oz) puff pastry (preferably homemade)
225 g (8 oz) Roquefort cheese
4 spring onions, trimmed and chopped
30 ml (2 tbsp) chopped walnuts
1 egg
120 ml (4 fl oz) double cream
salt and freshly ground black pepper
freshly grated nutmeg

Redcurrant and Walnut Dressing:
45 ml (3 tbsp) olive oil
15 ml (1 tbsp) walnut oil
15 ml (1 tbsp) balsamic vinegar
7.5 ml (1½ tsp) lemon juice
2.5 ml (½ tsp) French wholegrain mustard
30 ml (2 tbsp) redcurrant jelly
45 ml (3 tbsp) chopped walnuts

To Serve:
lamb's lettuce

Roll out the pastry on a lightly floured surface and use to line 4 individual 7.5 cm (3 inch) flan tins. Prick the bases with a fork, line with greaseproof paper and baking beans and bake blind in a preheated oven at 220°C (425°F) mark 7 for 8-10 minutes until firm. Remove the paper and beans and allow to cool.

Chop the Roquefort and mix with the spring onions and walnuts. In a bowl, whisk the egg and cream together. Season with pepper, nutmeg and a little salt. Stir in the cheese mixture and spoon into the flan cases. Bake in the oven for 15 minutes until risen and golden.

Meanwhile put all of the dressing ingredients into a screw-topped jar and shake vigorously to emulsify. Toss the lamb's lettuce in the dressing, then arrange a bed on each serving plate. Place the warm tartlets on top to serve.

Fiona Phelps

> *"One of the best dishes I have had."*
>
> Egon Ronay

Roquefort and Spring Onion Tartlets

CHEESE AND WALNUT SOUFFLÉ

50 g (2 oz) dry white breadcrumbs
100 ml (3½ fl oz) milk
30 g (1 oz) unsalted butter
15 g (½ oz) plain white flour
1 egg yolk
80 g (3¼ oz) mature soft cheese (eg chaumes, maroille, milleens)
3 egg whites
5 ml (1 tsp) lemon juice
75 g (3 oz) walnuts, chopped
salt and freshly ground pepper
60 g (2¼ oz) watercress, trimmed
45 ml (3 tbsp) walnut oil
15 ml (1 tbsp) white wine vinegar

Liberally butter 4 ramekins and coat with a generous layer of breadcrumbs.

Bring the milk to the boil in a small saucepan, then remove from the heat. In another saucepan, melt the butter, stir in the flour and cook for 1-2 minutes. Slowly add the milk, stirring constantly. Bring to the boil and simmer for 1 minute, stirring. Remove from the heat and stir in the egg yolk and soft cheese until smooth.

"A lovely dish."

Sonia Stevenson

Whisk the egg whites in a large mixing bowl with a pinch of salt, until soft peaks form. Add the lemon juice and continue whisking until the mixture is smooth and stiff. Beat about a quarter of the egg white into the cheese mixture, then fold in the remainder. Season with salt and pepper.

Half fill the ramekins with the soufflé mixture. Sprinkle 50 g (2 oz) of the chopped walnuts evenly over the surface, then cover with the remaining soufflé.

Stand the ramekins in a bain-marie (roasting tin containing enough water to come halfway up the sides of the dishes). Bake in a preheated oven at 180°C (350°F) mark 4 for 8 minutes. Leave to cool for 10 minutes. Shake the soufflés to loosen them from the ramekins, then turn them out carefully onto a lightly oiled baking sheet. Allow to cool for a further 10 minutes (or longer if more convenient).

Just before serving, return the soufflés to the oven and bake at the same temperature for 5 minutes until the crusts are crisp.

Meanwhile toss the watercress leaves in the walnut oil and wine vinegar and arrange on individual serving plates. Sprinkle with the rest of the chopped walnuts. Serve the hot soufflés on the bed of watercress leaves.

Ashley Wilson

STEAMED LEEKS WITH BACON

AND A TOMATO AND CORIANDER SAUCE

450 g (1 lb) baby cherry tomatoes
45 ml (3 tbsp) olive oil
5 ml (1 tsp) caster sugar
salt and freshly ground black pepper
900 g (2 lb) leeks, thoroughly cleaned
50 g (2 oz) butter
2 turnips
60 ml (2 fl oz) white wine
15 ml (1 tbsp) finely chopped coriander leaves
225 g (8 oz) lightly smoked bacon, cut into lardons
cayenne pepper, to taste

To Garnish:
tomato flowers (optional)

Arrange the cherry tomatoes in a shallow ovenproof dish and add 15 ml (1 tbsp) of the oil, the sugar and 2.5 ml (½ tsp) salt. Toss the tomatoes to ensure they are evenly coated. Bake in a preheated oven at 220°C (425°F) mark 7 for 30-40 minutes until the tomatoes begin to blacken and have released plenty of juice. Allow to cool in the dish.

Meanwhile prepare the leeks. Slice into 5 cm (2 inch) lengths and steam over boiling water for up to 12 minutes, depending on thickness, until just cooked, but still retaining some crispness. Transfer to a shallow dish and dot with the butter. Season with salt and pepper to taste; keep warm.

Peel the turnips, slice into fine julienne strips and place in a bowl of iced water.

For the sauce, press the cherry tomatoes through a conical sieve into a pan to remove the seeds and skin and yield a tomato coulis. Add the wine and bring to the boil. Allow to reduce for 1-2 minutes, then remove from the heat and add the chopped coriander. Keep warm.

To serve, heat the remaining oil in a pan and quickly fry the bacon lardons until tender and slightly browned. Drain on kitchen paper.

Using a 7.5 cm (3 inch) pastry cutter as a guide, arrange a round of turnip julienne in the centre of each plate. Slice the leek sections lengthwise into quarters and arrange these on top of the turnips in a stack. Pour the sauce around each stack and scatter the bacon lardons on the sauce. Sprinkle a little cayenne pepper over the leeks and garnish each serving with a tomato flower if you like. Serve at once.

Michael Gray

Cook's Note

To make a tomato flower, simply peel the skin from an unripe tomato, retaining a uniformly thick and intact skin. Roll the skin into a flower shape.

Ravioli of Ricotta and Boursin Cheese

with Fennel and Pine Nut Butter

Pasta Dough:

310 g (10½ oz) '00' flour
2.5 ml (½ tsp) salt
3 eggs (size 2)
25 ml (1 fl oz) olive oil (approximately)

Filling:

2 cloves garlic, crushed
15 ml (1 tbsp) olive oil
225 g (8 oz) ricotta cheese
175 g (6 oz) Boursin cheese
1 egg (size 2)
30 ml (2 tbsp) finely chopped basil

Topping:

75 g (3 oz) butter
60 ml (4 tbsp) olive oil
1 fennel bulb, cored and finely chopped
50 g (2 oz) pine nuts
3 ripe plum tomatoes, seeded and chopped
30 ml (2 tbsp) finely chopped basil
25 g (1 oz) Parmesan cheese, freshly grated

To Garnish:

basil leaves

To make the ravioli dough, put the flour, salt, eggs and olive oil in a food processor and process about 30 seconds until a smooth dough is formed. If necessary, add a little more olive oil to help the dough come together. Wrap in cling film and flatten. Leave to rest in the refrigerator for 30 minutes.

To make the ravioli filling, sauté the garlic in the olive oil until softened, then transfer to a bowl. Add all of the remaining ingredients and whisk with an electric beater until smooth.

Cut off about one quarter of the ravioli dough and re-wrap the remainder. Flatten the piece of dough slightly and dust with flour. Pass through a pasta machine on its widest setting, then fold the dough and pass through the machine repeatedly, narrowing the setting by one notch each time until you each the last but one setting. Dust lightly with flour, cover with a tea-towel and set aside. Repeat with the rest of the dough.

Using a 7.5 cm (3 inch) pastry cutter, cut 30 circles from the pasta dough. Place a rounded teaspoon of the filling in the centre of 15 circles. Moisten the edges of the other 15 circles and place over the filling. Press the edges together to seal. Leave the ravioli on a tea-towel and allow to dry slightly before cooking.

Meanwhile, prepare the topping. Heat the butter and 45 ml (3 tbsp) olive oil in a pan, add the fennel and sauté for 3 minutes or until soft; keep warm. Heat the remaining 15 ml (1 tbsp) olive oil in a frying pan and toast the pine nuts until browned. Warm the tomatoes through in a pan.

Cook the ravioli in a large pan of boiling water for 4-5 minutes until al dente (tender but firm to the bite). Drain and arrange on warmed serving plates. Top with the buttered fennel, pine nuts, chopped tomatoes and basil. Sprinkle the Parmesan on top and garnish with basil leaves. Serve immediately.

Holly Schade

NEUFCHÂTEL CHEESE

WITH A CARAMELISED RED PEPPER SAUCE

200 g (7 oz) fresh neufchâtel cheese
mixture of salad leaves (eg frisée and lamb's lettuce)

Dressing:
45 ml (3 tbsp) olive oil
15 ml (1 tbsp) wine vinegar
2.5ml (½ tsp) mustard
salt and freshly ground black pepper
pinch of sugar

Red Pepper Sauce:
125 ml (4 fl oz) dry white wine
125 ml (4 fl oz) vinegar
125 ml (4 fl oz) water
75 g (3 oz) granulated sugar
1 red pepper, cored, seeded and finely chopped

To Serve:
pumpernickel bread

Slice the cheese and arrange on individual serving plates with the salad leaves. Combine the ingredients for the dressing in a screw-topped jar and shake vigorously to blend. Spoon a little dressing over the salad leaves.

To make the red pepper sauce, put the wine, vinegar and water in a saucepan. Add the sugar and dissolve over low heat, then increase the heat and reduce by about two thirds until the mixture is forming tiny bubbles; this will take about 10 minutes. Before it begins to caramelise, remove from the heat and add the pepper. Leave for 1 minute, then pour over the cheese.

Let stand for 2 minutes before serving, with pumpernickel bread.

Nicholas Hocking

PARCELS OF MARINATED ORKNEY GOAT'S CHEESE

WITH DRESSED SALAD

225 g (8 oz) goat's cheese (preferably Lairobell)
45 ml (3 tbsp) extra-virgin olive oil
15 ml (1 tbsp) chopped parsley
15 ml (1 tbsp) chopped thyme
30 ml (2 tbsp) chopped chives
½ clove garlic, crushed
freshly ground black pepper
1 yellow pepper
1 red pepper
4-8 large spinach leaves

Salad:
selection of salad leaves (eg frisée, rocket, oakleaf lettuce)
30 ml (2 tbsp) extra-virgin olive oil
10 ml (2 tsp) raspberry vinegar
salt and freshly ground black pepper

Cut the cheese into four slices. Pour the oil into a shallow dish, add the chopped herbs, garlic and black pepper, and mix well. Add the cheese, turning to coat well. Cover and leave to marinate for 2 hours at room temperature, or overnight in the refrigerator.

Halve the peppers and place-cut side down under a preheated high grill for about 10-15 minutes until the skin is blistered and blackened. Cover with a tea-towel and leave until cool enough to handle, then skin, deseed and slice each pepper half into 6 strips.

Blanch the spinach leaves in boiling water for a few seconds only until pliable. Refresh in cold water, then drain well and dry on a tea-towel. Wrap each piece of cheese in a spinach leaf, brush with a little olive oil and place in an ovenproof dish. Cover with foil, and bake in a preheated oven at 220°C (425°F) mark 7 for 8 minutes.

Meanwhile combine the olive oil, raspberry vinegar, salt and pepper for the salad dressing in a screw-topped jar and shake well to combine. Toss the peppers in a little of the dressing; use the rest to dress the salad leaves. Arrange the salad leaves and peppers on individual plates. Top each with a goat's cheese parcel. Serve at once.

Katherine Rendall

Parcels of Marinated Orkney Goat's Cheese

Spiced Cornucopia of Wild Mushrooms

450 g (1 lb) assorted mushrooms
120 ml (4 fl oz) olive oil
10 ml (2 tsp) cumin seeds
10 ml (2 tsp) coriander seeds
120 ml (4 fl oz) white wine
75 ml (2½ fl oz) water
rosemary sprig
juice of ½ lemon
freshly ground black pepper
30 ml (2 tbsp) chopped coriander leaves
1 clove garlic, crushed
4 thin slices white bread
few salad leaves, to garnish

Clean the mushrooms thoroughly. Heat half of the olive oil in a saucepan, add the cumin and coriander seeds and sauté for 1 minute, then add the mushrooms and sauté for 2 minutes. Add the wine, water, rosemary and lemon juice and simmer for about 10 minutes. Turn up the heat and boil rapidly until the liquid has reduced by half. Season with pepper to taste. Stir in the chopped coriander and keep warm.

To make the cornucopias, mix the remaining olive oil with the garlic. Brush each slice of bread liberally with the garlic oil, then wrap around a cream horn tin and press the edges together, cutting off any excess, to achieve a horn shape. Place on a baking tray and bake in a preheated oven at 180°C (350°F) mark 4 for 10-15 minutes until light golden. Carefully remove the bread horns from the tins.

To serve, spoon some of the mushrooms into each bread horn, then lay on a serving plate. Spoon the rest of the mushrooms onto the plates so that they look as if they are spilling out of the cornucopias. Pour some of the mushroom juices around the plate and garnish with a few salad leaves. Serve at once.

Elaine Bates

Cook's Note

For this starter, use a mixture of different mushrooms – such as pied de moutons, chanterelles, oyster and button mushrooms – depending on whatever is available.

> *"Very, very nice."*
>
> Alan Yentob

Smoked Mushroom and Chilli Tamales

with Avocado and Tequila Salsa

50 g (2 oz) butter
225 g (8 oz) smoked mushrooms, chopped
15 ml (1 tbsp) chopped coriander
2 cloves roasted garlic, peeled (see cook's note)
salt and freshly ground black pepper
1 smoked chilli, finely chopped
30 ml (2 tbsp) masa harina (see cook's note)
125 g (4 oz) Monterey Jack cheese, grated
150 ml (¼ pint) vegetable stock (approximately)
8 large dried corn husks, pre-soaked in hot water

Avocado and Tequila Salsa:
1 green pepper, cored, seeded and finely chopped
1 avocado, peeled, stoned and chopped
juice of 2 limes
½ red onion, finely chopped
1 green chilli, finely chopped
15 ml (1 tbsp) chopped coriander
15 ml (1 tbsp) tequila
30 ml (2 tbsp) olive oil

First prepare the salsa. Combine all of the ingredients in a bowl and toss gently to mix. Cover and leave to stand for at least 1 hour.

Heat the butter in a frying pan, add the smoked mushrooms and fry gently until cooked. Allow to cool slightly, then transfer to a food processor and process on a very low speed until coarsely chopped. Transfer to a large mixing bowl and add the coriander, garlic, salt and pepper, chilli, masa harina and cheese. Stir well. Add the vegetable stock, a little at a time, until a soft dough is formed. You may not need to add all of the stock.

Open out a corn husk and place a dessertspoon of the dough in the centre. Roll to enclose the filling and form a cracker shape. Use extra thin pieces of husk to tie the ends together, or use string if preferred. Repeat with the rest of the corn husks. Place in a steamer and steam for 25 minutes. Serve the tamales with the salsa.

Abigail Barlow

Cook's Note

Masa harina is a special type of maize flour. You should be able to obtain masa harina and dried corn husks from Mexican food suppliers. For the roasted garlic, wrap the garlic cloves in foil and bake in a moderate oven for 20 minutes. For a milder flavoured salsa, remove the seeds from the chilli.

Cheese Choux Pastries

filled with Wild Mushrooms in Madeira

Choux Pastry:

65 g (2½ oz) strong plain flour
pinch of cayenne
150 ml (¼ pint) water
50 g (2 oz) butter, in pieces
2 eggs (size 1), beaten
65 g (2½ oz) Gruyère cheese, grated
beaten egg, to glaze

Filling:

15 g (½ oz) dried porcini mushrooms, chopped if large
40 g (1½ oz) butter
175 g (6 oz) onions, finely chopped
2 cloves garlic, crushed
175 g (6 oz) open cup mushrooms, chopped
175 g (6 oz) oyster mushrooms, chopped
2.5 ml (½ tsp) chopped thyme
salt and freshly ground black pepper
freshly grated nutmeg
150 ml (¼ pint) Madeira
90 ml (3 fl oz) double cream

To Serve:

1 small head frisée
2 oranges (preferably ruby-red)
30 ml (2 tbsp) extra-virgin olive oil

For the filling, put the dried mushrooms in a small bowl and pour on about 350 ml (12 fl oz) hot water. Leave to soak for 30 minutes.

To make the sauce, melt the butter in a saucepan, add the onions and garlic and cook gently for 5 minutes until softened and pale golden. Stir in all of the fresh mushrooms, then add the soaked mushrooms, together with their soaking water; there should be about 250 ml (8 fl oz). Add the thyme and season with salt, pepper and a generous grating of nutmeg. Pour in the Madeira and cover the pan with a tight-fitting lid. Let the mushrooms cook as slowly as possible for 1½ hours; the liquid should barely simmer; check from time to time that it hasn't evaporated and add a little more water if necessary.

To make the choux pastry, sift the flour with the cayenne and a pinch of salt onto a piece of paper. Put the water and butter in a medium saucepan over a gentle heat until the butter has melted and the mixture comes to the boil. Turn the heat off and immediately tip in the flour, beating vigorously with a wooden spoon. Continue beating until the mixture forms a smooth ball. Beat in the eggs a little at a time, until you have a smooth, shiny paste. (It should have a dropping consistency – you may not need to add all of the egg.) Fold in 50 g (2 oz) of the cheese and season with salt, pepper and cayenne.

Place heaped spoonfuls of the choux pastry on a lightly greased baking sheet, spacing them well apart, to make 12 buns. Brush with a little beaten egg, then sprinkle with the rest of the cheese. Bake near the top of a preheated oven at 200°C (400°F) mark 6 for 10 minutes. Increase the temperature to 220°C (425°F) mark 7, and bake for a further 20 minutes.

Meanwhile, prepare the salad. Roughly tear the frisée into a bowl. Peel the oranges, removing all white pith, then slice crosswise into thin rounds. Add to the frisée. Season with salt and pepper and toss with the oil.

Split the choux pastries horizontally. Stir the cream into the mushroom filling, then use to fill the choux buns. Serve with the frisée and orange salad.

James Doering

FISH & SHELLFISH

Pan-fried Fillet of Tuna

served with a Basil Salsa

4 tuna fillets, each about 175 g (6 oz), cut from the middle to the tapering end of the fillet if possible

Marinade:
60 ml (4 tbsp) extra-virgin olive oil
juice of 1 lemon
handful of fresh mixed herbs (bay, thyme, oregano, parsley, chervil)
2 cloves garlic, very roughly chopped
salt and freshly ground black pepper

Basil Salsa:
90 ml (3 fl oz) agrumato (see cook's note)
25 ml (1 fl oz) lemon juice
5 ml (1 tsp) coriander seeds, crushed
8 basil leaves, shredded
2 tomatoes, skinned, seeded and diced

To Finish:
a little oil for cooking

To Serve:
Potato Galettes (page 18)
Confit of Fennel and Olives (page 109)

Wipe the tuna fillets with kitchen paper, then place in a shallow dish. Mix together the ingredients for the marinade, then pour over the tuna to cover evenly. Cover the dish with cling film and leave to marinate for at least 2 hours.

To prepare the basil salsa, heat the oil gently in a small pan. Add the lemon juice. Remove from the heat, add the crushed coriander seeds and leave to infuse. Set aside the shredded basil and diced tomato.

To cook the tuna, heat a little oil in a heavy-based frying pan or griddle until searing hot. Lift the tuna out of the marinade, discarding any bits of herb that may be sticking to the fillets. Add the tuna to the pan, pressing down firmly to sear the fillets. Cook for 1 minute each side only; the tuna should still be pink in the centre.

To serve, place a warm potato galette on each large warmed serving plate and position a tuna fillet alongside. Add the basil and tomato to the basil salsa and spoon over the tuna and sparingly around the plate. Arrange the confit of fennel and olives on the plate and serve at once.

Gill Tunkle

Cook's Note

Agrumato is extra-virgin olive oil flavoured with pressed lemons. If unobtainable, use a good quality extra-virgin olive oil instead.

"I think it's an outstanding dish."

Willi Elsener

Pan-fried Fillet of Tuna served with a Basil Salsa

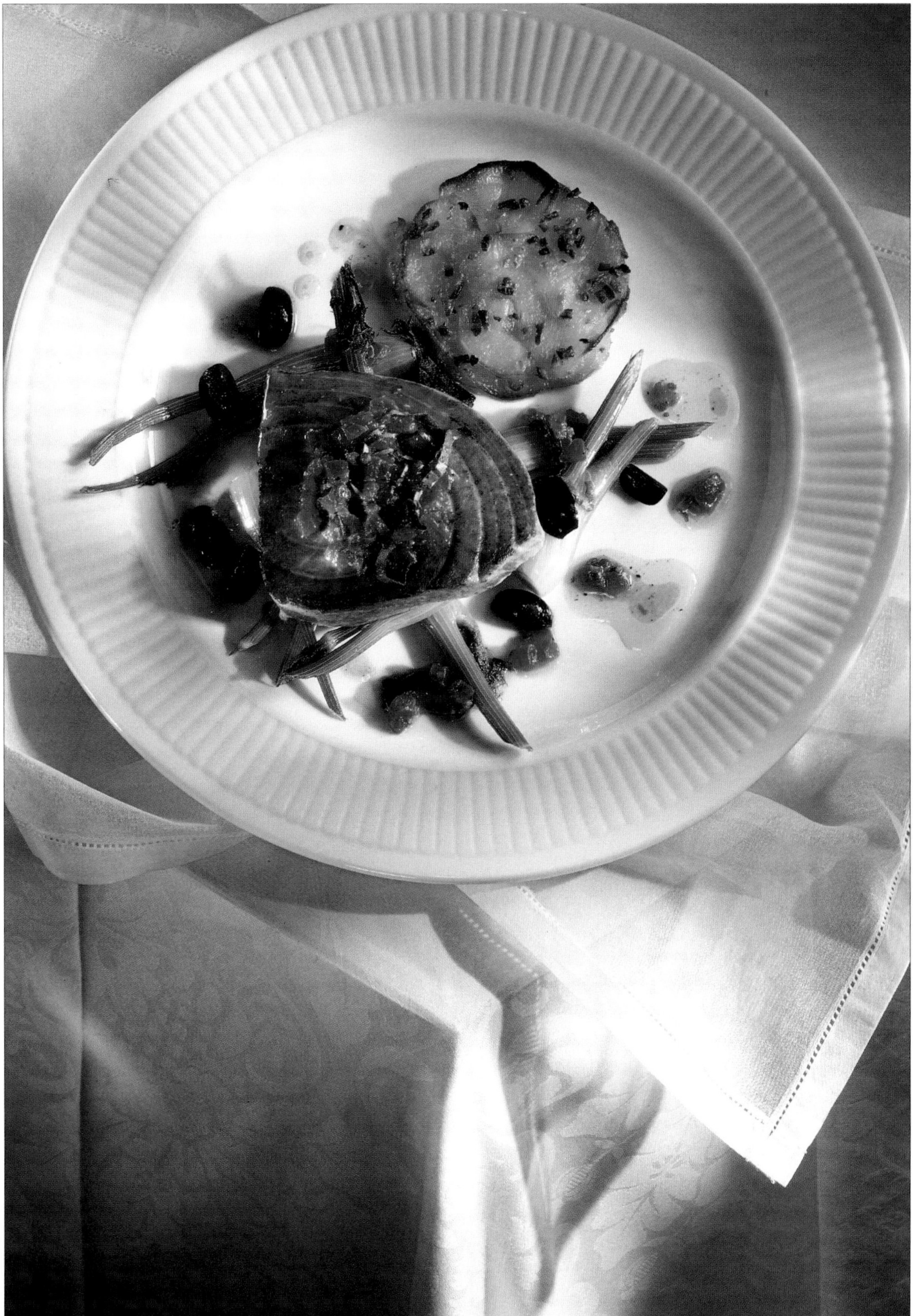

Seared Tuna Fillets

with a Slow-cooked Tomato Sauce

4 pieces fresh tuna fillet, each about 125 g (4 oz) and 1 cm (½ inch) thick
4 large basil leaves, torn
15 ml (1 tbsp) olive oil

Tomato Sauce:
450 g (1 lb) plum tomatoes
15 ml (1 tbsp) olive oil
5 ml (1 tsp) sugar
2 cloves roasted garlic (from the ½ head – see cook's note)

To Garnish:
basil leaves
½ head garlic, roasted (see cook's note)

Place the tuna fillets in a shallow dish, sprinkle with the torn basil leaves and olive oil and turn to coat. Cover and leave to marinate in the refrigerator for about 2 hours.

Meanwhile, make the tomato sauce. Immerse the tomatoes in a bowl of boiling water for 30 seconds, then remove and peel away the skins. Deseed and chop the tomato flesh. Heat the olive oil in a large pan. Add the chopped tomatoes and sugar and cook for 2-3 minutes. Reduce the heat and cook very gently for 40 minutes, stirring occasionally. Add the garlic and purée in a blender or food processor until smooth. Season with salt and pepper to taste.

To cook the tuna, preheat a griddle or heavy-based frying pan over a high heat for 3-4 minutes (without any oil) until very hot. Place the tuna fillets on the griddle (or in the pan) and cook for 1-2 minutes each side.

To serve, place the tuna fillets on warmed serving plates and top with the tomato sauce. Garnish with basil and roasted garlic. Serve with accompaniments of your choice.

Abigail Barlow

Cook's Note

To roast the garlic, wrap the ½ head in foil and bake in a moderate oven for 30 minutes. It is essential to preheat the griddle until it is very hot otherwise the tuna will stick.

"The tuna was wonderful... beautifully cooked."

Nick Nairn

Feuilleté of Fish

with a Lemon and Herb Sauce

350 g (12 oz) halibut steak
225 g (8 oz) salmon fillet
350 g (12 oz) fillet of Dover sole
bouquet garni
small piece each of leek, carrot, celery
1 lemon balm sprig
1 glass of white wine (eg Chardonnay)
1 egg, separated
150 ml (¼ pint) double cream, chilled
salt and freshly ground lemon pepper
30 ml (6 tsp) chopped mixed herbs (chives, parsley, lemon balm)
125 g (4 oz) prawns
450 g (1 lb) puff pastry (preferably homemade)
15 ml (1 tbsp) milk
melted butter, for brushing

Sauce:
150 g (5 oz) unsalted butter, chilled and diced
1 shallot, finely chopped
finely pared rind and juice of 1 lemon
150 ml (¼ pint) white wine (eg Chardonnay)

First make a fish stock. Remove any skin and bones from the fish and place the trimmings in a pan with the bouquet garni, leek, carrot and celery, and the lemon balm. Add the wine and an equal quantity of water. Bring to the boil, lower the heat and simmer for about 20 minutes. Strain through a fine sieve; set aside.

Put 50 g (2 oz) of the salmon and 125 g (4 oz) of the sole in a blender or food processor and work to a purée. With the machine running, add the egg white through the feeder tube, processing briefly until smooth. Pass the fish mousse through a sieve into a bowl. Gradually beat in the chilled cream, then season and add 10 ml (2 tsp) of the chopped mixed herbs. Cover and chill in the refrigerator.

Cut the rest of the fish into small chunks and place in a bowl along with the prawns and another 10 ml (2 tsp) of the herbs. Season with lemon pepper. Toss lightly to mix, cover and place in the refrigerator.

Roll out three quarters of the pastry to a 2 mm (1/10 inch) thickness and cut out four rounds, about 12 cm (5 inches) in diameter and large enough to fit 4 individual curved pie moulds. Line the moulds with the pastry, allowing it to overhang the rim by about 1 cm (½ inch). Beat the egg yolk with 15 ml (1 tbsp) milk to make a glaze. Brush the inside of the pastry with egg glaze, then spread a quarter of the fish mousse around the inside of each pastry case. Reserve a few pieces of the fish for garnish; fill the pastry cases with the rest.

Roll out the remaining pastry and cut out four rounds to cover the tops of the moulds; place in position and brush with egg glaze. Seal the overhanging pastry edges with glaze. Turn the feuilletés out of their moulds onto a baking sheet. Brush the outside with egg glaze and mark shallow spiral cuts with the point of a knife to decorate. Chill for about 30 minutes.

Meanwhile, make the sauce. Melt 25 g (1 oz) of the butter in a pan, add the chopped shallot and cook until softened. Add the lemon rind and half the juice, 150 ml (¼ pint) of the fish stock and two-thirds of the wine. Boil rapidly until reduced by half, then strain through a fine sieve into a clean saucepan. Return to a low heat and gradually whisk in the remaining butter, a piece at a time. Add the reserved pieces of fish and poach in the sauce for about 1 minute until cooked through. Season with salt and lemon pepper to taste. Add the remaining wine and keep warm.

Cook the feuilletés in a preheated oven at 200°C (400°F) mark 6 for about 15 minutes until the pastry is crisp and golden. Brush with some melted butter.

To serve, place one feuilleté, cut in half and opened out, in the centre of each warmed plate, then pour the sauce around. Sprinkle the sauce with the remaining chopped herbs. Serve at once.

Elaine Bates

Crispy Skin Salmon with Morels and Trompette de Mort

on a bed of Curly Kale with spiced Puy Lentils

575 g (1¼ lb) middle-cut salmon fillet, with skin
7.5 ml (1½ tsp) hazelnut oil
sea salt

Lentils:
125 g (4 oz) Puy lentils
25 g (1 oz) butter
50 g (2 oz) leek (white part only), shredded
1 clove garlic
2.5 ml (½ tsp) fennel seeds, freshly ground
2.5 ml (½ tsp) coriander seeds, freshly ground
2.5 ml (½ tsp) cardamom seeds, freshly ground
2.5 ml (½ tsp) cumin seeds, freshly ground
150 ml (¼ pint) chicken stock

Sauce:
12 small dried morels
12 dried trompette de mort
120 ml (4 fl oz) Noilly Pratt
150 ml (¼ pint) chicken stock
120 ml (4 fl oz) double cream
15 g (½ oz) butter

Kale:
5 ml (1 tsp) oil
25 g (1 oz) derinded bacon, finely chopped
125 g (4 oz) curly kale, finely chopped
4 juniper berries, crushed

Soak the lentils in cold water to cover for 2 hours. Cut the salmon fillet into four rectangular pieces and keep covered in a cool place until required.

To make the sauce, soak the dried mushrooms in warm water to cover for 30 minutes; drain. Simmer the Noilly Pratt in a pan until reduced by about two thirds. Add the stock and reduce again by about half. Add the cream and butter and bring to a simmer. Stir in the reconstituted mushrooms and cook gently until softened. Set aside to allow the flavours to infuse, until required.

To cook the lentils, melt the butter in a pan, add the leek and sauté until softened. Add the garlic and spices and cook for a further 1 minute. Drain the lentils and put into a saucepan with the stock and the leek and spice mixture. Cook for about 10 minutes until al dente, tender but firm to the bite.

To cook the curly kale, heat the oil in a wok, add the bacon and toss over a medium-high heat for 1 minute. Add the kale and juniper berries and toss over a moderate heat for 2-3 minutes until just wilted.

Meanwhile heat the hazelnut oil in a heavy-based frying pan until very hot. Place the salmon fillets, skin-side down, in the pan and cook for 1 minute then, using tongs, seal each of the other surfaces. Now place skin-side down for 2 minutes, turn and cook the opposite side for 1 minute, then turn again and cook skin-side down for a further 1-2 minutes; the skin should be dark brown and crisp.

To serve, place a mound of kale on each serving plate and scatter over the lentils. Position a portion of salmon on top and spoon the sauce and mushrooms around. Sprinkle the salmon with sea salt and serve at once.

Marion MacFarlane

> *"I think that salmon is most probably the best salmon I've ever tasted... it was absolutely magnificent."*
>
> Ken Livingstone

Crispy Skin Salmon with Morels and Trompette de Mort on a bed of Curly Kale with spiced Puy Lentils

PAN-FRIED FILLET OF SALMON

WITH A TOMATO AND BASIL VINAIGRETTE

15 ml (1 tbsp) butter
5 ml (1 tsp) chopped herbs
5 ml (1 tsp) crushed or finely chopped garlic
4 Scottish salmon fillets, skinned

Vinaigrette:
175 ml (6 fl oz) olive oil
60 ml (4 tbsp) cider vinegar
5 ml (1 tsp) honey
1 clove garlic, crushed
15 ml (1 tbsp) finely chopped tomato flesh
15 ml (1 tbsp) chopped basil
salt and freshly ground black pepper

To Garnish:
lemon wedges
basil sprigs

First make the vinaigrette. Place all the ingredients in a screw-topped jar and shake well. Season with salt and pepper.

Melt the butter in a heavy-based frying pan, add the herbs and garlic, then add the salmon fillets and cook over a high heat for about 10-15 seconds each side to seal. Turn the heat down to medium and cook for 6-8 minutes, until the salmon is just cooked and flakes easily when tested with a fork.

Place one salmon fillet in the middle of each warmed serving plate. Give the vinaigrette a good shake and spoon over the salmon. Garnish with lemon and basil to serve.

Betsy Anderson

COOK'S NOTE

This tomato and basil vinaigrette is equally good as a salad dressing. Store it in the refrigerator for up to 2 weeks and shake vigorously before use.

MOSAIC OF SALMON AND COD WITH SORREL SAUCE

2 thick cod fillets, skinned, each about 300 g (10 oz)
2 thick salmon fillets, skinned, each about 225 g (8 oz)
juice of 1 lemon
salt and freshly ground white pepper
16-20 large spinach leaves
Japanese dried seaweed, for steaming (optional)

Sorrel Sauce:
225 g (8 oz) sorrel
50 g (2 oz) butter
250 ml (8 fl oz) single cream
250 ml (8 fl oz) double cream
30-45 ml (2-3 tbsp) reduced fish stock
few drops of lemon juice

Trim the top of each fish fillet as necessary, to leave a flat fillet approximately 2 cm (¾ inch) thick. Cut each cod fillet lengthways into 8 strips, each about 10 x 2 x 2 cm (4 x ¾ x ¾ inch). If it isn't possible to cut 10 cm (4 inch) lengths, wrap shorter pieces together to achieve the required length. Cut each salmon fillet widthways into 8 strips, each about 2 cm (¾ inch) wide. Sprinkle with lemon juice and season with salt and white pepper.

Wash the spinach leaves thoroughly and remove the thick stalks. Blanch the spinach in boiling water for 1 minute or so until pliable. Drain thoroughly. Wrap each cod strip in a blanched spinach leaf. Weave four strips of each fish together to form a chequerboard, trimming the salmon as necessary. Season each mosaic well with salt and pepper.

If using seaweed, cover with cold water and leave to soak for 10 minutes, then drain. Half-fill a large frying pan with water and bring to the boil. Take a large steamer and line with the seaweed if using. Lay the fish in the steamer. Set over the frying pan. Cover and steam for about 8-10 minutes until the salmon flakes easily when tested.

"*Very dainty.*"

Michel Roux Jnr

Meanwhile prepare the sauce. Wash the sorrel leaves thoroughly and remove the thick stalks. Melt the butter in a saucepan, add the sorrel leaves and cook gently until wilted. In a separate pan, gently heat the creams together, taking care not to allow the mixture to boil. Add the fish stock and sorrel; stir well. Add the lemon juice and season with salt and pepper to taste.

To serve, place a mosaic on each warmed serving plate and pour on some of the sorrel sauce. Hand the extra sorrel sauce separately, in a small jug. Serve immediately, with wild rice and vegetable julienne.

Sara Douglas

Salmon with Coriander, Plums and Passion Fruit

700 g (1½ lb) salmon fillet, skinned and cut into 4 even-sized portions
50 g (2 oz) butter, in pieces
squeeze of lemon juice

Court Bouillon:
1 shallot or ½ medium onion
2 sticks celery
1 large carrot
300 ml (½ pint) white wine (approximately)
300 ml (½ pint) water (approximately)
10 ml (2 tsp) fennel seeds
salt and freshly ground pepper
handful of chopped coriander leaves

Plum and Passion Fruit Sauce:
2-3 passion fruit, halved
4-5 Victoria plums, stoned
10 ml (2 tsp) sugar
300 ml (½ pint) water

Garnish:
plum slivers
coriander leaves

For the court bouillon, cut the vegetables into large chunks and place in a pan which will be wide enough to hold the salmon steaks in a single layer. Add the remaining court bouillon ingredients and bring to the boil. Simmer for 20-30 minutes until the stock is a rich yellow colour. Strain off about 90-120 ml (6-8 tbsp) and reserve. Add extra wine and water to cover the vegetables if necessary.

Scoop out the seeds and pulp from the passion fruit. Chop the plums and place in a pan with the passion fruit, sugar and water. Cook until soft and jam-like in consistency. Press through a fine nylon sieve to yield a smooth sauce; set aside.

Lay the salmon on the vegetables in the court bouillon pan and allow to half steam/half poach for 4-5 minutes until cooked through, but still springy to touch.

Meanwhile reduce the reserved stock to about half of its original volume, then whisk in the butter, a piece at a time, until you have a smooth yellow sauce. Add lemon juice to taste. Lift a portion of salmon onto the centre of each plate. Spoon the court bouillon sauce on one side of the salmon and the plum and passion fruit sauce on the other side. Decorate the fruit sauce with slivers of plum. Scatter coriander leaves on the yellow sauce. Serve immediately.

Melanie Jappy

Salmon Fillet on a bed of Courgette and Ginger

with an Orange Butter Sauce

4 skinless salmon fillets, each about 140 g (4½ oz)
4 courgettes, about 525 g (1¼ lb) total weight
salt and freshly ground black pepper
olive oil and butter, for frying
10 ml (2 tsp) grated fresh root ginger
30 ml (2 tbsp) chopped chives
30 ml (2 tbsp) chopped tarragon

Dressing:
juice of 1 lime, ie 22 ml (1½ tbsp)
60 ml (4 tbsp) sunflower oil
10 ml (2 tsp) caster sugar
5 ml (1 tsp) coarse-grain mustard
freshly ground black pepper, to taste

Sauce:
120 ml (4 fl oz) fish stock (see right)
juice of 1 very large orange, ie 120 ml (4 fl oz)
15 ml (1 tbsp) wine vinegar
3 egg yolks
225 g (8 oz) unsalted butter
rind of 1 orange, removed in thin strips with a zester

To Garnish:
4-8 cherry tomatoes, halved and grilled
few steamed asparagus tips
fried courgette skin (see cook's note)

Coarsely grate the courgettes, place in a colander and sprinkle with salt. Leave to stand (over a plate to collect the degorged juices) for 2 hours.

Meanwhile, prepare the dressing. Put all of the ingredients into a screw-topped jar and shake well to combine; set aside. Prepare the garnish at this stage too.

For the sauce, put the fish stock and orange juice in a pan and boil to reduce by half. In a separate pan, bring the wine vinegar to the boil. Immediately pour onto the egg yolks, whisking constantly, preferably using a hand-held blender. Melt the butter in a pan, then very slowly add to the yolk mixture, whisking all the time; it will become very thick. Whisk in enough of the reduced stock and orange juice to give a smooth pouring consistency. Stir in the orange zest.

Season the salmon fillets liberally with salt and pepper. Brush with oil and cook under a preheated hot grill for 2-3 minutes each side. (Alternatively, fry in a little oil and butter for 1-2 minutes, then finish off under the grill for 1 minute).

Meanwhile, squeeze excess water from the courgettes, then toss with the ginger and steam for 1 minute to just heat through. Mix with the herbs and 30 ml (2 tbsp) of the dressing.

To serve, pile the courgette mixture onto warmed serving plates and surround with the sauce. Arrange the salmon on the courgette and top with the fried courgette skin. Garnish the plates with the cherry tomatoes and asparagus tips. Serve accompanied by Parsnip and Potato Cakes (page 120).

Clare Askaroff

Fish Stock: For this you will need about 1 kg (2 lb) washed fish bones and heads: use the bones from the salmon, plus plaice or sole bones. Heat 25 g (1 oz) unsalted butter in a large pan. Add 1 leek, chopped; 1 onion, finely chopped; 1 carrot, diced; and 1 stick celery, diced. Sweat the vegetables until soft, then add the fish heads and bones and cook for 1-2 minutes. Add 300 ml (½ pint) dry white wine, bring to the boil and boil for 1-2 minutes. Add 1.2 litres (2 pints) cold water, a small bunch of parsley and 2 bay leaves. Return to the boil and boil for 2 minutes, then skim the surface. Simmer for 20 minutes only. Let cool a little, then strain through a sieve. Strain again through a muslin-lined sieve. Makes about 1.2 litres (2 pints).

Cook's Note

To prepare the garnish, use a zester to remove strips of skin from 2 courgettes. Fry in sunflower oil until crisp; drain on kitchen paper.

Salmon Fillet on a bed of Courgette and Ginger with an Orange Butter Sauce

Wild Salmon Filled with Spinach Mousse in a Puff Pastry Parcel

4 fillets of wild salmon
1 egg, beaten
450 g (1 lb) ready-prepared puff pastry

Spinach Moulds:
1 kg (2¼ lb) trimmed baby spinach leaves
25 g (1 oz) butter, melted
200 ml (7 fl oz) crème fraîche
salt and freshly ground black pepper
2 egg whites (size 2)

Tomato Butter Sauce:
300 g (10 oz) ripe, full-flavoured tomatoes
40 g (1½ oz) unsalted butter, chilled and diced
5 ml (1 tsp) caster sugar
2.5 ml (½ tsp) cayenne pepper

To Garnish:
diced skinned tomato
8 baby spinach leaves

First prepare the spinach. Cook either in a steamer or in a covered pan with just the water clinging to the leaves after washing for 3 minutes. Refresh in cold water and squeeze dry. Thoroughly pat dry on kitchen paper.

Butter 4 individual moulds. Put the remaining butter in a pan on a high heat, add the spinach and cook for 2-3 minutes; do not allow to brown. Drain off any excess butter, then chop finely or purée in a food processor.

"I'd pick it every time."

Rick Wakeman

Put the crème fraîche in a small pan and reduce by one third over a medium heat. Add to the chopped spinach and season. In a bowl, whisk the egg whites until soft peaks form, then fold into the spinach. Set aside a small quantity for stuffing the salmon. Spoon the remaining mixture into the prepared moulds and place in a bain-marie, or roasting tin containing enough hot water to come halfway up the sides. Bake in a preheated oven at 180°C (350°F) mark 4 for 15-20 minutes.

Meanwhile make the salmon parcels. Roll out the pastry to a 3-5 mm (⅛-¼ inch) thickness. Cut out 4 rectangles large enough to wrap the salmon fillets in. Cut a slit in the centre of each salmon fillet and insert the reserved spinach mousse; do not overfill.

Place a stuffed salmon fillet on one side of each pastry rectangle. Brush the pastry edges with beaten egg and fold the pastry over the salmon to enclose and form a neat parcel. Press the edges together firmly. Brush the top of the parcel with more beaten egg. Decorate with shapes cut from the pastry trimmings. Brush with beaten egg to glaze. Make two small slits in the top of each parcel. Bake in a preheated oven at 200°C (400°F) mark 6 for 15 minutes or until the pastry is crisp and golden brown.

Meanwhile, make the tomato butter sauce. Halve, skin and deseed a third of the tomatoes. Place in a blender or food processor with the rest of the tomatoes and blend well. Pass the blended tomatoes through a sieve into a small pan, pressing them through with the back of a spoon. Warm gently over a low heat; do not to allow to boil or it will separate. Whisk in the butter, a piece at a time, on and off the heat. Taste and add sugar, salt and cayenne pepper.

To serve, place a salmon parcel on each warmed serving plate. Unmould a spinach mousse onto each plate and add a portion of tomato butter sauce. Garnish with diced tomato and spinach leaves. Serve at once.

Connie Stevens

Mousseline of Sea Trout

with a Coriander Hollandaise

575 g (2¼ lb) piece sea trout (middle-cut)
2-3 egg whites
300 ml (½ pint) double cream
squeeze of lime juice
squeeze of fresh ginger juice
1 clove garlic, crushed
salt and freshly ground pepper

Coriander Hollandaise:
450 ml (¾ pint) fish stock (see right)
200 g (7 oz) unsalted butter
5 egg yolks
squeeze of lemon juice (optional)
30 ml (2 tbsp) chopped coriander

To Garnish:
deep-fried leek strips (optional)

Skin and bone the sea trout, reserving the trimmings (to make a stock for the hollandaise). Lay the trout fillet out on a board and, using a suitable pastry cutter, cut 8 rounds to fit 4 ramekin dishes. Season four of the trout rounds lightly with salt and pepper and use to line the base of the buttered ramekin dishes. Place in the refrigerator, with the other rounds.

Put the rest of the sea trout in a food processor and process briefly until just smooth. With the machine running, gradually add the egg whites until the mixture is firm and smooth, then slowly add the cream. (If you have time, put the mixture in a bowl over a larger bowl of crushed ice before beating in the cream, a quarter at a time, refrigerating the mousseline for 15 minutes between each addition.) Add the lime juice, ginger juice, garlic and seasoning to taste. Chill in the refrigerator for at least 20 minutes.

"The mousseline itself was perfect."

Anna del Conte

Meanwhile, make the coriander hollandaise. Boil the fish stock to reduce down to about 15 ml (1 tbsp) liquid. Melt the butter in a pan and heat until it is bubbling. Whizz the egg yolks in a food processor, then add the reduced stock. With the machine running, gradually add the melted butter. Season with salt and pepper to taste. Stir in the coriander, and lemon juice if desired.

Spoon the chilled mousseline into the ramekins, dividing it equally between them. Smooth the surface and top with the other fish rounds. Cover each ramekin with a disc of buttered greaseproof paper and stand the dishes in a bain-marie (roasting tin containing enough boiling water to come halfway up the sides of the dishes). Bake in a preheated oven at 180°C (350°F) mark 4 for 10-12 minutes or until springy to the touch.

Run a knife around the edge of each mousseline and turn out onto individual serving dishes. Blot off any cooking juices with kitchen paper. Surround with the coriander hollandaise and garnish with thin strips of deep-fried leeks if desired. Serve at once, with accompaniments of your choice.

Alexandra Ives

Fish Stock: Put the fish trimmings in a large saucepan with 1 small onion or leek, halved; 1 carrot; 1 bay leaf and 1 small wine glass of dry white wine. Add 600 ml (1 pint) water and bring to the boil. Skim, then simmer, uncovered, for 20 minutes. Strain through a fine sieve.

Sea Bass with a Basil and Pine Nut Crust

25 g (1 oz) butter
1 shallot, chopped
3 cloves garlic, chopped
4 fillets of sea bass, each 125-150 g (4-5 oz)
1 bouquet garni
600 ml (1 pint) court bouillon (see right)

Basil and Pine Nut Crust:
50 g (2 oz) roasted pine nuts
30 ml (2 tbsp) olive oil
50 g (2 oz) fresh white breadcrumbs
20 basil leaves, finely chopped
sea salt and freshly ground black pepper

Sauce:
small bunch of flat-leaved parsley, finely chopped
75 g (3 oz) butter, in pieces
juice of 1 lemon

To Serve:
16 cherry tomatoes, skinned
basil leaves, to garnish

First prepare the basil and pine nut crust. Put the pine nuts and olive oil in a blender or food processor and work to a purée. Combine the breadcrumbs and chopped basil in a bowl, add the pine nut purée and mix thoroughly. Season with salt and pepper to taste.

Melt 25 g (1 oz) butter in a large frying pan, add the shallot and garlic, cover and sweat gently until softened. Place the sea bass fillets on the top and add the bouquet garni and court bouillon. Cover and simmer for about 5 minutes; it should be slightly undercooked at this stage. Transfer the fish to a shallow flameproof dish and spread the pine nut crust evenly on top. Cover the dish and keep warm.

"Light and subtle."

Loyd

To make the sauce, strain the cooking liquid into a saucepan and reduce by about half, then add the chopped parsley and whisk in the butter, a piece at a time. Add the lemon juice and season with salt and pepper to taste.

Place the fish under a preheated hot grill for a few minutes until the breadcrumbs are golden and the fish is cooked through. Place one fish fillet on each warmed serving plate and pour the sauce around. Garnish with cherry tomatoes and basil leaves. Serve at once.

Andrea Ferrari

Court Bouillon: Put 900 ml (1½ pints) water in a large saucepan with 1 carrot, sliced; 1 onion, sliced; 1 bouquet garni; 6 peppercorns; 2.5 ml (½ tsp) salt and 250 ml (8 fl oz) dry white wine. Bring to the boil, lower the heat and simmer gently for 30 minutes. Strain before use.

Sea Bass with a Basil and Pine Nut Crust

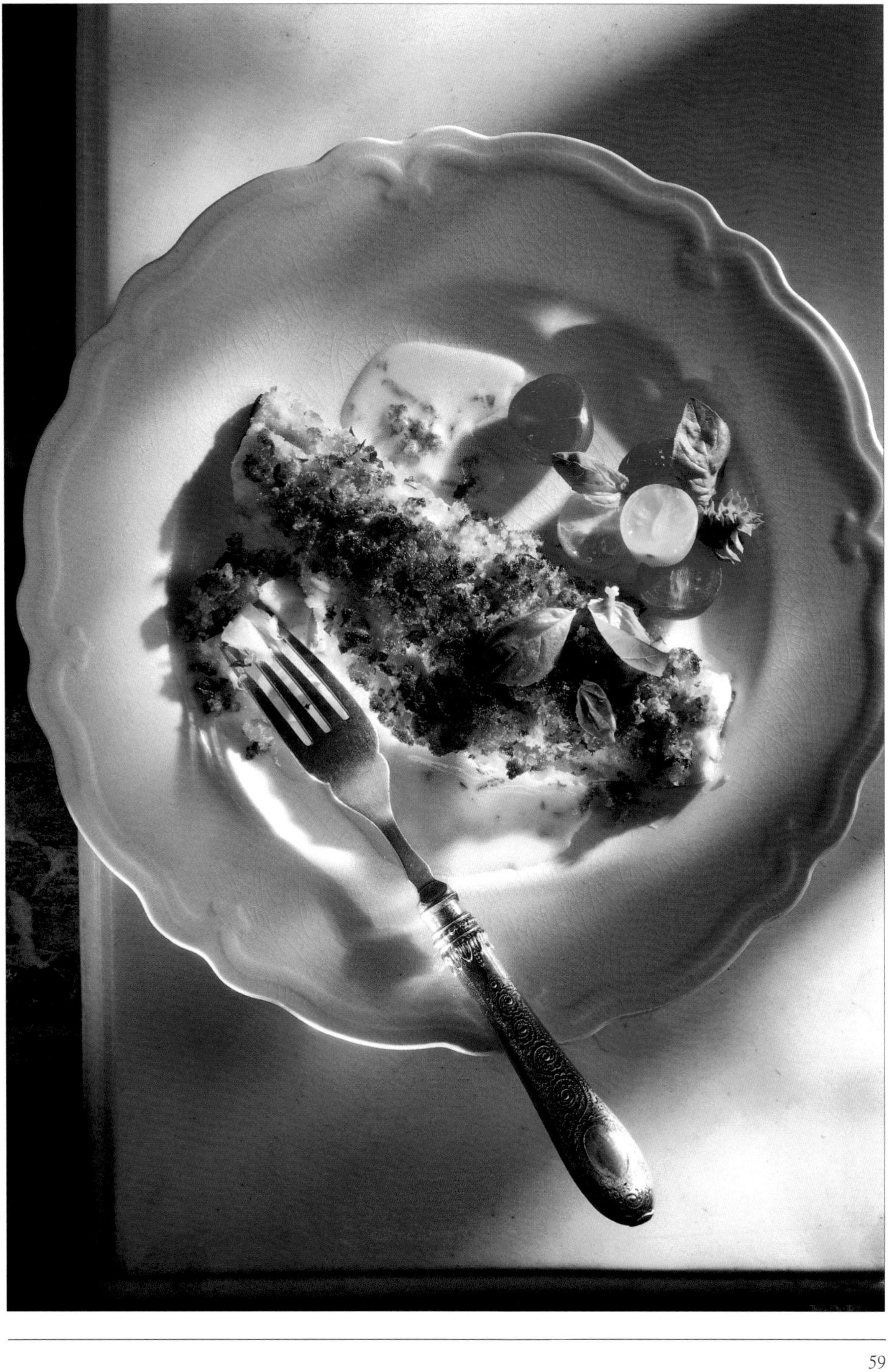

Rolled Fillets of Sole and Mixed Peppers

on a Cream and Chive Sauce

12 sole fillets, each about 50 g (2 oz), skinned
1 large lemon
½ red pepper
½ green pepper
½ yellow pepper

Sauce:
90 ml (3 fl oz) dry white wine
15 ml (1 tbsp) Noilly Prat
1 small shallot, finely chopped
250 ml (8 fl oz) fish stock
200 ml (7 fl oz) double cream
salt and freshly ground pepper
22 ml (1½ tbsp) finely chopped chives

To Garnish:
snipped chives

Place the sole fillets in a shallow dish. Grate 5 ml (1 tsp) zest from the lemon, then squeeze the juice and sprinkle the lemon juice and zest over the sole. Leave to marinate in a cool place for 2 hours.

Halve, core and deseed the peppers, then cut into thin strips. Blanch in boiling water for 3 minutes, then refresh under cold water.

To make the sauce, put the wine, Noilly Prat and shallot in a saucepan and simmer to reduce by half. Add the fish stock and reduce to one quarter. Stir in the cream and let the sauce simmer for 5 minutes until slightly thickened. Strain the sauce through a fine sieve or muslin and season with salt and pepper. Stir in the chopped chives.

Lay the sole fillets on a board and place 3 pepper strips, one of each different colour, on top. Roll up and place, seam-side down, in a steamer. Steam for 6-8 minutes.

To serve, ladle the chive sauce onto warmed serving plates and arrange the sole fillets on top. Serve immediately, garnished with chives.

James Doering

"The sole was perfect."

Stephen Bull

Sole Fillets Stuffed with Smoked Salmon Mousse

125 g (4 oz) smoked salmon
125 g (4 oz) salmon fillet
1 egg white
200 ml (8 fl oz) single cream
salt and freshly ground pepper
5 ml (1 tsp) chopped dill
8 sole fillets
45 ml (3 tsp) dry white wine
few dill sprigs
5 ml (1 tsp) tomato purée
lemon juice to taste
dill sprigs, to garnish

Cut half of the smoked salmon into strips; reserve for garnish. Chop the remaining smoked salmon and the fresh salmon, then work in a blender or food processor with the egg white, 30 ml (2 tbsp) cream and a pinch of salt. Stir in the chopped dill.

Lay the sole fillets on a board, season, then divide the salmon mixture between them. Roll up and place in a buttered shallow ovenproof dish. Pour over the wine and add the dill sprigs. Cover with foil and cook in a preheated oven at 180°C (350°F) mark 4 for about 20 minutes.

Carefully lift out the fish rolls and keep warm. Pour the cooking juices into a saucepan and boil rapidly until reduced by about half. Add the remaining cream and the tomato purée, stir well and boil for a few minutes. Season carefully, possibly adding a little lemon juice.

To serve, halve each rolled fillet and arrange on serving plates. Pour over the sauce and garnish with the reserved smoked salmon and dill.

Daphne Nelson

Fillet of Dover Sole with a Fish Mousseline

with Fish Puffs and a Watercress Sauce

2 Dover soles, each about 450 g (1 lb), skinned and filleted into 4 pieces

Fish Stock:
bones and white skin from the sole
15 g (½ oz) unsalted butter
1 small onion, chopped
50 ml (2 fl oz) dry white wine
bouquet garni (parsley, bay leaf, tarragon, fennel, chervil, white of leek, blade of mace)
1 shallot, finely chopped
3 thick lemon slices

Mousseline:
225 g (8 oz) whiting, filleted and skinned
1 egg white (size 3)
120 ml (4 fl oz) double cream
22 ml (1½ tbsp) chopped mixed herbs (parsley, tarragon, chervil)
salt and freshly ground black pepper

Pastry Fish:
150 g (5 oz) fresh puff pastry
egg yolk, to glaze

Watercress Sauce:
120 ml (4 fl oz) dry white wine
150 ml (¼ pint) double cream
1 bunch of watercress, stalks removed
15 ml (1 tbsp) cornflour

To Garnish:
tomato pieces
dill sprigs

To make the fish stock, melt the butter in a large saucepan, add the chopped onion and cook over a low heat for 2 minutes until soft but not coloured. Add the fish bones and cook for a further 2 minutes. Add the fish skin, 900 ml (1½ pints) water, the wine and bouquet garni. Bring to the boil, reduce the heat and simmer, uncovered, for 20 minutes.

> *"I enjoy those sensitive flavours."*
>
> Ian McCaskill

To prepare the mousseline, place the whiting and egg white in a food processor and blend for 2-3 minutes. Press through a sieve into a bowl set over a bowl of ice. Gradually fold the cream into the mixture. Stir in the chopped herbs and season well. Put the mixture into a piping bag fitted with a large plain nozzle.

Place each sole fillet on a board, boned-side uppermost. Pipe some of the mousseline across the centre of each fillet. Gently roll up and secure each one with a wooden cocktail stick. Place in a greased roasting tin with the shallot and lemon slices. Pour in enough fish stock to cover the base of the tin. Cover the tin with greased greaseproof paper and set aside in a cool place.

To make the pastry fish, roll out the pastry on a lightly floured surface to a rectangle. On the lower half of the pastry, pipe 8 small portions of mousseline. Fold over the top half of the pastry and press gently together around the mousseline. Cut out 8 fish shapes (see note), making sure the filling is in the centre of each fish. Place on a baking sheet, brush with beaten egg yolk to glaze and sprinkle with salt crystals. Bake in a preheated oven at 200°C (400°F) mark 6 for 8-10 minutes until golden.

Cook the fish in the oven at the same temperature for 15 minutes.

For the watercress sauce, put 300 ml (½ pint) of the remaining fish stock and the wine in a pan. Bring to the boil and boil steadily until reduced by half. Stir in the cream and cook for 1 minute. Place the sauce and the watercress leaves in a blender or food processor and blend for 1 minute. Return the sauce to the pan. Mix the cornflour to a paste with 10 ml (2 tsp) cold water. Stir into the sauce and cook, stirring, until thickened and smooth.

To serve, remove the cocktail sticks from the sole. Serve on warmed plates, on a pool of watercress sauce with the fish pastries. Garnish with tomato and dill sprigs.

Elizabeth Truscott

Cook's Note

If possible, get your fishmonger to bone the fish for you, remembering to ask for the bones which you will need for the stock. You may find it easier to use a template, cut from paper or card, as a guide when shaping the pastry fish.

MEDALLIONS OF SKYE MONKFISH

WITH A TROMPET AND TARRAGON SAUCE

700 g (1½ lb) monkfish
16 cherry tomatoes
25 g (1 oz) dried trompets (or other dried mushrooms)
300 ml (½ pint) wine fish stock
200 ml (⅓ pint) double cream
maldon salt
freshly ground white pepper
175 g (6 oz) spinach, thoroughly cleaned
tiny knob of butter
lemon juice, to taste
40 g (1½ oz) tarragon, chopped

Potato and Courgette Topping:
175 g (6 oz) potatoes, peeled
2 courgettes
oil for deep-frying

To Garnish:
tarragon sprigs

Cut the monkfish into medallions, ½-1 cm (¼-½ inch) thick, and pat dry with kitchen paper; cover and set aside in a cool place.

Place the cherry tomatoes on an oiled baking tray and roast in a preheated oven at 150°C (300°F) mark 2 for 2-3 hours.

Meanwhile soak the mushrooms in warm water to cover for 20 minutes. Transfer to a small pan and cook until the mushrooms are tender and the liquid has evaporated. In another pan, heat the fish stock. Stir in the cream and adjust the seasoning. Add the mushrooms to the sauce.

"Absolutely sensational."

Loyd

To prepare the potato and courgette topping, using a vegetable peeler, finely pare thin strips from the potatoes. Repeat with the courgettes. Pat dry with kitchen paper. Heat the oil in a deep-fryer to 190°C (375°F). Add the potato strips and fry until they just stop bubbling and begin to change colour. Remove and drain on kitchen paper; keep warm. Repeat with the courgette strips; keep warm.

Remove any tough stalks from the spinach. Place a frying pan over moderate heat. Add the butter, then the spinach and cook, turning constantly, until tender. Season with salt and pepper, and add lemon juice to taste. Set aside; keep warm.

To cook the monkfish, place a heavy-based frying pan over a high heat. Add a few drops of oil, then place the fish medallions in the pan, moving them a little initially to prevent sticking (then don't move again). Cook for about 1 minute, then turn and cook for 45 seconds. (The cooking time will depend on the thickness of the fish.) Season with salt and pepper, and sprinkle with a little lemon juice; keep warm.

Bring the sauce to the boil and stir in the chopped tarragon. Place a bed of spinach on each warmed serving plate and arrange the monkfish on top. Place 2 cherry tomatoes at each end of the fish and pour the sauce around. Sprinkle the crispy courgette and potatoes on top of the fish. Serve immediately, garnished with tarragon sprigs.

Gerry Goldwyre

Medallions of Skye Monkfish with a Trompet and Tarragon Sauce

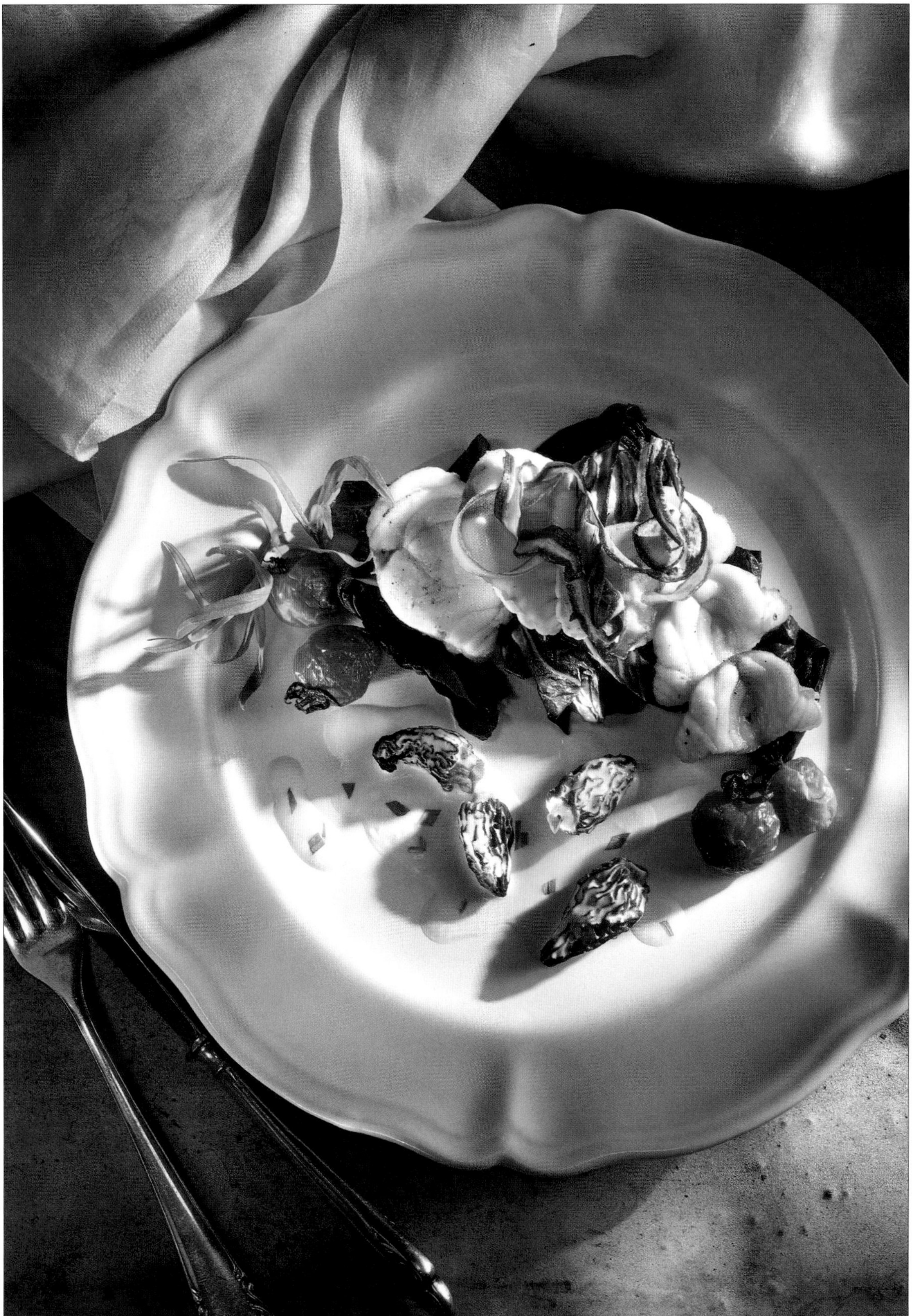

Gingered Crab and Sole Layer

with a Rhubarb Sauce

100 g (3½ oz) filo pastry
30 g (1 oz) butter
450 g (1 lb) filleted white fish (eg sole, plaice, cod)
100 g (3½ oz) young spinach leaves
15 ml (1 tbsp) crème fraîche
2 pieces preserved stem ginger in syrup, finely chopped
15 ml (1 tbsp) stem ginger syrup
225 g (8 oz) dressed crab meat
salt and freshly ground white pepper
cayenne pepper, to taste

Rhubarb Sauce:
450 g (1 lb) rhubarb
75 g (3 oz) sugar
30 ml (2 tbsp) stem ginger syrup

First make the sauce. Put the rhubarb and sugar in a saucepan with 200 ml (7 fl oz) water. Place over a low heat until the sugar is dissolved, then bring to the boil. Lower the heat and simmer for 10-15 minutes. Strain the sauce through a sieve, pressing through as much juice from the rhubarb as possible. Add the stem ginger syrup and set aside.

Place 3 sheets of filo pastry one on top of another, brushing each sheet with melted butter, then cut out 8 rectangular or diamond shapes, each about 8 x 5 cm (3 x 2 inches). Place on a greased baking sheet and bake in a preheated oven at 200°C (400°F) mark 6 for 5-10 minutes until golden and crisp.

Meanwhile, cut the fish into eight similar-sized pieces. Blanch the spinach in boiling water for 1 minute; drain thoroughly. In a bowl, mix the crème fraîche, ginger and ginger syrup with the crab and season with salt, pepper and cayenne to taste.

Place 4 pieces of fish on a foil-lined baking sheet and cover with half of the spinach. Spoon the crab meat on top, then cover with the remaining spinach. Lay the other fish pieces on top to form 4 neat stacks. Bake in a preheated oven at 200°C (400°F) mark 6 for 10 minutes until the fish is just cooked. Meanwhile reheat the sauce.

Sandwich each 'fish stack' between the cooked filo pastry pieces and serve on warmed plates on a pool of rhubarb sauce, with accompaniments of your choice.

Ashley Wilson

Fillets of John Dory

with a Cardamom Butter Sauce

1 John Dory, weighing about 1.4 kg (3 lb), filleted

Fish Stock:
25 g (1 oz) butter
fish trimming and bones
2 carrots, chopped
½ leek, chopped
1 stick celery, chopped
½ onion, chopped
1 clove garlic, chopped
½ bottle medium dry white wine
1 bay leaf
1 parsley sprig
1 thyme sprig

To Finish Sauce:
10 cardamom pods, crushed
few saffron threads
dash of lemon juice
salt and freshly ground black pepper
40 g (1½ oz) butter, in pieces

To Garnish:
¼ green pepper, cored, seeded and finely sliced
8 chives

Cook's Note

Ask your fishmonger to skin and fillet the fish – to provide 4 fillets. Remember to take the skin and bones for the stock.

First make the fish stock. Heat the butter in a wide pan and add the fish trimmings, with the chopped vegetables, garlic and herbs. Cover and sweat over a low heat until the vegetables are softened. Add the wine, herbs and 900 ml (1½ pints) water. Bring to the boil, then simmer until the stock is reduced by two thirds. Strain the stock and return to the pan.

Carefully add the fish fillets to the stock and poach gently for 10 minutes or until just cooked through. Lift out and keep warm in a covered dish. Add the crushed cardamom pods to the pan, with the saffron and a little lemon juice to lift the flavour. Reduce slightly, season to taste with salt and pepper, then whisk in the butter. Strain through a fine sieve.

Divide the sauce equally between 4 warmed serving plates and arrange the fish fillets on top. Garnish with fine slices of green pepper and chives. Serve immediately.

Roger Hemming

Turbot with a Herb Topping

on a Beurre Blanc

4 turbot steaks, each 150-175 g (5-6 oz)
30 ml (2 tbsp) chopped parsley
15 ml (1 tbsp) chopped dill
15 ml (1 tbsp) chopped thyme
5 ml (1 tsp) finely chopped rosemary leaves
600 ml (1 pint) fish stock

Sauce:
60 ml (4 tbsp) reduced fish stock
15 ml (1 tbsp) white wine vinegar
1 shallot, chopped
225 g (8 oz) unsalted butter, chilled and cut into small pieces
salt and freshly ground black pepper
juice of ½ lemon, or to taste

Mix the chopped herbs together and press 15 ml (1 tbsp) onto the top of each turbot steak. Bring the fish stock to the boil in a steamer.

To make the sauce, put the stock, vinegar and shallot in a wide pan and bring to the boil, then boil to reduce to about 30 ml (2 tbsp). Strain and return to the pan. Place over a low heat and whisk in the butter, a piece at a time, until the sauce is thick and creamy. Season with salt and pepper to taste and add enough lemon juice to sharpen the sauce. Transfer to a bowl set over a pan of hot, but not boiling, water to keep warm for no longer than 15 minutes, whisking gently from time to time.

Meanwhile, steam the turbot over the fish stock for 8-10 minutes, depending on thickness. The fish should be just opaque in the middle. Remove the skin from the fish and take out the central bone, taking care to avoid disturbing the topping too much.

To serve, spread some of the sauce on each warmed serving plate and place the turbot on top. Serve at once, with accompaniments of your choice.

Judy Geisler

"It worked very well because the fish was treated with such respect and simplicity"

Stephen Bull

POULTRY & GAME

CHICKEN BREAST FILLED WITH SUN-DRIED TOMATO AND BASIL

WRAPPED IN AUBERGINE ON A TOMATO SALSA

4 chicken breasts
12 pieces of sun-dried tomato in oil, drained
12 basil leaves, roughly torn
1 aubergine, preferably a long one
salt and freshly ground black pepper
1 chicken stock cube
olive oil, for shallow-frying

Tomato Salsa:
30 ml (2 tbsp) sun-dried tomato oil
4 shallots, thinly sliced
4 medium ripe tomatoes, skinned, seeded and sliced
8 pieces of sun-dried tomato in oil, drained
500 ml (16 fl oz) passata (sieved tomatoes)
20 ml (4 tsp) red pesto
pinch of caster sugar

To Garnish:
basil leaves

Make a deep horizontal slit in the side of each chicken breast to form a pocket. Stuff the pocket with the sun-dried tomato pieces and torn basil leaves. Wrap firmly in greaseproof paper and set aside in a cool place.

Cut two lengthwise slices from the aubergine, each about 5 mm (¼ inch) wide and place on a plate. Sprinkle with salt and leave for about 20 minutes to degorge the bitter juces.

Bring a medium pan of water to the boil and crumble in the chicken stock cube. Seal the wrapped chicken breasts in boiler bags and add to the boiling stock. Immediately turn the heat down and simmer for approximately 30 minutes.

Meanwhile, wash the aubergine slices and pat dry thoroughly. Shallow-fry in olive oil until brown on both sides; the slices should still be soft. Drain well on kitchen paper.

For the salsa, heat the sun-dried tomato oil in a pan and fry the shallots for 5 minutes, until just turning brown. Add the fresh tomato slices, the sun-dried tomato pieces and the passata, the pesto and salt, pepper and sugar to taste. Simmer for 12-15 minutes.

Lift the chicken out of the stock and unwrap. When cool enough to handle, wrap each piece of chicken in a slice of aubergine, and secure with a cocktail stick.

Place on a greased baking tray and brush the chicken and aubergine with 30 ml (2 tbsp) olive oil. Place in a preheated oven at 180°C (350°F) mark 4 for about 7-10 minutes to heat through.

To serve, remove the cocktail sticks from the chicken breasts. Ladle some tomato salsa on to each warmed serving plate and position the chicken in the centre. Garnish with basil leaves.

Katie Targett-Adams
(Junior MasterChef)

"Oh! It's delicious."

Lady Claire Macdonald

Chicken Breast filled with Sun-dried Tomato and Basil

Chicken Roulé with a Sun-dried Tomato and Mushroom Stuffing

SERVED WITH A LEMON SAUCE

4 boneless chicken breasts, skinned
175 g (6 oz) shiitake mushrooms, finely chopped
4 shallots, finely chopped
12 sun-dried tomato pieces in oil, drained and finely chopped
150 ml (¼ pint) white wine
8 rashers lightly smoked streaky bacon
salt and freshly ground black pepper
4 knobs of butter
60 ml (4 tbsp) chicken stock

Lemon Sauce:
65 g (2½ oz) butter
15 ml (1 tbsp) plain flour
120 ml (4 fl oz) chicken stock
60 ml (4 tbsp) lemon juice
120 ml (4 fl oz) double cream

For the stuffing, put the mushrooms, shallots and sun-dried tomatoes in a small pan with 90 ml (6 tbsp) of the wine and cook for about 5 minutes until the shallots are softened.

Place the chicken breasts between layers of cling film and beat with a mallet until flattened to about a 1 cm (½ inch) thickness.

Divide the mushroom mixture between the chicken breasts, spreading it to 2 cm (¾ inch) from the edge. Roll each chicken breast up fairly tightly, like a Swiss roll. Wrap each in 2 rashers of streaky bacon to hold them together.

Place each roll on a piece of foil, season and add a knob of butter. Add 15 ml (1 tbsp) wine and 15 ml (1 tbsp) stock to each parcel and wrap the foil around the chicken to enclose.

Place on a baking sheet and cook in a preheated oven at 200°C (400°F) mark 6 for 45 minutes until tender. Turn off the oven and leave to rest inside the oven for 10 minutes.

Meanwhile, make the sauce. Melt the butter in a pan and add the flour; stir well to a smooth paste and cook for 30 seconds. Gradually add the chicken stock and lemon juice, stirring continuously. Bring to the boil, and simmer for 3 minutes. Reduce the heat and stir in the cream. Heat gently; do not boil.

Slice the chicken rolls and arrange on warmed serving plates to reveal the swirls of stuffing. Serve with the sauce and accompaniments of your choice.

Helen Deacon

"*Very inventive.*"

Ainsley Harriot

Macadamia and Sesame Chicken

500 g (1 lb) chicken fillets
30 ml (2 tbsp) light soy sauce
125 g (4 oz) macadamia nuts, finely chopped
75 ml (5 tbsp) sesame seeds
1 egg white
salt
30 ml (2 tbsp) cornflour
peanut oil, for shallow-frying

To Serve:
Thai-style salad (see page 111)
red chillies, to garnish
soy sauce flavoured with chilli slices, for dipping

COOK'S NOTE

Macadamia nuts are small round buttery nuts with a delicious flavour. If unavailable, substitute cashew nuts.

Cut the chicken into thin slices and place in a shallow dish. Add the soy sauce, turn to coat and leave to marinate for 1 hour.

Combine the chopped nuts and sesame seeds in a flat dish. Beat the egg white with a pinch of salt until light and frothy. Dip the chicken pieces into the cornflour, then in the egg white. Finally coat with the nut mixture, pressing it on firmly.

"The flavour of the chicken was outstanding."

Egon Ronay

Heat the oil for shallow-frying in a frying pan until a heat haze rises. Shallow-fry the chicken in batches until golden brown. Drain well on kitchen paper and keep warm while cooking the remainder.

To serve, divide the salad between serving plates and top with the warm chicken. Garnish with chillies and serve at once, accompanied by the dipping sauce.

Alison Fiander

Chicken Breasts Stuffed with Red Peppers

4 medium chicken breasts, skinned and boned
90 ml (6 tbsp) plain flour
1 egg (size 1), beaten
75 g (3 oz) ground almonds
30 ml (2 tbsp) roasted, blanched almonds, chopped
butter or oil, for shallow-frying

Red Pepper Stuffing:
2 large red peppers
2 onions
2 garlic cloves
30 ml (2 tbsp) demerara sugar
30 ml (2 tbsp) red wine vinegar
15 ml (1 tbsp) olive oil
30 ml (2 tbsp) pine nuts

Cook's Note

Make the red pepper stuffing well in advance as it has a better taste and texture when it has been refrigerated for several hours.

To make the red pepper stuffing, roughly chop the vegetables and then put everything, except the pine nuts, into a small saucepan over a low heat. Cook very gently for about 1½ hours until it forms a glossy, rich mixture. Allow to cool before adding the pine nuts. Chill until needed.

Carefully cut a large slit in the side of each chicken breast and fill with as much of the stuffing as possible. Secure the opening with cocktail sticks, then roll the chicken breasts in the flour. Next dip in the egg and finally coat the chicken breasts in the ground and chopped roasted almonds.

Heat the butter or oil in a large non-stick frying pan until it is gently bubbling, then carefully place each chicken piece in the pan. Fry over a medium heat for about 10 minutes, then turn over and fry the other side for 10 minutes until golden brown and cooked through. Drain well on kitchen paper. Serve immediately, with accompaniments of your choice.

Katherine Smith
(Junior MasterChef)

Duck Breast with Dried Cherry and Orange Sauce

3-4 duck breasts
salt and freshly ground black pepper
45 ml (3 tbsp) cherry preserve

Sauce:
350 ml (12 fl oz) duck or brown stock
350 ml (12 fl oz) red wine
125 ml (4 fl oz) port
2.5 ml (½ tsp) thyme leaves
30 ml (2 tbsp) grated orange rind
juice of ½ orange
75 g (3 oz) dried cherries
10 ml (2 tsp) arrowroot

To make the sauce, boil the stock to reduce by half, then add the rest of the ingredients except the dried cherries and arrowroot. Simmer until reduced by half, then add the cherries and cook for a further 10 minutes. Mix the arrowroot with 5 ml (1 tsp) water, then add to the sauce and stir over a medium heat until thickened. Keep warm until ready to serve.

Rub the fat side of the duck breasts with salt and pepper, then spread with the cherry preserve. Preheat a heavy-based frying pan, then add the duck breasts, skin-side down, and sear over a high heat for 2 minutes. Turn the duck breasts over and sear the other side for 2 minutes. Transfer to a roasting tin and cover lightly with foil.

Cook the duck in a preheated oven at 200°C (400°F) mark 6 for 10-15 minutes until cooked through but still pink in the centre. Slice the duck breasts and fan out on warmed individual serving plates. Pour on the sauce and serve at once, with Potato Rösti (page 118), and courgettes flavoured with thyme.

Holly Schade

Cook's Note

Dried cherries are now readily available from delicatessens and larger supermarkets. They lend a superb flavour to both sweet and savoury dishes.

"The duck breasts were perfectly cooked... a very, very nice dish."

Willi Elsener

Duck Breast with Dried Cherry and Orange Sauce

Duck Breast in a Pastry Lattice

with Grapes and Green Lentils

2 Barbary ducks
45 ml (3 tbsp) olive oil
½ carrot, diced
½ small onion, diced
5 cm (2 inch) white part of leek, diced
½ celery stick, diced
1 thyme sprig
1 glass dry white wine
450 ml (¾ pint) good chicken stock
15 g (½ oz) butter
125 g (4 oz) seedless grapes, peeled

Pastry:
125 g (4 oz) plain flour
pinch of salt
75 g (3 oz) butter, chilled
beaten egg yolk, to glaze

For the Lentils:
50 g (2 oz) green lentils, soaked in cold water for 4 hours
1 thyme sprig
½ carrot, very finely diced
½ celery stick, very finely diced
5 cm (2 inch) piece white part of leek, very finely diced
15 g (½ oz) butter

Remove the breast fillets from the ducks; discard the skin and any excess fat. Set aside.

Chop the duck legs and carcasses and place in a roasting tin containing 30 ml (2 tbsp) of the oil. Roast in a preheated oven at 220°C (425°F) mark 7 for 20 minutes, then add the diced vegetables and thyme and roast for a further 10 minutes. Pour off the fat, then add the wine to the roasting tin and reduce over a moderate heat. Add the chicken stock and simmer, uncovered, for 20 minutes, skimming occasionally to remove any impurities as they rise to the surface. Remove the bones and strain the sauce through a fine sieve. Whisk in the butter and season with salt and pepper to taste.

Season the duck breast fillets with salt and pepper. Heat the remaining 15 ml (1 tbsp) oil in a heavy-based frying pan, add the duck breasts and seal quickly on both sides.

Meanwhile make the pastry. Sift the flour and salt into a bowl. Grate in the butter and mix together with a round-bladed knife, adding a little cold water if necessary to bind the dough. Wrap in cling film and leave the pastry to rest in the refrigerator for 20 minutes.

Cut the pastry into 4 equal portions and roll each one out to a rectangle, 3mm (⅛ inch) thick and large enough to wrap around the duck breast fillets. Roll each rectangle with the lattice roller to make 4 pastry lattices. Wrap each duck breast fillet in a pastry lattice and brush with beaten egg yolk. Cover with cling film and leave to rest in the refrigerator for 20 minutes.

Drain the lentils and cook in boiling salted water, with a sprig of thyme added, for 15 minutes. Sweat the finely diced vegetables in the butter until tender. Drain the lentils, add to the vegetables and stir to mix. Season with salt and pepper to taste.

Meanwhile cook the duck breast parcels in a preheated oven at 220°C (425°F) mark 7 for 8 minutes or until golden. Leave to rest on a rack in a warm place for 4 minutes before serving.

Just before serving, add the grapes to the sauce and heat through. Spoon a portion of lentils onto each warmed serving plate. Place a duck breast alongside and pour around some of the sauce. Hand the remaining sauce separately. Serve accompanied by mangetouts, carrots and turnips, tossed in butter.

Katherine Rendall

Cook's Note

To make the pastry lattice you will need a lattice roller. This is a plastic or perspex cylinder with 'blades' set in it available from kitchen shops and mail order cookware suppliers. As you roll the lattice roller over the pastry it cuts slits. When the pastry is lifted from the worksurface, these slits open up to form the lattice.

Pan-fried Breast of Gressingham Duck

with a Jasmine-scented Sauce

2 Gressingham ducks
15 g (½ oz) unsalted butter
15 g (½ oz) caster sugar
150 ml (¼ pint) orange juice
5 ml (1 tsp) soy sauce
120 ml (4 fl oz) cherry brandy
juice of ¼ lime
salt and freshly ground black pepper
1 jasmine tea bag
15 ml (1 tbsp) clarified butter

Remove the breasts from the ducks, discard the skin, then set aside.

Chop the duck carcasses and place in a roasting tin. Roast in a preheated oven at 230°C (450°F) mark 8 for about 20 minutes until well browned. Transfer to a large pan and add water to cover. Bring to the boil, then lower the heat and simmer for about 30 minutes. Pass through a sieve into a clean pan, then reduce over a moderate heat to 200 ml (7 fl oz). Skim off any fat from the surface.

Melt the butter in a separate pan, add the sugar and dissolve over a low heat. Increase the heat and cook until caramelised. Add the orange juice and soy sauce and reduce by about half.

Pour the cherry brandy into another pan and reduce over a moderate heat by two thirds. Add to the orange sauce with the duck stock and reduce to the desired consistency. Add the lime juice and check the seasoning.

Heat the clarified butter in a heavy-based frying pan and fry the duck breasts, skinned-side down, for 5 minutes. Turn and cook the other side for about 3 minutes until browned. Cover and leave to rest in a warm place for a few minutes. Immerse the tea bag in the sauce for a few seconds just before serving.

> "A distinctive and delicious taste."
>
> Loyd

Carve the duck breasts into thin slices and arrange on warmed serving plates. Serve with Parmesan Parsnips (page 118), and seasonal vegetables, such as new potatoes, leeks, carrots and fine green beans.

Graham Underwood

Cook's Note

Gressingham ducks are small, lean, birds prized for their full flavour and texture. They are becoming increasingly widely available.

Duck Breast with Basil and Lemon

with Mediterranean Salsa and Potato Rösti

3 duck breasts, skinned
45 ml (3 tbsp) olive oil
juice of 1 lemon
15 ml (1 tbsp) chopped basil
salt and freshly ground black pepper
a little olive oil, for frying

Salsa:
4 baby sweet peppers, cored and seeded
3 sun-dried tomatoes
few green olives, stoned
1 large clove garlic, peeled
finely grated rind of 1 lemon
45 ml (3 tbsp) set yogurt

Rosti:
2 baking potatoes
30 ml (2 tbsp) melted butter

To Garnish:
basil sprigs

Put the duck breasts in a shallow dish with the olive oil, lemon juice and basil. Turn to coat, then leave to marinate for 1½-2 hours.

To prepare the salsa, chop the peppers, sun-dried tomatoes, olives and garlic. Place in a bowl with the lemon rind and yogurt. Mix well and season with salt and pepper to taste. Set aside.

Peel and grate the potatoes for the rösti. Dry in a tea-towel to remove excess moisture, then place in a bowl. Stir in the melted butter and season liberally with salt and pepper. Divide the mixture into 4 portions.

Heat a large heavy-based frying pan until it is very hot. Add the rosti, pressing each one into a flat round cake, using the back of a fish slice. Cook for about 5 minutes until golden brown underneath, then turn the rösti and cook the other side until crisp and golden brown. Transfer to a warmed plate and keep hot in a warm oven.

Meanwhile, remove the duck breasts from the marinade. Heat a little olive oil in a heavy-based frying pan, add the duck breasts, skin-side down, and fry over a moderate heat for 6-8 minutes. Turn the duck breasts over, lower the heat and cook for 6-8 minutes until tender but still pink inside. Remove from the pan, wrap in foil and leave to rest for 5 minutes.

To serve, carve the duck breasts crosswise into thick slices. Place a rösti on each warmed serving plate and arrange the slices of duck alongside. Spoon the salsa on top of the rosti and garnish with basil sprigs. Serve at once, accompanied by braised leeks and carrots.

Sarah Dyson

"That worked really well."

Pat MacDonald

Duck Breast with Basil and Lemon, with Mediterranean Salsa and Potato Rösti

STUFFED GUINEA FOWL BREAST

2 guinea fowl
2 carrots, finely chopped
4 shallots, finely chopped
2 garlic cloves, finely chopped
salt and freshly ground black pepper
120 ml (4 fl oz) Vin Santo (strong sweet Tuscan wine), or a sweet Sauternes
5-10 ml (1-2 tsp) chopped mixed herbs (thyme, rosemary and marjoram), to taste
pinch of dried oregano
1 egg

Garlic Butter:
25 g (1 oz) butter, melted
½ garlic clove, crushed

Beurre Rouge Sauce:
15 g (½ oz) butter
2 shallots, finely chopped
175 ml (6 fl oz) red wine
75-100 g (3-4 oz) butter, chilled and diced

Skin the guinea fowl, then carefully remove the breasts by slicing down each carcass from the breastbone; set aside. Strip the flesh from the wings, legs and carcasses, discarding any fatty tissue. Chop this meat for the stuffing.

To prepare the stuffing, sprinkle the chopped carrots, shallots and garlic over the base of a baking dish. Add the reserved chopped guinea fowl flesh. Season with salt and pepper and sprinkle with 60 ml (2 fl oz) of the wine. Cover and cook in a preheated oven at 180°C (350°F) mark 4 for 15 minutes.

Allow the mixture to cool slightly, then transfer to a food processor. Add the herbs and egg and work to a coarse cream.

To prepare each guinea fowl breast, hold down on the work surface with one hand and, using a sharp knife, slice into the breast horizontally to make a pocket, but do not cut right through. Open up carefully, then cover with a sheet of greaseproof paper. Beat with a meat mallet or rolling pin until it is almost 12 cm (5 inches) in diameter, without splitting in half.

Mound 2 tablespoonfuls of the stuffing into each pocket, then roll up and tie neatly with string; reserve the remaining stuffing. Put the guinea fowl breasts in the baking dish (used for the stuffing).

For the garlic butter, mix the melted butter with the garlic. Brush the guinea fowl breasts with garlic butter and season with salt and pepper. Sprinkle with the remaining wine. Cook in the oven at 180°C (350°F) mark 4 for 20 minutes.

To make the beurre rouge sauce, melt the butter in a pan, add the shallots and sauté gently for 2 minutes. Meanwhile press the reserved stuffing through a fine sieve to extract the juices. Add this liquid to the pan with the red wine and bring to the boil. Boil the sauce until it is well reduced and the shallots are just visible.

Remove the pan from the heat and whisk in the butter a piece at a time, making sure each piece is thoroughly incorporated before adding the next. Continue whisking until the sauce is the consistency of mayonnaise.

Remove the string from the guinea fowl breasts and replace with blanched chive strips. Place on warmed serving plates and spoon on the sauce. Serve immediately, with the Celeriac Rösti (page 117), mangetouts and carrots.

Derek Johns

GUINEA FOWL IN RED WINE WITH CHESTNUTS

4 guinea fowl breasts

Stock:
30 ml (2 tbsp) olive oil
2 guinea fowl carcasses
2 onions, roughly chopped
2 carrots, roughly chopped
½ bottle full-bodied red wine
5 ml (1 tsp) juniper berries
1 bay leaf
bouquet garni

To Finish:
15 ml (1 tbsp) olive oil
¼ bottle full-bodied red wine
300 ml (½ pint) guinea fowl stock
30 ml (2 tbsp) black treacle
1 bay leaf
225 g (8 oz) frozen chestnuts, defrosted
salt and freshly ground black pepper
10 ml (2 tsp) arrowroot

COOK'S NOTE

Get your poulterer or butcher to bone the guinea fowl for you, remembering to ask for the carcasses which you will need for the stock.

First make the stock. Heat the oil in a large pan, add the guinea fowl carcasses and brown well. Add the onions and carrots and sauté until lightly browned. Add 600 ml (1 pint) water and all the other stock ingredients. Bring to the boil, lower the heat and simmer gently for about 3 hours.

Strain the stock into a bowl and allow to cool. Refrigerate when cold so that the fat sets on the surface. Discard this fat layer before use.

To cook the guinea fowl, heat the oil in a heavy-based frying pan over a medium-high heat. Add the guinea fowl breasts and brown on both sides. Add the wine, stock, treacle, bay leaf, chestnuts and salt and pepper. Bring to the boil, lower the heat and simmer for 15-20 minutes.

Mix the arrowroot to a paste with a little cold water. Remove the guinea fowl breasts from the pan and keep warm. Add the arrowroot paste to the sauce, stirring continuously. Cook, stirring, for 2-3 minutes.

To serve, slice the guinea fowl breasts and arrange on warmed individual serving plates with the chestnuts. Spoon over the sauce and serve at once, with accompaniments.

Keely Smith

Pan-fried Breast of Wood Pigeon

with a Wild Rowanberry Sauce

4 wood pigeons, plucked and drawn

Marinade:

¼ bottle full-bodied red wine
30 ml (2 tbsp) olive oil
1 clove garlic, crushed
2 bay leaves
1 thyme sprig or 5 ml (1 tsp) dried thyme
6 black peppercorns
salt and freshly ground black pepper

Sauce:

150 ml (¼ pint) well-flavoured pigeon stock (see right)
30 ml (2 tbsp) rowan jelly
½ square dark bitter chocolate
40 g (1½ oz) unsalted butter, in pieces

Croûtons:

4 slices wholemeal bread
25 g (1 oz) butter
15 ml (1 tbsp) hazelnut oil

To Garnish:

lamb's lettuce
12 steamed sugar snap peas

Remove the breasts from the pigeons, using a sharp knife. Use the carcasses to make the stock (see right).

For the marinade, combine the red wine, olive oil, garlic, bay leaves, thyme, black peppercorns and a pinch of salt in a large bowl. Add the pigeon breasts, turn to coat and leave to marinate for at least 5 hours, preferably overnight.

Shortly before serving, prepare the croûtons. Using a mug or similar sized guide, cut a disc from each slice of wholemeal bread. Melt the butter in a frying pan with the hazelnut oil. When hot, add the bread rounds and fry, turning once, until crisp and golden brown on both sides. Drain on kitchen paper and keep warm.

Lift the pigeon breasts out of the marinade and pat dry with kitchen paper. Strain the marinade and reserve. Place a non-stick frying pan over a moderate heat (without any fat). When it is very hot, add the pigeon breasts and sear for 2-3 minutes each side. Remove, cover with foil and leave to rest in a warm place.

Add the strained marinade to the pan, stirring with a wooden spoon to scrape up any sediment. Transfer to a saucepan and add the pigeon stock. Slowly bring to the boil, skim, then add the rowan jelly and stir until melted. Add the chocolate and again stir until incorporated. Simmer to reduce by one third or until the sauce has a syrupy consistency. Whisk in the butter, a piece at a time, and season with salt and pepper to taste.

To serve, slice each pigeon breast horizontally in two. Pool the sauce on the warmed serving plates and float a croûton in the centre. Arrange the pigeon slices on the croûton and top with a little lamb's lettuce. Garnish with sugar snap peas and serve with accompaniments.

Roger Hemming

Pigeon Stock: Chop the pigeon carcasses, place in a roasting tin and roast in a preheated oven at 450°C (230°F) mark 8 for 30 minutes until well browned. Transfer to a large saucepan and add 1.2 litres (2 pints) water, 1 chopped onion, 1 chopped carrot, 1 chopped celery stick and a bouquet garni. Bring to the boil and simmer for 3-4 hours; Strain.

Salmis of Pheasant with Chestnuts and Redcurrants

2 pheasants
16 fresh chestnuts (or vacuum-packed chestnuts)
175 g (6 oz) unsalted butter
10 ml (2 tsp) sugar
600 ml (1 pint) pheasant stock (see right)
salt and freshly ground black pepper
15 ml (1 tbsp) red wine vinegar
30 ml (2 tbsp) brandy
150 ml (¼ pint) red wine (eg Burgundy)
10 ml (2 tsp) redcurrant jelly
50 g (2 oz) redcurrants

Remove the breasts and wing tips from the pheasants by scraping a knife between the bone and the breast along to the wing, cutting through the bone at the wing end if necessary. Use the carcasses to make the stock (see right).

If using fresh chestnuts, make a slit in their shells, then add to a pan of boiling water and cook for about 30 minutes. Drain and cool slightly, then peel off the shells and skins.

Melt 50 g (2 oz) butter in a non-stick pan, then add the sugar, chestnuts and 60 ml (2 fl oz) pheasant stock. Cook over a very low heat, turning occasionally, until the liquid has almost evaporated and the chestnuts are glazed.

Season the pheasant breasts with salt and pepper. Heat 50 g (2 oz) of the butter in a large pan. Add the pheasant breasts, skin-side down, and cook until golden brown, then turn and brown the underside. Add the wine vinegar, then the brandy and half of the stock. Bring to the boil, reduce the heat and simmer gently for 10-15 minutes, depending on the thickness of the breasts, until just slightly pink in the middle. Remove from the pan and keep warm.

Add the rest of the stock to the pan with the wine and redcurrant jelly and boil rapidly until reduced by half. Whisk in the remaining 50 g (2 oz) butter, a piece at a time, until the sauce is glossy. Stir in the redcurrants.

To serve, cut the pheasant breasts into fine slices, leaving a portion attached to the wing. Fan the slices out on warmed serving plates. Garnish with the chestnuts and spoon the sauce around. Serve at once, accompanied by Wild Rice with Lemon Grass (page 121) and Braised Celery Hearts (page 113).

Elaine Bates

Pheasant Stock: Heat 30 ml (2 tbsp) oil in a large pan and brown the pheasant carcasses. Roughly chop 2 onions and 2 carrots; add these to the pan and brown. Add a sprig of thyme and 600 ml (1 pint) water. Bring to the boil, then lower the heat and simmer for 10 minutes. Add a bottle of full-bodied red wine (eg Burgundy), 5 ml (1 tsp) juniper berries, a bay leaf and a bouquet garni. Bring back to the boil, lower the heat and simmer gently for about 3 hours. At this stage, there should be about 600 ml (1 pint). Strain the stock into a bowl and allow to cool. Refrigerate when cold so that the fat sets on the surface. Remove this before use.

Salmis of Pheasant with Chestnuts and Redcurrants

Pan-fried Breast of Pheasant

with a Date and Red Wine Sauce

4 pheasant breasts
25 g (1 oz) butter
30 ml (2 tbsp) olive oil
salt and freshly ground black pepper

Date and Red Wine Sauce:
knob of butter
4 shallots, finely chopped
3 cloves garlic, finely chopped
75 ml (5 tbsp) red wine
30 ml (2 tbsp) brandy
6 fresh dates, stoned and roughly chopped
24 peppercorns, crushed
15 ml (1 tbsp) plain flour
600 ml (1 pint) chicken stock (see right)

To Garnish:
4 fresh dates

First make the sauce. Melt the knob of butter in a saucepan, add the shallots and garlic, cover and sweat gently until softened. Add the red wine and reduce until the wine has almost completely evaporated. Add the brandy and reduce again.

Add the chopped dates and crushed peppercorns; cook for 2-3 minutes. Add the flour and mix well, then stir in the chicken stock. Allow to simmer for 10 minutes, then pass through a conical sieve into a clean saucepan, pressing the ingredients through to extract as much flavour as possible. Check the seasoning. Keep warm while cooking the pheasant.

To cook the pheasant breasts, heat the butter and oil in a large frying pan. When sizzling, add the pheasant breasts and fry, turning constantly, for 8-10 minutes or until cooked through. Transfer to a warmed plate, season with salt and pepper and leave to rest in a low oven for a few minutes.

To serve, place the pheasant breasts on warmed serving plates and pour over the sauce. Serve immediately, garnished with dates.

Chris Rand

"That works rather well."

Carol Thatcher

Chicken Stock: Put 1.4 kg (3 lb) chicken wings in a large saucepan and pour on about 1.7 litres (3 pints) water. Bring to the boil and skim. Add 2 carrots, peeled and quartered; 1 stick celery, chopped; 2 leeks, sliced; 2 small onions quartered; salt, pepper and a bouquet garni. Lower the heat, cover and simmer for 2 hours. Strain and use as required.

Pan-fried Fillet of Wild Rabbit

in a Juniper and Hermitage Sauce

8 fillets of wild rabbit
15-30 ml (1-2 tbsp) light olive oil, for frying

Marinade:
60 ml (4 tbsp) Hermitage red wine
30 ml (2 tbsp) port
30 ml (2 tbsp) cognac
2 thyme sprigs
2 bay leaves
salt and freshly ground black pepper

Sauce:
600 ml (1 pint) well-flavoured stock
reserved marinade ingredients
12 juniper berries
125 g (4 oz) button mushrooms, chopped
10 ml (2 tsp) rowan jelly
15 g (½ oz) unsalted butter, chilled and diced
25 g (1 oz) chanterelles

Cook's Note

For the sauce, make a well-flavoured stock using rabbit and veal bones if possible.

Mix together the ingredients for the marinade in a shallow dish. Add the rabbit fillets and turn to coat with the marinade. Cover and leave in the refrigerator for at least 1½ hours. Remove the rabbit fillets, reserving the marinade.

Pour the stock into a saucepan and add the marinade ingredients, juniper berries, mushrooms and rowan jelly. Bring to the boil, lower the heat and simmer, uncovered, for 20-30 minutes. Strain the sauce into a clean saucepan. Reduce by half, tossing in the chanterelles towards the end of the reduction. Just before serving, whisk in the butter, a piece at a time, and check the seasoning.

To cook the rabbit, heat the oil in a heavy-based frying pan. Add the rabbit fillets and fry, turning constantly, over a high heat for 3-4 minutes. Remove from the pan, wrap in foil and leave to rest in a warm place for 5-10 minutes.

To serve, slice the rabbit fillets at an angle to give long thin slices and arrange in rosettes on warmed serving plates. Spoon the sauce and chanterelles around the rabbit. Serve at once, accompanied by the vegetables of your choice.

Elaine Ford

FILLET OF HIGHLAND HARE

WITH WILD MUSHROOMS IN A CREAMY MARSALA SAUCE

2 saddles of hare
10 ml (2 tsp) hazelnut oil
8 dried morels
175 g (6 oz) mixed wild and cultivated mushrooms (eg chanterelles, boletus, pied de mouton, chestnut mushrooms)
salt and freshly ground black pepper
10 ml (2 tsp) olive oil
40 g (1½ oz) unsalted butter
300 ml (½ pint) hare stock
120 ml (4 fl oz) Marsala
150 ml (¼ pint) double cream

Forcemeat Balls:
50 g (2 oz) reserved hare meat
50 g (2 oz) chestnut mushrooms
7.5 ml (1½ tsp) double cream
salt and freshly ground black pepper

To Garnish:
chervil sprigs

Carefully remove the fillets and the tiny fillets mignon from the saddles of hare, reserving the carcasses to make the stock. Place the meat in a shallow dish, drizzle with the hazelnut oil and rub in. Leave to marinate for about 24 hours. Trim the ends off the fillets; reserve the trimmings and the fillets mignon for the forcemeat balls.

The next day soak the dried morels in warm water to cover for 30 minutes; drain, straining and reserving a little of the liquid. Slice all of the fresh mushrooms and set aside.

To make the forcemeat balls, put the reserved hare meat and mushrooms in a food processor and process until finely chopped. Mix with the cream and season with salt and pepper. Divide into 4 equal portions and roll into balls. Cover and keep in a cool place until needed, then bake in a preheated oven at 190°C (375°F) mark 5 for 5-6 minutes until set.

Season the hare fillets with salt and pepper. Heat the oil and a knob of butter in a frying pan. When hot, add the hare fillets and sear on both sides over a high heat for 3-5 minutes, depending on size; the fillets should still be quite pink. Remove and keep warm.

Pour off the fat then add the remaining butter to the pan and sauté the fresh mushrooms for a few minutes. Season with salt and pepper, remove from the pan and keep warm. Add the stock and reserved morel soaking liquid. Reduce almost by half, then add the Marsala and reduce again. When the alcohol has evaporated, add the cream and reduce until the sauce thickens. Add the morels and heat through.

To serve, carve the hare fillets into 6-7 collops and arrange on warmed serving plates in a circle around a mound of stir-fried leeks. Garnish with the mixed mushrooms and spoon over the sauce. Position a forcemeat ball on the leeks and garnish the plates with chervil.

Marion MacFarlane

COOK'S NOTE

It is essential to use a young hare. Remember that you will need to marinate the fillets for 24 hours before cooking.

Sliced Fillet of Venison with Damson Sauce

450 g (1 lb) boned loin of venison
150 ml (¼ pint) good red wine
5-10 ml (1-2 tsp) juniper berries, lightly crushed
2.5 ml (½ tsp) sea salt
freshly ground black pepper
15 ml (1 tbsp) sunflower oil

Damson Sauce:
25 g (1 oz) damson cheese (or damson jam), cut into small pieces
10 ml (2 tsp) crème fraîche

To Garnish:
flat-leaved parsley

Cut the venison into 4 equal slices. Place in a shallow dish and pour over the red wine. Add the juniper berries, salt and a generous grinding of pepper. Stir, then cover and leave to marinate for 2 hours.

Remove the meat from the marinade and pat dry with kitchen paper; strain the marinade through a fine sieve and set aside. Heat the oil in a sauté pan over a high heat until smoking. Add the meat and cook quickly, turning constantly, for 4 minutes. Remove the meat from the pan and keep warm.

Add the marinade to the pan with the damson cheese. Simmer gently until the cheese has melted. Adjust the seasoning, remove from the heat and stir in the crème fraîche.

To serve, place the venison slices on warmed serving plates and pour on the damson sauce. Garnish with parsley and serve with accompaniments of your choice.

Derek Morris

Fillet of Spiced Venison with Mulled Fruits

4 venison fillets, trimmed
16 dried figs or prunes
16 dried apricots
600 ml (1 pint) red wine
2 sachets of mulling spices (or 3 cinnamon sticks, 8 crushed juniper berries and 12 cloves)
15 ml (1 tbsp) olive oil
salt and freshly ground black pepper

To Serve:
Grilled Polenta (page 121)

Cook's Note

For this recipe, you really need to marinate the venison and fruits 24 hours ahead.

Lay the venison fillets in a shallow dish with the dried fruits. Pour in the wine and add the spices. Cover and leave to marinate for 24 hours.

Lift the venison fillets out of the marinade. Remove and discard the spices from the marinade. Heat the olive oil in a frying pan, add the venison fillets and cook for about 3 minutes each side, depending on the thickness of the meat. Ideally it should still be quite pink inside. Remove the meat from the pan; cover and keep warm.

Add the marinade and fruit to the pan, stirring to scrape up the sediment. Allow the sauce to simmer, uncovered, for about 15 minutes, until reduced by half and slightly thickened. Season with salt and pepper to taste.

Cut each venison fillet into 6 slices and return to the pan. Heat through for 1-2 minutes, then arrange the venison slices in a fan-shape on each warmed serving plate. Surround with the mulled fruits and sauce. Serve at once, accompanied by the Grilled Polenta and steamed asparagus or mangetouts.

Andrea Ferrari

Fillet of Spiced Venison with Mulled Fruits

Medallions of Venison in a Rich Red Wine Sauce

575 g (1¼ lb) venison fillet (plus the bones from the saddle)
salt and freshly ground black pepper
a little oil, for cooking

Marinade:
30 ml (2 tbsp) olive oil
50 g (2 oz) shallots, finely chopped
50 g (2 oz) carrots, diced
125 g (4 oz) celery, diced
50 g (2 oz) mushrooms, diced
45 ml (3 tbsp) red wine vinegar
500 ml (16 fl oz) full-bodied red wine
5 ml (1 tsp) juniper berries
small bunch of thyme sprigs
1 bay leaf
2 cloves garlic, finely chopped

Sauce:
30 ml (2 tbsp) dark treacle or molasses
60 ml (4 tbsp) light soy sauce

To Garnish:
thyme sprigs

Cook's Note

This dish is better if the venison is allowed to marinate for 2-3 days. If time is short you can use roe deer to avoid marinating. Ask your butcher to fillet the saddle and chop the bones into small pieces.

To prepare the marinade, heat the oil in a heavy-based pan until hot, then brown the venison bones. Transfer to a large bowl. Add the shallots, carrots, celery and mushrooms to the pan and cook until golden. Deglaze the pan with the vinegar, transfer to the bowl and allow to cool. Cut the venison into 4 equal portions and add to the bowl, with the wine, juniper berries, thyme, bay leaf and garlic. Leave to marinate in the refrigerator for up to 3 days.

Remove the venison from the marinade, pat dry and set aside in a cool place. Transfer the marinade (including the bones and vegetables) to a pan, bring to the boil and reduce by half. Stir in the treacle or molasses, 200 ml (7 fl oz) water and the soy sauce. Simmer for 1 hour or until reduce to a shiny sauce-like consistency.

About 20 minutes before the sauce has finished reducing, cut the venison into medallions, about 2.5 cm (1 inch) thick. Flatten slightly with the palm of your hand and season with salt and pepper. Heat a thin film of oil in a frying pan until very hot, add the medallions and seal on each side. Transfer to a lightly oiled baking tray then roast in a preheated oven at 190°C (375°F) mark 5 for about 5 minutes; keep warm.

Strain the sauce through a fine sieve and season with pepper to taste.

Arrange the venison medallions on warmed serving plates and pour the sauce over and around them. Garnish with thyme and serve with accompaniments of your choice.

Michael Deacon

Tuscan-style Venison

15 g (½ oz) dried porcini mushrooms
700-900 g (1½-2 lb) venison
salt and freshly ground black pepper
flour, for coating
olive oil and butter, for cooking
125 g (4 oz) pancetta, derinded and chopped
1-2 cloves garlic, chopped
2 onions, finely chopped
2 carrots, finely chopped
2 sticks celery, finely chopped
500 ml (16 fl oz) dry red wine
500 ml (16 fl oz) passata
a little stock (optional)

Dolce Forte:
125 ml (4 fl oz) red wine vinegar
40 g (1½ oz) raisins
25 g (1 oz) pine nuts
40 g (1½ oz) plain chocolate chips
15 ml (1 tbsp) sugar

Soak the dried porcini in 150 ml (¼ pint) hot water for 20 minutes; drain.

Cut the venison into chunks and toss in seasoned flour to coat. Heat some olive oil and butter together in a heavy-based pan or braising pot, then brown the venison in batches on all sides, adding more oil and butter as necessary. Remove and set aside.

Add the pancetta and the garlic to the pan and sauté briefly, then add the oinions and sauté for a few minutes. Add the porcini, carrots and celery and cook, stirring, for a few minutes. Add the red wine and cook for about 5 minutes. Stir in the passata and cook, uncovered, for about 15 minutes.

Return the venison to the pan and cook for 15 minutes. Add the *dolce forte* ingredients and cook for a further 5 minutes. Leave the lid off the pot throughout the cooking time. If the sauce is too thick, thin with a little stock.

Serve accompanied by creamed potatoes flavoured with snipped chives, and green beans.

Alison Fiander

Venison with Black Pudding

and a Mushroom Sauce

4 venison fillets, each about 150 g (5 oz)
30 ml (2 tbsp) olive oil

Marinade:
150 ml (¼ pint) olive oil
150 ml (¼ pint) red wine
30 ml (2 tbsp) balsamic vinegar
1 celery stalk, chopped
20 juniper berries, crushed
salt and freshly ground black pepper

Mushroom Sauce:
15 ml (1 tbsp) demerara sugar
15 ml (1 tbsp) balsamic vinegar
475 ml (15 fl oz) chicken stock
120 ml (4 fl oz) well-flavoured mushroom stock
10 ml (2 tsp) redcurrant jelly

Black Pudding Purée:
225 g (8 oz) black pudding
30 ml (2 tbsp) olive oil
50 ml (2 fl oz) chicken stock (approximately)

"The black pudding made the venison more interesting...it lent a richness and a different texture."

Loyd

Mix all the marinade ingredients together in a shallow dish. Add the venison fillets, cover and leave to marinate in the refrigerator for 2-4 hours.

Meanwhile, make the sauce. Melt the sugar in a small heavy-based saucepan over a low heat, then continue to cook over a medium heat without stirring until caramelised. Carefully add the balsamic vinegar and about 30 ml (2 tbsp) of the stock (protect your hand with a cloth as the mixture will boil and spurt furiously). Continue heating and stirring until the caramel has dissolved; if necessary, stubborn pieces of caramel can be removed with a slotted spoon and discarded. Add the rest of the stock, and the redcurrant jelly. Bring to the boil and reduce to approximately 300 ml (½ pint). Strain through a fine sieve and season with salt and pepper to taste.

Steam the black pudding for 10 minutes, then transfer to a food processor or blender with the olive oil. Process, adding sufficient stock to make a fairly smooth purée (the purée will not be perfectly smooth but should be processed long enough to be reasonably so).

Heat the olive oil in a heavy-based frying pan, add the venison fillets and fry over a medium-high heat for 2 minutes on each of the four sides. Wrap in foil and leave to rest in a warm place for 5-10 minutes. Reheat the sauce and the black pudding purée. Slice each venison fillet into 6 or 8 pieces. Arrange the venison slices on a bed of swede purée, fanned out and sandwiched with a little of the black pudding. Serve surrounded by a pool of sauce.

Ashley Wilson

MEAT DISHES

Fillet of Beef with a Herb Crust

750 g (1 lb 10 oz) middle-cut fillet of beef, in one piece
freshly ground black pepper
45 ml (3 tbsp) olive oil
1 egg yolk, beaten

Herb Crust:
4 slices smoked back bacon
25 g (1 oz) pistachio nuts
2 slices granary bread
60 ml (4 tbsp) chopped parsley
50-75 g (2-3 oz) butter, melted
1 clove garlic, crushed
5 ml (1 tsp) coarse-grain mustard
5 ml (1 tsp) Worcestershire sauce
freshly ground black pepper

Sauce:
15 ml (1 tbsp) olive oil
1 onion, chopped
2 large mushrooms, chopped
300 ml (½ pint) brown beef stock
120 ml (4 fl oz) red wine
15 ml (1 tbsp) sherry
salt and freshly ground black pepper

To Serve:
25 g (1 oz) butter
50 g (2 oz) wild mushrooms, or shiitake
squeeze of lemon juice

Begin by making the sauce. Heat the olive oil in a pan, add the onion and mushrooms and cook until golden brown. Pour on the stock and red wine and bring to the boil. Simmer until reduced to a shiny sauce consistency. Strain into a clean pan and add the sherry. Season well. Set aside until ready to serve.

To prepare the herb crust, grill the bacon until crispy; let cool, then chop finely in a food processor. Place in a large shallow dish. Finely chop the nuts in the food processor; add to the bacon. Whizz the bread in the processor to make fine breadcrumbs; add to the dish with the parsley. Mix the melted butter with the garlic, mustard and Worcestershire sauce. Pour onto the crumb mixture, season well with pepper and mix thoroughly. (The bacon will probably add sufficient salt.) Set aside.

Season the meat liberally with pepper. Heat the olive oil in a frying pan and quickly seal the meat on all sides, over a high heat. Cool a little, then brush the top and sides with beaten egg yolk. Coat with the crumb mixture, pressing it very firmly onto the meat to ensure it adheres. Place in a roasting tin and roast in a preheated oven at 190°C (375°F) mark 5 for about 30 minutes to give a rare meat.

Shortly before serving, reheat the sauce. Heat the butter in another pan and sauté the mushrooms until they have just softened. Add a squeeze of lemon juice and pepper to taste.

Leave the beef to rest for a few minutes after cooking, then carve into thick slices, allowing 2-3 per person. Arrange on warmed serving plates with the wild mushrooms. Pour on the sauce and serve accompanied by a Warm Spinach Salad (page 108) and Sweet Potato Bakes (page 120).

Clare Askaroff

"The crust on that beef was wonderful, and the sauce was really, really spectacular."

William Waldegrave

Fillet of Beef with a Herb Crust

Fillet of Beef with Oriental Mushrooms

575 g (1½ lb) fillet of beef, in one piece
15 g (½ oz) dried wild ceps or porcini
40 g (1½ oz) butter
225 g (8 oz) mixed fresh mushrooms (eg shiitake, oyster and brown cap)
2 cloves garlic, crushed
30 ml (2 tbsp) rich soy sauce
7.5 ml (1½ tsp) sweet chilli sauce
45 ml (3 tbsp) black bean sauce
10 ml (2 tsp) yellow bean sauce
10 ml (2 tsp) oyster sauce
5 ml (1 tsp) five-spice powder
salt and freshly ground black pepper
2.5-5 ml (½-1 tsp) sugar

Put the dried mushrooms in a bowl, pour on 175 ml (6 fl oz) hot water and leave to soak for 20 minutes.

Melt 25 g (1 oz) of the butter in a pan, add the fresh mushrooms and garlic and cook over a medium heat for 3-4 minutes. Drain the soaked mushrooms, reserving the liquid, add to the pan and cook for 2 minutes. Stir in the oriental sauces, then add the five-spice powder and cook for a further 1 minute. Season with salt and pepper, and add sugar to taste. Add the reserved mushroom soaking liquid and cook over a medium heat until the sauce is reduced and thickened. Add 175 ml (6 fl oz) water and reduce once more, until thickened.

Insert a long pointed knife into one end of the beef fillet to make a slit through to the centre. Repeat from the other end – hopefully meeting in the middle – to form a cavity for the stuffing. With a slotted spoon, remove some of the mushrooms from the sauce and use to fill the beef fillet cavity. Either sew up both ends or secure with skewers.

Melt the remaining butter and brush over the stuffed beef fillet. Place under a preheated medium grill for 7 minutes, turning occasionally to seal on all sides. Transfer to a baking tray and cook in a preheated oven at 180°C (350°F) mark 4 for 20 minutes for rare meat, or longer if preferred.

When cooked, cover the beef and leave to stand in a warm place for 5 minutes. Meanwhile, reheat the mushroom sauce. Cut the beef into thick slices and place on warmed serving plates. Pour the mushrooms and sauce over and around the beef. Serve at once, with the accompaniments.

Connie Stevens

Beef Olives in an Onion and Herb Sauce

12 thin slices Aberdeen Angus sirloin beef, about 150 g (5 oz) total weight
salt and freshly ground black pepper
olive oil for frying

Marinade:
60 ml (4 tbsp) extra-virgin olive oil
10 ml (2 tsp) golden syrup
juice of 1 lemon
6 spring onions, finely chopped
30 ml (2 tbsp) chopped parsley
leaves from 2 rosemary sprigs, chopped

Stuffing:
50 g (2 oz) butter
6-8 spring onions, chopped
125 g (4 oz) mushrooms, sliced
chopped thyme and parsley leaves, to taste
fresh breadcrumbs from 3 slices of granary bread

Sauce:
30 ml (2 tbsp) vegetable oil
1 large onion, finely sliced
2 handfuls button mushrooms, finely chopped
2 cloves garlic, finely chopped or crushed
leaves from 6 thyme sprigs
450 ml (¾ pint) vegetable stock
7.5 ml (1½ tsp) Dijon mustard
7.5 ml (1½ tsp) tomato purée
7.5 ml (1½ tsp) cornflour, blended with a little milk or water

To Garnish:
finely chopped parsley

Season the beef slices with salt and pepper and place in a shallow dish. Mix the marinade ingredients together, pour over the beef and turn the slices to coat evenly. Cover and leave to marinate overnight in the refrigerator.

To prepare the stuffing, melt the butter in a heavy-based frying pan and gently fry the spring onions for a minute or two. Add the mushrooms to the pan, keep stirring, then add the thyme leaves, chopped parsley, breadcrumbs, and salt and pepper. Fry gently for a few minutes. Transfer to a bowl.

Remove the beef slices from the marinade. Divide the stuffing equally between the slices of beef. Roll each one up and secure with a cocktail stick.

Heat a little olive oil in a frying pan, add the beef olives and brown rapidly on all sides. Transfer to a warmed ovenproof dish, cover and place in a preheated oven at 200°C (400°F) mark 6 while making the sauce.

Heat the oil in a pan and fry the onion until softened, but not browned, stirring from time to time. Add the mushrooms, garlic, thyme leaves, stock, mustard, tomato purée and a little salt and pepper. Bring to the boil, lower the heat and simmer for 2 minutes.

Pour the sauce over the beef olives, cover tightly with foil and cook in the middle of the oven for 1 hour. About 10 minutes before the end of cooking, stir in the blended cornflour to thicken the sauce. Taste and adjust the seasoning.

Remove the cocktail sticks from the beef olives and serve garnished with chopped parsley.

Miranda Tetley
(Junior MasterChef)

Harvester Steak with a Green Pepper Sauce

4 sirloin steaks, each about 175 g (6 oz)
150 g (5 oz) blue Stilton cheese, crumbled
1 large apple, peeled, cored and grated
finely chopped herbs (basil, thyme, oregano), to taste
salt and freshly ground black pepper
4 rashers back bacon
50 g (2 oz) clarified butter

Sauce:
250 ml (8 fl oz) red wine
75 ml (5 tbsp) chicken or beef stock
pinch of grated fresh horseradish root
10 green peppercorns or juniper berries, crushed
150 ml (¼ pint) double cream or natural yogurt

With a sharp knife, make an incision lengthways in each steak and fill with the cheese and grated apple. Sprinkle with finely chopped herbs, and season with salt and pepper.

Remove the rind from the bacon, and wrap a bacon rasher around each steak to hold the filling in place. Secure the opening with a wooden cocktail stick if necessary.

Melt the clarified butter in a frying pan, add the steak parcels and cook each side for approximately 4 minutes. Remove and keep warm.

"Quite a British product."

Antony Worrall-Thompson

For the sauce, pour the red wine into the juices in the pan and simmer to reduce a little. Add the stock, grated horseradish and crushed peppercorns or juniper berries. Simmer for 2-3 minutes, then stir in the cream.

Serve the sauce either poured over the steaks or separately.

Sam Goss
(Junior MasterChef)

Cook's Note

Clarified butter can be heated to a higher higher temperature than ordinary butter without burning. To prepare, melt butter in a pan over a low heat, then skim froth from surface. Remove from heat and allow to stand until the sediment settles on the bottom of the pan. Carefully pour the clarified butter into a bowl, leaving the sediment behind.

FILLET OF BEEF POACHED IN ST EMILION

WITH A CONFIT OF SHALLOTS

450 g (1 lb) pink shallots
50 g (2 oz) unsalted butter
30 ml (2 tbsp) olive oil
1 bottle of St Emilion, or other full-bodied red wine
450 g (1 lb) fillet of beef, in one piece
1 carrot, sliced
2 pieces streaky bacon, derinded and chopped
1 thyme sprig
600 ml (1 pint) beef stock
salt and freshly ground black pepper

Finely slice the shallots, reserving 15 ml (1 tbsp) for later. In a small saucepan, melt 25 g (1 oz) of the butter with 15 ml (1 tbsp) of the olive oil. Add the shallots and cook until beginning to soften and turn golden. Increase the heat and add 150 ml (¼ pint) of the wine. Bring to the boil, then simmer over a very low heat for about 45 minutes until the shallots have absorbed all of the wine and are very soft.

Meanwhile, heat the remaining oil in a large heavy-based pan. Add the beef and seal on all sides over a high heat, then remove. Add the reserved spoonful of shallots to the pan with the carrot, bacon and thyme; fry until browned. Add half the remaining wine, bring to the boil and reduce by half. Strain into a small saucepan and reserve for the sauce.

Meanwhile, pour the stock and remaining wine into a large saucepan and bring to the boil. Add the beef, reduce the heat to a gentle simmer and cook for about 10-15 minutes, depending on the thickness of the meat; it should still be pink in the middle. Lift out the meat, cover with foil and rest for 15 minutes.

Reheat the wine reduction reserved for the sauce and add a similar amount of cooking liquid from the beef. Reduce again until a good consistency is obtained and taste for seasoning. Whisk in a knob of butter.

To serve, slice the beef into 12 thin rounds. Place a mound of shallots in the centre of each serving plate and arrange three slices of beef to one side. Serve with Savoy cabbage and baby carrots.

Elaine Bates

COOK'S NOTE

A good full-bodied wine is essential for this dish.

"Absolutely beyond reproach."

Loyd

Fillet of Beef poached in St Emilion with a Confit of Shallots

Fillet Steaks in Black Bean Sauce

4 Aberdeen Angus fillet steaks, each about 150 g (5 oz)
20 ml (4 tsp) fermented black beans
1 small garlic clove, peeled
4 cm (1½ inch) cube of fresh root ginger, peeled and roughly chopped
dash of rice wine
450 ml (15 fl oz) well-flavoured reduced beef stock
15 ml (1 tbsp) olive oil
60 ml (2 fl oz) red wine
salt and freshly ground black pepper

Ginger and Coriander Crisps:
150 g (5 oz) fresh root ginger
about 30 coriander leaves
sunflower oil for deep-frying

> "The meat was extremely good, a good combination of flavour."
>
> Albert Roux

Trim the fillet steaks and set aside.

Rinse the fermented black beans well and pat dry with kitchen paper. Put half into a mortar. Add the garlic and ginger and pound with the pestle until smooth; the mixture should be quite dry and thick. Add a dash of rice wine and mix to a smooth paste. Warm the stock in a saucepan, then add the black bean paste. Turn off the heat and leave to infuse.

To make the ginger and coriander crisps, peel the ginger, cutting off any knobbly bits and trim to a good even shape. Slice extremely thinly across the diagonal to make 24-32 crisps. Rinse the coriander leaves and pat dry. Heat the oil for deep-frying to 160°C (325°F). Deep-fry the crisps in batches until golden, then drain on kitchen paper; they will crisp up as they cool. Deep-fry the coriander leaves for about 1 minute; do not overcook. Drain on kitchen paper.

To cook the steaks, heat the olive oil in a heavy-based pan or griddle. Add the steaks and cook for 3 minutes each side for medium rare. Remove from the pan and keep warm. Deglaze pan with the wine, then add the stock and black bean paste. Let bubble for a few moments, then strain and return to the pan. Add the whole black beans and check seasoning.

Carve each steak into 5mm (¼ inch) thick slices. Arrange on warmed plates and pour over the sauce. Sprinkle the ginger crisps and coriander leaves on top. Serve with accompaniments of your choice.

Gill Tunkle

Fillet of Beef stuffed with Oysters

with a Claret and Oyster Sauce

575 g (1¼ lb) fillet of beef
salt and freshly ground black pepper
12 oysters
juice of 1 lemon, or to taste
30 ml (2 tbsp) olive oil

Claret and Oyster Sauce:
25 g (1 oz) butter
1 shallot, chopped
1 clove garlic, bruised
2 strips of finely pared lemon rind, each 2.5 x 1 cm (1 x ½ inch)
pinch of freshly grated nutmeg
pinch of cayenne pepper
50 g (2 oz) mushrooms, chopped
2 anchovy fillets, pounded
325 ml (11 fl oz) beef stock
375 ml (13 fl oz) claret
450 ml (¾ pint) double cream
lemon juice, to taste

To Garnish:
watercress sprigs

Trim the beef of all fat, then make a lengthways cut along the side of the beef, three quarters through. Open out and season with salt and pepper.

Open the oysters and reserve the beards and liquor. Lay about six of the oysters, overlapping along the open fillet to within 2 cm (¾ inch) of each end. (Reserve the other oysters for the sauce.) Sprinkle the oysters and fillet with lemon juice. Reshape meat, to enclose oysters and tie at 2.5 cm (1 inch) intervals with string. Cover and set aside.

To make the sauce, melt the

butter in a pan. Add the shallot, garlic, lemon rind, nutmeg and cayenne. Cook over a low heat for 2-3 minutes until the onions are soft. Add the mushrooms and cook for 1 minute. Stir in the anchovies, oyster beards and liquor. Simmer for 2 minutes.

Add the reserved oysters and poach gently in the liquor for 1-2 minutes or until the edges begin to curl. Remove with a slotted spoon and set aside.

Add the beef stock and all but 45 ml (3 tbsp) claret to the pan and reduce by half, or until the liquid is of a syrupy consistency. Add the cream and reduce again until the sauce is thick enough to coat the back of a spoon. You should have about 400 ml (14 fl oz). Strain the sauce through a fine sieve into a clean bowl and keep warm over a steamer.

Purée the reserved oysters in a blender or food processor with the remaining 45 ml (3 tbsp) claret. Stir into the sauce. Add lemon juice, salt and pepper to taste.

To cook the beef, heat the oil in a heavy-based frying pan. Season the fillet with salt and pepper, then add to the pan and sear over a high heat on all sides. Transfer to a rack over a roasting tin, containing 150 ml (¼ pint) warm water.

Roast in a preheated oven at 220°C (425°F) mark 7 for 15-20 minutes. Cover and leave to stand in a warm place for 20 minutes, before carving into slices.

To serve, spoon a little of the sauce on to each plate and arrange the beef slices on top. Garnish with watercress.

Tony Purwin

Pan-fried Calves Liver with Grilled Pineapple

1 small pineapple
125 ml (4 fl oz) plum wine
125 ml (4 fl oz) Japanese rice wine vinegar
10 ml (2 tsp) olive oil
5 ml (1 tsp) unsalted butter
700 g (1½ lb) calves liver
flour, for coating

Sauce:
125 ml (4 fl oz) red wine
125 ml (4 fl oz) port
30 ml (2 tbsp) rice vinegar
60 ml (4 tbsp) veal stock
50 g (2 oz) chilled unsalted butter, in pieces
large pinch of ground cinnamon
salt and freshly ground black pepper

To Garnish:
16 chives, with flowers if possible
5 ml (1 tsp) jalapeno peppers, chopped (optional)

Cut the top and base off the pineapple, then cut away the skin and remove the brown 'eyes'. Cut four 1 cm (½ inch) slices from the centre of the pineapple; chop the rest, discarding the hard central core and set aside 125 g (4 oz) for the garnish. Combine the plum wine and rice vinegar in a shallow dish. Add the pineapple rings, turn to coat with the mixture and leave to marinate for 15 minutes.

Meanwhile prepare the sauce. Put the red wine, port and rice vinegar in a small pan and boil until reduced by half. Add the veal stock and boil to reduce until the sauce starts to thicken. Whisk in the butter, cinnamon and salt and pepper to taste until smooth. Keep warm.

Drain the pineapple rings and cook under a preheated hot grill, turning occasionally, until golden brown on both sides.

Meanwhile cut the liver into 5 mm (¼ inch) thick slices – to give 2-3 slices per serving. Drizzle with a little olive oil. Toss in flour to coat evenly. Heat the butter and remaining olive oil in a heavy-based frying pan. When it is very hot, add the liver slices and sauté over a high heat for no longer than 1 minute each side.

To serve, toss the chopped fresh pineapple in the sauce. Arrange the liver slices and grilled pineapple slices on warmed serving plates. Garnish with the chives, and peppers if using. Serve with the sauce.

David Chapman

VEAL MEDALLIONS WITH ONION MARMALADE

4 onions, sliced
salt and freshly ground black pepper
750 ml (1¼ pints) chicken stock
22 ml (1½ tbsp) red wine vinegar
350 ml (12 fl oz) double cream
8 veal medallions, each 75 g (3 oz)
flour, for dusting
30 ml (2 tbsp) sunflower oil
50 g (2 oz) butter
250 ml (8 fl oz) port

To Garnish:
sage leaves

Put the onions in a medium saucepan with seasoning. Add 500 ml (16 fl oz) of the chicken stock and the vinegar. Cook, covered, over a moderate heat for about 15 minutes until the liquid is almost totally evaporated.

In a separate small pan, bring the cream to the boil and boil steadily to reduce to 60-75 ml (4-5 tbsp). Add the cream to the onions and bring back to the boil. Check the seasoning and remove from the heat.

Season the veal with salt and pepper and dust all over with flour. Heat the oil and half of the butter in a large heavy-based frying pan. Add the veal and sauté for 3-4 minutes on each side until browned, but pink inside. Remove and keep warm.

Pour off any remaining fat from the pan, then add the port to deglaze, scraping up any sediment from the base of the pan. Add the remaining chicken stock, bring to the boil and boil to reduce to 60-75 ml (4-5 tbsp). Gradually whisk in the remaining 25 g (1 oz) butter, a piece at a time, to yield a smooth glossy sauce.

To serve, gently reheat the onions and spoon a portion onto each warmed serving plate. Top with the veal and spoon on the sauce. Garnish with sage and serve with Sage Tagliatelle (page 121) and French beans.

Holly Schade

FILLETS OF LAMB WRAPPED IN SPINACH AND PROSCIUTTO

2 loin of lamb fillets, each about 225 g (8 oz)
10 ml (2 tsp) olive oil
salt and freshly ground black pepper
8-10 large spinach leaves, stalks removed
5 ml (1 tsp) French mustard
5 ml (1 tsp) Dijon mustard
2.5 ml (½ tsp) wholegrain mustard
2.5 ml (½ tsp) chopped dill
4-6 slices prosciutto or Parma ham
2-3 shallots, finely chopped
1 clove garlic, finely chopped
200 ml (7 fl oz) rosé wine
250 ml (8 fl oz) well-flavoured veal or lamb stock
2.5 ml (½ tsp) tomato purée

Heat the olive oil in a heavy-based pan, add the lamb fillets and seal on all sides over a high heat. Season with salt and pepper and set aside. (Don't rinse the pan).

Plunge the spinach leaves into a pan of boiling water, then remove immediately so as not to overcook them. Lay them out on a clean teatowel to drain. Spread out, overlapping the leaves slightly to form two 'sheets' of spinach.

Mix the mustards together with the dill. Spread all but 2.5 ml (½ tsp) evenly on both sheets of spinach.

Place a lamb fillet on each spinach sheet and wrap the spinach around the lamb to enclose completely. Lay out the prosciutto slices, overlapping them slightly to form two 'sheets'. Place the lamb fillets on top and fold the prosciutto around each fillet to enclose. The prosciutto should adhere to itself and hold together, but if at all concerned, tie at intervals with cotton string to hold it in place. (Wrap in cling film and left to rest in a cool place until ready to cook.)

Roast the lamb in a preheated oven at 220°C (425°F) mark 7 for 15-20 minutes, depending on how you like your lamb. Meanwhile make the gravy. Reheat the oil remaining in the pan used to seal the lamb, add the shallots and garlic and cook until softened. Deglaze with the rosé wine, stirring to scrape up the sediment. Simmer to reduce by one third then add the stock and reduce again by about a third.

Strain the sauce through a conical sieve or pass through a mouli to purée the shallot and garlic. Return to the pan, add the tomato purée and if necessary, reduce to the desired consistency. Add a little of the reserved mustard mixture to taste.

Cover the lamb lightly with foil and let rest for at least 5 minutes.

To serve, slice each lamb fillet into 3 or 4 medallions, depending on size. Arrange on warmed plates and serve with the sauce and accompaniments of your choice.

Joanna Crossley

Fillets of Lamb wrapped in Spinach and Prosciutto, served with Potato Rösti

Char-grilled Loin of Lamb Fillet

with Glazed Turnips and a Cassis and Madeira Sauce

2 lamb loin fillets (plus reserved bones), total weight about 675 g (1½ lb)

Marinade:
180 ml (6 fl oz) red wine (eg Claret)
180 ml (6 fl oz) crème de cassis
juice of 1 lemon
1 large clove garlic, chopped
30 ml (2 tbsp) olive oil
few mixed herbs (eg bay leaf, parsley sprig, rosemary sprig)
1 tomato, chopped
salt and freshly ground black pepper

Sauce:
30 ml (2 tbsp) olive oil
reserved lamb bones
1 stick celery, with leaves
1 large carrot, chopped
1 medium onion, chopped
15 ml (1 tbsp) tomato purée
10 ml (2 tsp) Dijon mustard
50 ml (2 fl oz) Madeira
5 ml (1 tsp) redcurrant jelly
a little crème de cassis, to taste (optional)

Glazed Turnips:
4 turnips, sliced
5 ml (1 tsp) light brown sugar
30 ml (2 tbsp) crème de cassis
25 g (1 oz) butter
15 ml (1 tbsp) muscovado sugar

To Garnish:
herb sprigs
handful of blackcurrants, glazed in sugar syrup (optional)

Mix all the ingredients for the marinade together in a shallow dish. Add the lamb fillets and turn to coat. Cover and leave to marinate in a cool place overnight or for several hours at least.

The next day, remove the lamb from the marinade and set aside; reserve the marinade.

To prepare the sauce, heat the oil in a large saucepan. Add the lamb bones, celery, carrot and onion and fry, stirring, for a few minutes until browned; do not burn. Add the reserved marinade and 250 ml (8 fl oz) water. Bring to the boil and simmer for 30-45 minutes. Increase the heat and reduce the liquid by two thirds.

Meanwhile, prepare the glazed turnips. Put the turnips in a pan with 250 ml (8 fl oz) water, the light brown sugar, crème de cassis and seasoning. Bring to the boil, cover and cook for about 30 minutes until tender. Drain the turnips, adding the cooking liquor to the sauce. Add the butter and muscovado sugar to the turnips and toss over a moderate heat to glaze; keep warm.

When the sauce has reduced, remove from the heat and strain into another pan. Add the tomato purée, mustard, Madeira and redcurrant jelly. Check the seasoning and add a little more crème de cassis if needed; keep warm.

Meanwhile, preheat the grill to high (or a griddle). Place the lamb on the grill rack (or griddle) and cook for 3-5 minutes each side, until browned on the outside but still pink in the middle.

To serve, thinly slice the lamb and arrange alternate pieces of lamb and turnip on the serving plate. Spoon around the sauce and garnish with herbs and glazed blackcurrants if desired.

Jill O'Brien

Medallions of Lamb with Redcurrant and Port Sauce

1.2 kg (2½ lb) best end of lamb, boned (plus reserved bones)
salt and freshly ground black pepper
30 ml (2 tbsp) olive oil

Sauce:
300 ml (½ pint) lamb stock (made from the reserved bones)
150 ml (¼ pint) ruby port
125 g (4 oz) redcurrant jelly
juice of 1 orange
5 ml (1 tsp) arrowroot (optional)

To Garnish:
redcurrants (optional)

Cook's Note

For both recipes on this page, get your butcher to bone the lamb for you, remembering to ask for the bones which you will need for the sauce.

Trim the lamb if necessary and season with salt and pepper.

To make the sauce, pour the lamb stock into a saucepan and bring to the boil. Boil steadily until reduced by about half. Add the port and boil to reduce further. Whisk in the redcurrant jelly until amalgamated, then add the orange juice. The sauce should be thick enough to lightly coat the back of a spoon. If it requires thickening, mix the arrowroot with a little water, stir into the sauce and cook, stirring, for 1-2 minutes until thickened and translucent. Set aside.

"The lamb works well with a sweet sauce."

Terry Laybourne

Heat the oil in a heavy-based pan until hot, then add the lamb and quickly seal until browned on all sides. Transfer the meat to an ovenproof tin and cook in a preheated oven at 230°C (450°F) mark 8 for 15-20 minutes. Wrap in foil and leave to rest in a warm place for 5-10 minutes.

To serve, carve the lamb into slices and arrange on warmed serving plates. Garnish with redcurrants if desired.

Jenni Guy

Rosette of Welsh Lamb with Pistou Sauce

2 fillets of Welsh lamb, each about 225-300 g (8-10 oz)
25 g (1 oz) butter
15 ml (1 tbsp) olive oil
salt and freshly ground black pepper

Pistou Sauce:
handful of basil leaves
12 stems of parsley
30 ml (2 tbsp) pine nuts
1 clove garlic
300 ml (½ pint) well-flavoured homemade lamb stock
125 g (4 oz) butter

Vegetables:
4 carrots
½ swede
1 leek
unsalted butter, for cooking
2 potatoes
5 ml (1 tsp) freshly grated nutmeg

To Garnish:
basil sprigs

"I thought the lamb with pistou was absolutely fabulous."

Loyd

To make the pistou sauce, blanch the herbs in boiling water for 15 seconds, then refresh in iced water. Drain and chop finely. Press through a sieve. Toast the pine nuts, then grind with the garlic. Place the stock, butter, herbs and garlic mixture in a saucepan. Bring to the boil and reduce by half; keep warm.

To prepare the vegetables, 'turn' the carrots and swede by cutting into classic barrel shapes of uniform size. Cook in boiling salted water until tender; drain and keep warm. Cut the leek into julienne strips. Sweat the leek in a pan with a knob of butter until tender.

To prepare the potato rösti, grate the potatoes and mix with the nutmeg and seasoning. Melt 40 g (1½ oz) butter in a heavy-based frying pan. Set four 7.5 cm (3 inch) metal rings in the pan. Divide the potato mixture evenly between the rings, pressing well down. Cook over a moderate heat for about 5 minutes until the underside is crisp and golden brown. Turn and cook the other side until crispy. Drain on kitchen paper.

Season the lamb fillets with salt and pepper. Heat the butter and olive oil in a heavy-based frying pan, add the lamb fillets and fry, turning frequently, for 5-6 minutes depending on thickness; they should still be pink inside. Remove from the pan, cover and leave to rest in a warm place for 5 minutes.

To serve, cut the lamb into noisettes. Position a rösti on each serving plate and top with leek julienne. Arrange the noisettes on top. Surround with the pistou sauce and vegetables. Garnish with basil.

Gareth Richards

Braised Lamb Shanks

8 small or 4 medium lamb shanks
45 ml (3 tbsp) olive oil
1 onion, chopped
4 cloves garlic, crushed
50 g (2 oz) tomato purée
2 carrots, sliced
125 g (4 oz) canned chopped tomatoes
350 ml (12 fl oz) red wine
350 ml (12 fl oz) lamb stock
5 ml (1 tsp) finely chopped rosemary leaves
5 ml (1 tsp) finely chopped thyme leaves
2.5 ml (½ tsp) allspice
salt and freshly ground black pepper
5-10 ml (1-2 tsp) arrowroot, mixed with a little water
thyme sprigs, to garnish

Heat half of the olive oil in a heavy flameproof casserole. Add the onion and sauté for 3-4 minutes until soft. Add the garlic and cook for a further 2 minutes. Add the tomato purée, carrots, tomatoes, wine, stock, herbs, allspice and seasoning. Bring to the boil.

Meanwhile, heat the remaining olive oil in a heavy-based frying pan and brown the lamb shanks on all sides. Add the lamb to the casserole, cover and cook in a preheated oven at 180°C (350°F) mark 4 for 1½-2 hours, stirring from time to time, until the meat comes away from the bone easily. Lower the oven temperature to 110°C (225°F) mark ¼.

Lift the lamb shanks out of the casserole and place in an ovenproof dish; keep warm in the oven. Strain the sauce into a saucepan and boil steadily until reduced by about half. Add the arrowroot to thicken the sauce slightly if necessary, and heat, stirring, until thickened.

Place the lamb on warmed serving plates and pour on the sauce. Garnish with thyme and serve with minted carrots and Colcannon (page 113).

Holly Schade

Lamb with Pumpkin Risotto

450 g (1 lb) boned loin of lamb
coarse sea salt and freshly ground black pepper
30 ml (2 tbsp) extra-virgin olive oil
45-60 ml (3-4 tbsp) red or white wine
45-60 ml (3-4 tbsp) lamb stock

Pumpkin Risotto:
90 ml (6 tbsp) extra-virgin olive oil
2 onions, chopped
2 cloves garlic, chopped
2 large red chillis, deseeded and chopped
300 g (10 oz) Arborio rice
250 ml (8 fl oz) white wine (eg Australian Semilion Chardonnay)
5 ml (1 tsp) turmeric
about 1.2 litres (2 pints) chicken stock
250 g (9 oz) butternut squash or pumpkin, finely chopped
100 g (3½ oz) goat's cheese, cut into small pieces
100 g (3½ oz) pine nuts, toasted

First prepare the risotto. Heat the olive oil in a frying pan, add the onions and garlic and fry until softened. Stir in the chopped chillis. Add the rice and cook for 2-3 minutes, then add the wine and stir gently until the liquid is absorbed. Stir in the turmeric.

Gradually start adding the chicken stock, stirring constantly over a low heat. Continue adding the stock, a ladleful at a time, as each addition is absorbed. Once half the stock has been absorbed, add the pumpkin. Continue to stir in the stock until the rice is plump and tender but still retains a bite. The maximum cooking time is 30 minutes; you may not need to use all of the stock.

When the risotto is nearly ready, cook the lamb. Season the meat with the pepper. Heat the oil in a frying pan, add the lamb and fry over a very high heat for 2-3 minutes each side. Transfer to a warmed dish and allow to stand briefly before carving. Meanwhile, deglaze the pan with the wine and stock, stirring to scrape up the sediment.

When the risotto is cooked, stir in the goat's cheese, turn off the heat and cover the pan to encourage the cheese to melt.

To serve, season the meat with salt and pepper and slice thinly. Fold most of the pine nuts into the risotto. Spoon the risotto onto warmed serving plates and arrange the lamb slices alongside. Moisten the meat with a little of the deglazed pan juices. Sprinkle the remaining pine nuts over the risotto and serve at once, accompanied by the chicory and watercress salad.

Alison Fiander

Lamb with Pumpkin Risotto

Saddle of Jacob Lamb with a Black Pudding Stuffing

1 boned saddle of lamb, about 575 g (1¼ lb)

Stuffing:
50 g (2 oz) skinless chicken breast fillet
1 egg
175 g (6 oz) black pudding
1 rosemary sprig, leaves only, finely chopped
salt and freshly ground black pepper

Sauce:
150 ml (¼ pint) blackberry wine, or fruity red wine
300 ml (½ pint) good lamb stock
8 blackberries, squashed
4 peppercorns
5 ml (1 tsp) blackberry jelly
few knobs of butter

Caramelised Apple:
1 Granny Smith apple
25 g (1 oz) unsalted butter
1 large pinch of caster sugar

To Garnish:
16 blackberries

To make the stuffing, process the chicken meat with the egg in a food processor until smooth, then add the black pudding and process until fairly smooth. Add the chopped rosemary and process until evenly mixed.

Spread the stuffing into the boned saddle, roll up and tie at 2.5 cm (1 inch) intervals with cotton string. Keep in a cool place until ready to cook. Place in a roasting tin and cook in a preheated oven at 180°C (350°F) mark 4 for 40 minutes. Remove from the oven, cover loosely with foil and leave to rest in a warm place for 10-15 minutes.

Meanwhile make the sauce. Simmer the blackberry wine until reduced by half. Add the lamb stock and reduce again by half. Add the squashed blackberries and the peppercorns. Leave to infuse for 10 minutes. Add the blackberry jelly and stir until melted. Strain, return to the pan and whisk in the butter to finish the sauce.

"Absolutely brilliant."

Raymond Blanc

To caramelise the apple, peel the apple and cut into wedges. Melt the butter with the sugar in a small frying pan, then add the apple and cook quickly over a high heat until golden brown.

To serve, carve the lamb into 2 cm (¾ inch) slices and arrange on warmed serving plates. Garnish with the caramelised apple and blackberries and carefully spoon the sauce around. Serve at once, with vegetable purées.

Marion MacFarlane

Cook's Note

Jacob lamb is an ancient breed of four-horned sheep. The meat is lean with a superb 'gamey' taste and texture. You could however use traditional Scottish lamb instead. Get your butcher to bone out the saddle for you and remember to ask for the bones which you will need to make a stock.

Best End of Lamb with Roasted Beetroot

and Garlic

2 best ends of neck of lamb
350-450 g (¾-1 lb) extra lamb bones, chopped up
salt and freshly ground black pepper
3-4 rosemary sprigs
15 g (½ oz) butter, softened
3-4 thyme sprigs, leaves only

Beetroot Jus:
1 raw beetroot, cut into small pieces
12 black peppercorns
6 cloves
2 bay leaves
5 ml (1 tsp) wine vinegar
5 ml (1 tsp) caster sugar

Roasted Beetroot and Garlic:
4-6 raw baby beetroots (unpeeled but washed)
60 ml (4 tbsp) extra-virgin olive oil
150 ml (¼ pint) milk
8 garlic cloves, unpeeled
8 shallots, peeled
4 thyme sprigs
30 ml (2 tbsp) caster sugar
15 ml (1 tbsp) sherry vinegar

To Finish Sauce:
50 g (2 oz) cold unsalted butter, diced

First make the beetroot jus. Place all the ingredients in a pan with 300 ml (½ pint) cold water and bring to the boil. Lower the heat and simmer for 20 minutes. Cool, then strain. If necessary, make up to 150 ml (¼ pint) with cold water. Set aside until required for the sauce.

Season the lamb bones liberally, then place in a roasting tin with the rosemary sprigs. Roast in the oven at 200°C (400°F) mark 6 for 30-45 minutes.

Meanwhile, rub the meat all over with the softened butter. Season liberally with salt and pepper and press the thyme leaves into the meat. Leave to stand for a while.

Cut the beetroot into quarters, place in a roasting tin and drizzle with 30 ml (2 tbsp) olive oil. Roast in the oven for 10 minutes. Meanwhile bring the milk to the boil, add the garlic and cook for 1 minute. Drain and skin the garlic cloves. Add to the roasting tin containing the beetroot. Add the shallots, thyme and remaining 30 ml (2 tbsp) olive oil. Season generously with salt and pepper, baste well and return to the oven for 20 minutes.

Stand the meat on top of the lamb bones and roast in the oven for 10-15 minutes. Transfer the meat to a warmed dish, cover with foil and leave to rest in a warm place.

Sprinkle the roasted vegetables with the sugar and sherry vinegar. Place on the hob and allow to sizzle for about 1 minute to caramelise. Transfer to a warmed serving dish with a slotted spoon. Keep warm. Deglaze the roasting tin with half of the beetroot jus.

Remove the lamb bones from their roasting tin and deglaze the tin with the remaining beetroot jus. Strain the liquids from both roasting tins into a saucepan. Boil to reduce a little, then whisk in the butter a little at a time until the sauce is glossy and a little thicker. Adjust the seasoning.

Carve the meat into thick slices and arrange on warmed serving plates. Surround with the caramelised vegetables. Pour on the sauce and serve with accompaniments of your choice.

Clare Askaroff

> *"The main course was absolutely superb."*
>
> Sue MacGregor

Cook's Note

For this recipe, you need well trimmed French-style best ends of lamb, with their bones scraped clean.

Fillet of Lamb with Tarragon Marsala Sauce

2 lamb (loin) fillets, each about 225 g (8 oz)
15 g (½ oz) unsalted butter
20-30 rashers sweet-cured streaky bacon, derinded
125 g (4 oz) spinach leaves
30-45 ml (2-3 tbsp) tarragon mustard

Sauce:
300 ml (½ pint) lamb stock
15 g (½ oz) chopped tarragon
150 ml (¼ pint) Marsala
15-30 ml (1-2 tbsp) redcurrant jelly
15 ml (1 tbsp) crème fraîche or mascarpone

To Garnish:
tarragon sprigs

Melt the butter in a frying pan, add the lamb fillets and brown evenly; remove and drain.

Stretch the bacon rashers with the back of a knife. Arrange them overlapping on a board to form 2 sheets (the same length as the lamb fillets). Blanch the spinach leaves in boiling water for 30 seconds, plunge into cold water to refresh, then drain thoroughly. Spread a thin layer of mustard over the bacon. Arrange the spinach leaves in a layer on top.

Place a lamb fillet at one end of each spinach and bacon 'sheet', then roll up. Wrap loosely in foil and set aside until required.

Place the lamb parcels in a roasting tin and cook in a preheated oven at 190°C (375°F) mark 5 for 20-25 minutes, according to taste.

Meanwhile, prepare the sauce. Put the stock in a pan with half of the chopped tarragon and boil to reduce by half. Add the Marsala and, again, reduce by half. Strain through a fine sieve into a clean pan, pressing the tarragon with the back of a wooden spoon to extract the juices.

Allow the cooked lamb to rest for 5 minutes before carving. Add the juices from the roasting tin to the sauce. Add the redcurrant jelly and heat, stirring, to dissolve. Whisk in the crème fraîche or mascarpone and reduce to the desired consistency. Stir in the remaining tarragon.

To serve, cut each lamb fillet into 6 slices. Arrange 3 slices on each warmed serving plate and surround with the sauce. Garnish with tarragon and serve with accompaniments of your choice.

Gillian Humphrey

Devilled Pork Tenderloin in a Port Sauce

14 prunes (preferably Agen), stoned
600 ml (1 pint) port
2 pork tenderloins, each 225-300 g (8-10 oz)
25 g (1 oz) butter
salt and freshly ground black pepper
12 rashers rindless streaky bacon (dry-cure)
30 ml (2 tbsp) olive oil

Sauce:
reserved port (see recipe)
2 shallots, peeled
300 ml (½ pint) reduced homemade chicken stock
15 g (½ oz) unsalted butter, in pieces

Put the prunes in a bowl with the port and leave to soak for 1 hour. Remove the prunes with a slotted spoon, reserving the port.

To prepare the pork, split each tenderloin lengthways with a sharp knife, without cutting all the way through. Open out and put a row of 7 prunes down the middle of each tenderloin. Bring up the sides of the meat to form a sausage and secure temporarily with cocktail sticks; smear with the butter and season with salt and pepper.

Place a line of 6 bacon rashers close together on the work surface. Lay the pork on top of the bacon and bring the rashers over the top of the pork, crossing over if necessary. Repeat with the other piece of pork. Cut 12 pieces of string slightly longer than the bacon rashers and tie the meat at regular intervals to secure the bacon.

Put the olive oil in a roasting tin and heat in a preheated oven at 200°C (400°F) mark 6. Add the pork tenderloins, turning quickly to brown. Bake in the oven for 45 minutes or until cooked through and brown.

Meanwhile, make the sauce. Set aside 45 ml (3 tbsp) of the port. Put the rest in a pan with the shallots and simmer over a low heat until reduced to one third of the original volume. Strain the port through a fine sieve and discard the shallots. Heat the reduced stock and add to the port; if necessary strain the sauce through a fine sieve again to obtain a smooth consistency. Add the reserved port and whisk in the butter.

After cooking, leave the pork to rest in a warm place for 10 minutes, then carve into 1 cm (½ inch) thick slices. Serve with the port sauce, garlic roast potatoes and seasonal vegetables.

Nicola Kidd

Devilled Pork Tenderloin in a Port Sauce

Tenderloin of Pork with a Surprise Stuffing

on a Beetroot Sauce

2 pork fillets (tenderloin), each about 350 g (12 oz)
about 60 ml (4 tbsp) olive oil
12 shallots
300 ml (½ pint) white wine

Stuffing:
225 g (8 oz) spinach, trimmed, steamed for 4 minutes and chopped
2 cloves garlic, crushed
2 spring onions, chopped
50 g (2 oz) cooked smoked ham, chopped
30 ml (2 tbsp) pine nuts
6 sun-dried tomatoes, sliced
30 ml (2 tbsp) freshly grated Parmesan cheese
freshly ground black pepper
30 ml (2 tbsp) oil from sun-dried tomatoes

Sauce:
600 ml (1 pint) homemade ham stock
3 cooked beetroot
3 bay leaves
5 ml (1 tsp) cloves
squeeze of lemon juice
50 g (2 oz) butter
15 ml (1 tbsp) plain flour

To Garnish:
flat-leaf parsley

The day before serving, bring the ham stock to simmering point. Remove from the heat and add two of the cooked beetroots cut into chunks, the bay leaves, cloves and lemon juice. Leave to infuse for 24 hours to extract flavour and colour from the beetroots.

The next day, strain the stock and discard the beetroot, spices and bay leaves.

To make the stuffing, mix all the ingredients together, binding the mixture with the oil from the sun-dried tomatoes.

Cut the pork tenderloins in half widthways and slit each piece lengthways, but do not cut right through. Open out each piece like a book and spread with the stuffing. Fold over to enclose and tie securely at intervals with string.

Heat the olive oil in a sauté pan with a lid, add the shallots and sauté until browned. Add the meat and seal on all sides. Add the white wine, bring to the boil, then simmer, covered, for 20 minutes, turning once.

Meanwhile make the sauce. Bring the strained stock to the boil. Knead the butter with the flour to make a beurre manié. Whisk into the stock a little at a time, adding just enough to thicken the sauce.

Cut half of the remaining cooked beetroot into thin strips for the garnish; cut the other half into a few rough chunks. Stir the latter into the sauce to add colour.

To serve, carve each piece of meat into about 5 slices. Strain the sauce and pool some on each warmed serving plate. Place the slices of meat on top of the sauce, and arrange the shallots and beetroot around. Garnish with parsley and serve with accompaniments of your choice.

Camilla Askaroff
(Junior MasterChef)

Pork Fillet in Rich Onion and Madeira Sauce

2 pork fillets (tenderloin), each about 350 g (12 oz)
60 ml (4 tbsp) olive oil
1 large onion, finely chopped
2 cloves garlic, crushed
large handful of thyme leaves
1 vegetable stock cube, dissolved in 450 ml (¾ pint) boiling water
7.5 ml (1½ tsp) Dijon mustard
7.5 ml (1½ tsp) tomato purée
45 ml (3 tbsp) Madeira
salt and freshly ground black pepper
125 g (4 oz) button mushrooms
7.5 ml (1½ tsp) cornflour
a little milk (if necessary)

Marinade:
60 ml (4 tbsp) extra-virgin olive oil
5 ml (1 tsp) golden syrup
6 spring onions, chopped
30 ml (2 tbsp) chopped parsley
2 rosemary sprigs
10 ml (2 tsp) thyme leaves
juice of ½ lemon

Split the pork fillets lengthways and cut any membrane and fat away. Place the pieces of pork in a glass dish. Mix the marinade ingredients together and pour over the pork. Leave overnight in the refrigerator.

Preheat the oven to 200°C (400°F) mark 6, and put a casserole dish in the oven to warm.

Remove the pork from the marinade and pat dry. Heat the olive oil in a frying pan, add the pork and fry quickly over a high heat, turning to seal and brown on all sides. Transfer to the warmed casserole dish.

Fry the onion gently in the fat remaining in the frying pan to soften. Add the garlic and thyme leaves, and fry for 1 minute. Add the stock, mustard, tomato purée, Madeira and black pepper to taste. Bring to the boil, lower the heat and simmer for 2-3 minutes.

Add the sauce to the meat in the casserole, mix well, then cover with foil. Cook in a preheated oven for 30 minutes.

Add the button mushrooms to the casserole and stir in. Return to the oven for 15 minutes.

Mix the cornflour with a little milk or water, and stir into the casserole. Taste for seasoning.

Return to the oven for at least another 15 minutes.

To serve, slice the pork and fan out on warmed serving plates. Pour on the sauce and serve with accompaniments of your choice.

Miranda Tetley
(Junior MasterChef)

Stuffed Tenderloin of Pork Roasted with Shallots

Served with a Soured Cream Sauce

2 pork fillets (tenderloins), each about 350 g (12 oz)
salt and freshly ground black pepper
30 ml (2 tbsp) olive oil
40 g (1½ oz) butter, softened
10 ml (2 tsp) fresh thyme leaves
8 shallots

Marinade:
60 ml (4 tbsp) olive oil
juice of 1 lemon
6 spring onions, finely chopped

Stuffing:
50 g (2 oz) butter
1 small onion, diced
20 ml (4 tsp) thyme leaves
20 ml (4 tsp) chopped parsley
12 button mushrooms, sliced
12 pistachio nuts, chopped
50 g (2 oz) sultanas
1 large slice Granary bread, made into breadcrumbs
grated rind of 1 large lemon

Sauce:
25 g (1 oz) butter
1 small onion, diced
8 organic brown mushrooms, sliced
250 ml (8 fl oz) soured cream

Trim the pork fillets and place in a dish. Mix the marinade ingredients together and pour over the pork. Cover and leave to marinate overnight in the refrigerator.

To make the stuffing, melt the butter in a frying pan, add the onion and herbs, and fry, stirring, for a few minutes. Stir in the remaining stuffing ingredients, with salt and pepper to taste. Transfer to a bowl and leave to cool for 1 minute.

Slit the pork fillets lengthwise, without cutting right through. Open out, like a book, and season well on the inside. Place the stuffing along one half of the meat, then fold the other half over to enclose and secure with wooden cocktail sticks.

> *"Moist pork and very pleasant stuffing."*
>
> Michel Roux

Heat the olive oil in a frying pan, add the pork fillets and seal quickly on all sides over a high heat. Transfer to a heated roasting tin and smear with the butter. Sprinkle with the thyme leaves, then put into the middle of a preheated oven at 200°C (400°F) mark 6. Cook for 1 hour, basting fairly frequently, adding the shallots to the tin halfway through cooking.

To make the sauce, melt the butter in a pan and fry the onion gently to soften and brown lightly. Add the mushrooms and fry for 2-3 minutes until softened. Add the soured cream and salt and pepper to taste. Warm through; do not boil.

To serve, slice the pork and fan out on warmed serving plates. Add the shallots and serve with the soured cream sauce.

Miranda Tetley
(Junior MasterChef)

ACCOMPANIMENTS

Salad Leaves in a Herb Vinaigrette

about 100 g ($3\frac{1}{2}$ oz) endive (frisée or batavia)
about 100 g ($3\frac{1}{2}$ oz) radicchio leaves

Herb Vinaigrette:
75 ml (5 tbsp) olive oil
1 shallot, crushed
1 thyme sprig
1 basil leaf
4 rosemary sprig needles
1 chervil sprig
15 ml (1 tbsp) white wine vinegar
45 ml (3 tbsp) cold water
1.25 ml ($\frac{1}{4}$ tsp) salt
1.25 ml ($\frac{1}{4}$ tsp) white pepper
1.25 ml ($\frac{1}{4}$ tsp) caster sugar

To make the herb vinaigrette, combine the olive oil, shallot and herbs together in a small saucepan. Bring to a simmer, then remove from the heat. Leave to stand for 2 hours. Strain the mixture through a fine sieve into a bowl. Whisk in the vinegar, water, salt, pepper and sugar.

Just before serving, toss the salad leaves in the dressing.

Chris Rand

Rocket Salad with a Lime and Sherry Vinegar Dressing

selection of salad leaves (preferably mainly rocket, with red chicory and feuille de chêne)
few flat-leaf parsley sprigs
few tarragon sprigs

Dressing:
30 ml (2 tbsp) sherry vinegar
60 ml (4 tbsp) extra-virgin olive oil
10 ml (2 tsp) Dijon mustard
1-2 drops of lime oil
freshly ground black pepper
5 ml (1 tsp) tomato purée

Croûtons:
1 slice Granary bread
olive oil, for shallow frying

To Serve:
freshly pared Parmesan cheese

For the dressing, mix all the ingredients together in a screw-topped jar and shake well to combine.

To make the croûtons, remove the crusts from the bread and cut into little squares. Heat the olive oil in a small frying pan, add the bread squares and fry, turning, until brown and crisp. Drain well on kitchen paper.

Arrange the salad and herb leaves on individual plates or toss together in a large salad bowl and pour over the dressing evenly. Sprinkle with the croûtons and some shavings of Parmesan.

Camilla Askaroff
(Junior MasterChef)

Cook's Note

Like other citrus oils, lime oil is extracted from the rind of the fruit and has a very strong flavour. A drop or two is all that is required to impart the flavour and aroma to this dressing.

Rocket Salad with a Lime and Sherry Vinegar Dressing

Warm Spinach Salad

350 g (12 oz) spinach leaves
25 g (1 oz) sun-dried tomatoes in oil, drained and roughly chopped
25 g (1 oz) pecan nuts, roughly chopped
1 clove garlic, crushed
2 spring onions, sliced
15 g (½ oz) freshly grated Parmesan cheese
30 ml (2 tbsp) oil from the sun-dried tomatoes
black pepper

To Garnish:
2 parsnips
few flat-leaved parsley sprigs
groundnut oil, for deep-frying
coarse sea salt

To prepare the garnish, peel the parsnips and pare long thin shreds, using a zester. Mix with a few sprigs of flat-leaved parsley. Heat the oil for deep-frying, then deep-fry the parsnip shreds and parsley, in batches, for about 1 minute until crispy. Remove with a slotted spoon and drain on kitchen paper. Immediately season with freshly ground salt; keep warm.

Meanwhile, steam the spinach for about 4 minutes until just wilted, then chop roughly. Place in a bowl with the rest of the ingredients and mix well. Served while still warm, or at room temperature; do not refrigerate. Pile the deep-fried parsnips and parsley on top of the salad to serve.

Clare Askaroff

Cook's Note

You can, of course, omit the deep-fried parsnip garnish altogether. Alternatively, sprinkle with crisp-fried snippets of bacon instead.

Chicory and Watercress Salad

1 bunch of watercress
2 heads of chicory

Vinaigrette:
15 ml (1 tbsp) tarragon vinegar
45 ml (3 tbsp) walnut oil
salt and freshly ground black pepper

Trim the watercress; rinse and drain thoroughly. Separate the chicory leaves. Put the watercress and chicory into a bowl.

To make the vinaigrette, put the vinegar and oil in a screw-topped jar with salt and pepper to taste. Shake vigorously to combine.

Pour the dressing over the salad leaves and toss lightly. Serve at once.

Alison Fiander

Tomato and Basil Salad

4 tomatoes
salt and freshly ground black pepper
30-45 ml (2-3 tbsp) finely shredded basil
30 ml (2 tbsp) red wine vinegar
60 ml (4 tbsp) olive oil
basil sprigs, to garnish

Slice the tomatoes, season with salt and pepper to taste and layer in a bowl with the shredded basil.

In a small bowl, whisk together the vinegar and oil, season and pour over the tomatoes, turning them carefully once or twice to ensure they are well coated with dressing.

Cover and set aside for at least 1 hour before serving.

Angela Geary

Cook's Note

This salad should be left at room temperature – not in the refrigerator for at least 1 hour before serving to allow the flavours to develop.

Mixed Peppers with Coriander and Lemon Juice

1 red pepper
1 green pepper
1 yellow pepper
1 orange pepper
15 ml (1 tbsp) lemon juice
25 g (1 oz) butter
15 ml (1 tbsp) coriander seeds, finely ground
pinch of sugar, to taste

Halve the peppers, remove the core and seeds, then thinly slice the flesh. Bring a pan of salted water to the boil. Add the peppers and simmer for 1-2 minutes only. Drain and toss with the lemon juice, butter, coriander and sugar to taste. Serve at once.

Jill O'Brien

Confit of Fennel and Olives

4 young thin fennel bulbs
salt and freshly ground black pepper
25 ml (1 fl oz) olive oil
8 black olives, halved and stoned (see cook's note)

Trim the young fennel bulbs and leave whole; if using bulbous fennel, trim, core and cut into 5 mm (¼ inch) slices. Blanch in boiling salted water for 3 minutes, then quickly refresh in a bowl of cold water. Drain, pat dry and place in a clean pan with the olive oil. Gently heat through, then add the olives. Season with pepper to taste.

Gill Tunkle

Cook's Note

For this accompaniment, use the young thin fennel shoots if available, rather than the rounded bulbs. For optimum flavour, use olives which have been preserved in wild fennel flavoured olive oil; use the oil in the recipe too.

Caesar Salad

2 small gem lettuces, trimmed
50 g ($1\frac{3}{4}$ oz) can anchovies, drained

Garlic Croûtons:
4 thick slices white bread, crusts removed
30-45 ml (2-3 tbsp) olive oil
2 cloves garlic, crushed
50 g (2 oz) Parmesan cheese, freshly grated

Dressing:
1 egg yolk
1 clove garlic
60 ml (2 fl oz) sherry or wine vinegar
120 ml (4 fl oz) olive oil
dash of Worcestershire Sauce

To Serve:
finely pared or grated Parmesan cheese

Slice the lettuces crosswise and place in a salad bowl. Cut the anchovies into small pieces.

To prepare the croûtons, cut the bread into small cubes. Heat the olive oil in a frying pan with the crushed garlic. Add the bread cubes and fry until golden brown. Drain on absorbent kitchen paper and allow to cool. Add the croûtons to the lettuce with the anchovies and Parmesan and toss lightly.

Combine the ingredients for the dressing in a screw-topped jar and shake vigorously to emulsify. Pour the dressing over the salad and toss lightly. Scatter over the Parmesan.

David Chapman

Caesar Salad

THAI-STYLE SALAD

125 g (4 oz) sugar snap peas
125 g (4 oz) baby sweetcorn, halved lengthways
¼ Chinese cabbage
½ red pepper, cored and deseeded
½ bunch spring onions, trimmed
2 carrots, peeled
¼ fresh pineapple, peeled and cored
125 g (4 oz) oyster mushrooms
handful (¼ cup) coriander leaves, roughly torn

Dressing:
45 ml (3 tbsp) groundnut oil
45 ml (3 tbsp) rice wine vinegar
5 ml (1 tsp) wasabi paste
5 ml (1 tsp) sugar
salt and freshly ground black pepper

Blanch the sugar snap peas and baby sweetcorn separately in boiling water for 1 minute. Drain and refresh under cold water; then drain thoroughly.

Finely shred the cabbage; finely slice the red pepper. Cut the spring onions into thin strips, on the diagonal. Pare the carrots into thin strips, using a vegetable peeler. Cut the fresh pineapple into finger-sized sticks. Combine all of these salad ingredients in a bowl.

Sauté the oyster mushrooms briefly in the groundnut oil for the dressing. Remove with a slotted spoon and add to the salad. Add the rest of the ingredients for the dressing to the pan and stir well. Pour over the salad, add the coriander leaves and toss well to serve.

Alison Fiander

Lemon-glazed Carrots and Courgettes

225 g (8 oz) carrots, peeled and cut into batons
225 g (8 oz) courgettes, trimmed and chopped
salt and freshly ground black pepper
15 g (½ oz) butter
10 ml (2 tsp) sugar
juice of ½ lemon

Add the carrots to a pan of boiling salted water and cook for 5-6 minutes. Add the courgettes and cook for 2-3 minutes. Drain thoroughly and return to the pan. Add the butter, sugar and lemon juice. Toss over a moderate heat for 2-3 minutes to glaze. Check the seasoning and serve at once.

Gillian Humphrey

Stir-fried Leeks

2 small leeks
sunflower oil, for frying

Slice the leeks into rounds and wash well. Drain thoroughly. Heat a little oil in a wok or frying pan, add the leeks and stir-fry for 2-3 minutes until just cooked. Serve at once.

Marion MacFarlane

Spinach Purée

450 g (1 lb) young spinach leaves
1 small clove garlic
60 ml (2 fl oz) double cream
knob of butter
freshly grated nutmeg
salt and freshly ground black pepper

Remove the stalks and tough central veins from the spinach, then wash thoroughly. Cook the spinach in a covered pan with just the water clinging to the leaves after washing, and the garlic until just wilted. Drain in a sieve or colander, pressing out excess water.

Transfer to a food processor or blender and chop finely. Add the cream, butter, and nutmeg, salt and pepper to taste. Serve piping hot.

Marion MacFarlane

Leeks in Vermouth

350 g (12 oz) leeks, thinly sliced
25 g (1 oz) butter
60 ml (2 fl oz) dry vermouth

Melt the butter with the vermouth in a saucepan. Add the leeks and cook, stirring, for 2-3 minutes until the leeks are tender and the liquid has evaporated. Serve at once.

Judi Geisler

Braised Red Cabbage

30 ml (2 tbsp) olive oil
1 onion, very finely shredded
15 ml (1 tbsp) sugar
1 large apple, peeled, cored and sliced
½ red cabbage, very finely shredded
2 bay leaves
15 ml (1 tbsp) sherry vinegar
4 juniper berries
60 ml (2 fl oz) water
salt and freshly ground black pepper

Heat the olive oil in a large heavy based pan. Add the onion and sauté until golden brown. Add the sugar and apple slices and cook, stirring frequently, until a rich caramel colour is obtained and the apple slices are fluffy.

Stir in the red cabbage, bay leaves, vinegar, juniper berries and water. Season well. Cover with a tight-fitting lid and cook at a gentle simmer for about 1 hour, or until the cabbage is tender.

Sophie Buchmannn

Cabbage with Garlic and Juniper

450 g (1 lb) Savoy cabbage, cored and finely shredded
30 ml (2 tbsp) olive oil
75 g (3 oz) onion, very finely sliced
6 juniper berries
1 clove garlic, finely chopped
salt and freshly ground black pepper

Heat the olive oil in a large pan, add the onion and fry until golden. Meanwhile crush the juniper berries using a pestle and mortar (or with the back of a spoon on a flat surface). Add the juniper berries and garlic to the onion and fry for about 1 minute. Add the cabbage and stir until well coated with the oil. Season with salt and pepper, then cover and cook for about 10 minutes, stirring occasionally.

Michael Deacon

Colcannon

6 medium potatoes
1 green cabbage, cored and chopped
185 ml (6 fl oz) double cream
75 g (3 oz) butter
2 cloves garlic, crushed
salt and freshly ground black pepper

Peel and quarter the potatoes, then cook in boiling salted water until tender. Drain well and mash with the cream, using a potato ricer or masher.

Meanwhile, steam the cabbage for 5 minutes. Heat the butter in a large heavy-based saucepan and sauté the garlic for about 2 minutes until softened. Add the cabbage and cook for about 5 minutes until soft.

Purée the cabbage in a food processor, then add to the creamed potato and mash well. Season with salt and pepper to taste. Serve hot.

Holly Schade

Braised Celery Hearts

2 heads of celery
5 ml (1 tsp) chopped thyme
salt and freshly ground black pepper

Discard the outer celery stalks, then cut off the top half of the remaining stalks. Halve each celery heart, then place in a single layer in a saucepan. Add sufficient water to cover. Add the thyme and salt and pepper. Cook gently for about 15 minutes; the celery should still be slightly crunchy. Drain and serve.

Elaine Bates

Clapshot with Fresh Herbs

450 g (1 lb) potatoes
350 g (12 oz) swede
salt
25 g (1 oz) butter
25 ml (1 fl oz) virgin olive oil
15 ml (1 tbsp) finely chopped chives
15 ml (1 tbsp) finely chopped parsley
10 ml (2 tsp) finely chopped celery or lovage leaves
freshly grated nutmeg, to taste

Cut the potatoes and swede into 2.5 cm (1 inch) cubes. Place in a saucepan and add water to cover. Bring to the boil and cook until soft. Drain well and mash until smooth. Add the butter, olive oil, herbs and celery leaves. Sprinkle with grated nutmeg to serve.

Marion MacFarlane

Cook's Note

This is a traditional Scottish dish of "chappit neeps and tatties", or mashed swede and potatoes. The addition of herbs and olive oil transforms it into a wonderful 90's dish.

Medley of Green Vegetables

with a Dill Dressing

125 g (4 oz) fine green beans
125 g (4 oz) sugar snap peas or mangetouts
125 g (4 oz) courgettes
125 g (4 oz) broccoli florets
salt
15 g (½ oz) slightly salted butter
10 ml (2 tsp) lemon juice
freshly ground mixed peppercorns
30 ml (2 tbsp) chopped fresh dill

Trim the beans and sugar snap peas. Trim the courgettes and thinly slice lengthwise, using a swivel vegetable peeler, to form fine ribbons. Divide the broccoli into small even-sized florets.

Cook the broccoli in a large pan of boiling salted water for 1 minute. Add the beans and sugar snap peas and cook for 2 minutes. Add the courgette ribbons and, as soon as the water returns to the boil, remove the pan from the heat. Drain the vegetables in a colander and refresh with cold water.

Melt the butter in a large frying pan over a moderate heat until sizzling. Add the vegetables and cook, shaking the pan constantly, for 1 minute. Add the lemon juice and freshly ground peppercorns to taste. Stir in the dill and serve at once.

Elizabeth Truscott

Medley of Green Vegetables with a Dill Dressing

MEDITERRANEAN VEGETABLES

1 aubergine
sea salt and freshly ground black pepper
3 courgettes
1 onion
1 green pepper, cored and deseeded
1 red pepper, cored and deseeded
1 yellow pepper, cored and deseeded
4 plum tomatoes
olive oil, for frying
1 clove garlic, chopped

Cut the aubergine into 5 mm (¼ inch) slices and layer in a colander, sprinkling with salt. Place a small plate on top and weight down. Leave to drain.

Slice the remaining vegetables to about the same thickness as the aubergine. Heat a little olive oil in a heavy-based frying pan and sauté the onion and garlic until almost soft; remove from the pan and set aside.

Rinse the aubergine slices under cold running water and pat dry. Heat a little more olive oil in the pan, add the aubergines and fry on both sides until golden brown.

Blanch courgettes and peppers in boiling water, or microwave on high for 1-2 minutes until softened.

Position four 7.5 cm (3 inch) metal ring moulds on a baking tray. Layer the vegetables in the moulds, starting with the aubergine slices and finishing with the tomato slices. Drizzle a generous 5 ml (1 tsp) olive oil on top of each one. Bake in a preheated oven at 190°C (375°F) mark 5 for about 25 minutes. Lift onto warmed serving plates, using a fish slice, and remove the metal rings. Serve at once.

Joanna Crossley

Celeriac with Coriander

1 celeriac root, about 675 g (1½ lb)
juice of 1 lemon
salt and freshly ground black pepper
25-50 g (1-2 oz) butter
30 ml (2 tbsp) soured cream
10 ml (2 tsp) coarse-grain mustard
1 spring onion, finely chopped
30-45 ml (2-3 tbsp) chopped coriander leaves

Peel the celeriac and cut into chunks. Quickly immerse in a bowl of cold water with the lemon juice added to prevent discolouration.

Cook the celeriac in boiling salted water for 10-15 minutes until tender; drain well. Roughly mash the celeriac with the butter. Add all the rest of the ingredients and season liberally. Stir well and serve piping hot.

Clare Askaroff

Carrots with Fresh Ginger

350 g (12 oz) carrots, cut into matchsticks
salt and freshly ground black pepper
15 g (½ oz) butter
15 g (½ oz) fresh root ginger, peeled and finely chopped
15 ml (1 tbsp) sugar

Cook the carrots in boiling salted water for 5-10 minutes until just tender. Drain, then plunge into a bowl of cold water to refresh. Drain and return to the pan with the butter, ginger and sugar. Stir over a low heat until the carrots are well coated with the mixture. Cover and simmer for 2 minutes, then check the seasoning and serve.

Judi Geisler

Caramelised Shallots

10-20 shallots (unpeeled)
20 g (¾ oz) butter
4 large pinches of caster sugar
salt and freshly ground black pepper

Add the shallots to a pan of boiling water and cook for 2-3 minutes. Drain and leave until cool enough to handle, then remove the skins.

Place the shallots, butter and sugar in a heavy-based pan. Cover with a tight-fitting lid and cook over a low heat for about 10 minutes until tender and caramelised, shaking the pan from time to time to prevent sticking.

Gillian Humphrey

Mashed Turnips with Crispy Shallots

700 g (1½ lb) turnips, peeled and diced
50 g (2 oz) butter, plus 15 ml (1 tbsp)
6 large shallots, thinly sliced
150 ml (¼ pint) double cream
pinch of freshly grated nutmeg
salt and freshly ground black pepper
15 ml (1 tbsp) finely chopped parsley

Cook the turnips in a pan of simmering water for about 10 minutes until tender. Drain and purée in a food processor.

Melt 50 g (2 oz) butter in a heavy-based pan and gently sauté the shallots until golden brown and crisp; this may take at least 15 minutes. Drain on kitchen paper and keep warm.

Put the cream and 15 ml (1 tbsp) butter in a saucepan and bring to the boil. Add the turnips and stir briskly. Season generously with the nutmeg, salt and pepper, then stir in the chopped parsley. Serve immediately, topped with the crispy shallots.

Sophie Buchmann

Swede Purée

100 g (3½ oz) butter
200 g (7 oz) onions, coarsely chopped
650 g (1½ lb) swede
250 ml (8 fl oz) chicken stock
salt and freshly ground black pepper

Melt the butter in a heavy-based saucepan, add the onions and cook gently until soft. Add the swede and the stock and bring to the boil. Turn the heat down to very low and cover the pan with a sheet of greaseproof paper and a tight-fitting lid. Cook for 30 minutes. Transfer the contents of the pan to a blender or food processor and work until smooth. Season with salt and pepper to taste.

Ashley Wilson

Turnip, Potato and Walnut Purée

350 g (12 oz) turnip, peeled and chopped
125 g (4 oz) potato, peeled and chopped
75 g (3 oz) butter
25 g (1 oz) walnuts, chopped
freshly grated nutmeg
salt and freshly ground black pepper

Cook the turnip and potato in boiling salted water until tender. Drain and purée in a food processor or blender with the butter. Return to the pan and add the walnuts and nutmeg, salt and pepper to taste. Reheat gently to serve if necessary.

Marion MacFarlane

Spiced Pumpkin Purée

1 small butternut squash
salt and freshly ground black pepper
freshly grated nutmeg
15-30 ml (1-2 tbsp) mascarpone cheese

Peel and dice the squash. Place in an ovenproof dish, cover and bake in a preheated oven at 180°C (350°F) mark 4 for about 45 minutes, until soft.

Mash the squash, adding salt, pepper and nutmeg to taste. Beat in the mascarpone cheese to give a creamy texture. Serve piping hot.

Gillian Humphrey

Cook's Note

I prefer the flavour of butternut squash to that of English pumpkin. Baking enhances its sweet flavour, and doesn't result in a mushy texture.

Parsnips Streamers

4 large parsnips, peeled
oil for deep-frying
salt and freshly ground black pepper

Using a swivel vegetable peeler, pare the parsnips into long thin strips. Heat the oil in a deep-fryer or deep saucepan to 180°C (350°F), or until a cube of bread dropped into the oil turns golden brown in 1 minute. Deep-fry the parsnip strips in batches for about 5 minutes until crisp and brown. Drain on kitchen paper and keep warm while frying the rest. Season with a little salt and pepper and serve piping hot.

Ashley Wilson

Celeriac Rösti

1 celeriac
salt and freshly ground black pepper
25 g (1 oz) butter

Peel and quarter the celeriac, then grate coarsely into a bowl. Season with salt and pepper. Divide the mixture into 4 portions. Press each portion into a muffin ring or 7.5 cm (3 inch) plain metal cutter, resting on a fish slice or spatula.

Melt the butter in a frying pan and carefully slide the rings into the pan. Press the celeriac well down in the rings and fry for 3-4 minutes until crisp and golden brown underneath.

Turn the rösti, carefully remove the metal rings and cook the other side for 3-4 minutes until golden brown and cooked through. Drain on kitchen paper.

Derek Johns

Parmesan Parsnips

450 g (1 lb) parsnips, peeled and quartered
salt
60 ml (4 tbsp) olive oil
freshly grated nutmeg
125 g (4 oz) Parmesan cheese, freshly grated

Heat the oil in a roasting tin in a preheated oven at 180°C (350°F) mark 4. Meanwhile, parboil the parsnips in salted water for about 5 minutes. Drain and transfer to the roasting tin. Sprinkle with nutmeg and bake for 20 minutes.

Sprinkle with the Parmesan and bake for a further 20 minutes or until crisp and brown. Serve immediately.

Keely Smith

Hot Grated Beetroot

2 boiled beetroot
25 g (1 oz) butter
2.5 ml (½ tsp) sugar
5 ml (1 tsp) red wine vinegar, or to taste
salt and freshly ground black pepper

Remove the skin from the beetroot, then grate, using a medium grater. Melt the butter in a pan, add the beetroot and heat through. Add the sugar and vinegar to taste. Season with salt and pepper to taste.

Marion MacFarlane

Potato Rösti

4 large potatoes
1 medium sweet potato (orange-fleshed)
1 onion, finely chopped
salt and freshly ground black pepper
15 ml (1 tbsp) lemon juice
50 g (2 oz) butter, melted
15 ml (1 tbsp) clarified butter, for cooking

Peel all of the potatoes, cut into quarters and cook in boiling water for 5 minutes. Drain and rinse in cold water to stop further cooking. Allow to cool for 15 minutes.

Grate the cooled potatoes and place in a bowl with the onion, seasoning, lemon juice and melted butter. Mix thoroughly.

Heat the clarified butter in a heavy-based frying pan. Place heaped spoonfuls of the potato mixture in the pan and shape into rounds, about 7.5 cm (3 inches) in diameter. Cook over a moderate heat for about 5 minutes, pressing down firmly with a spatula to hold their shape. Turn the rösti over and cook the other side until golden brown and crisp. Drain on kitchen paper and serve at once.

Holly Schade

Potato Galettes

4 medium potatoes
1 clove garlic, finely chopped
1 shallot, finely chopped
salt and freshly ground black pepper
25 g (1 oz) butter
150 ml (¼ pint) fish stock

Grease a 12 inch (30 cm) oval gratin dish. Peel the potatoes and cut into wafer-thin slices; do not rinse them, as the starch in the potato helps the gratin stick together.

Shape 4 potato galettes in the gratin dish. Start by overlapping 5 potato slices in a circle to form a base to each galette. Sprinkle with half of the garlic, shallot and salt and pepper, then make another slightly smaller potato layer on top. Sprinkle over the remaining garlic and shallot and dot with a few small knobs of butter. Carefully pour in the fish stock which should just cover the base of the gratin dish.

Cook uncovered in a preheated oven at 160°C (325°F) mark 3 for about 50 minutes until the galettes are golden brown and crisp, and slightly charred at the edges. Serve at once.

Gill Tunkle

POTATOES DAUPHINOISE

25 g (1 oz) butter
1 small onion, thinly sliced
1 clove garlic, crushed
450 g (1 lb) King Edward potatoes, peeled and thinly sliced
150 ml (¼ pint) double cream
a little milk
salt and freshly ground black pepper

Melt half of the butter in a saucepan, add the onion and garlic and cook until soft.

Grease a suitable dish with the remaining butter. Layer a third of the potatoes in the base of the dish. Cover with half of the onion and garlic, then pour on half of the cream and milk; season liberally. Repeat these layers and finish with a layer of potatoes.

Cover with foil and bake in a preheated oven at 180°C (350°F) mark 4 for 45 minutes. Remove the foil and bake for a further 15 minutes until brown. Serve immediately.

Keely Smith

"The dauphinoise were good."

Nicky Clarke

Parsnip and Potato Cakes

225 g (8 oz) parsnips
225 g (8 oz) floury potatoes (eg King Edward)
1 small clove garlic, crushed
15 g (½ oz) butter, plus extra if necessary
5 ml (1 tsp) dry mustard
salt and freshly ground black pepper
60 ml (4 tbsp) seasoned plain flour
2 eggs, beaten
3 slices wholemeal bread
30 ml (2 tbsp) sesame seeds
sunflower oil, for deep-frying (see note)

Peel the parsnips and potatoes, then cut into chunks. Cook in boiling salted water until soft.

Meanwhile cook the crushed garlic gently in the butter.

Drain the parsnips and potatoes. Mash until smooth, then beat in the garlic butter and mustard. Add a little more butter if necessary. Season well. Let cool, then chill the mixture for about 20 minutes.

Have ready 3 bowls: one containing the seasoned flour; one containing the beaten eggs. Process the bread to make breadcrumbs and mix with the sesame seeds in the third bowl.

Shape the parsnip and potato mixture into 10 small balls. Roll each ball first in the flour, then in the beaten egg, then finally in breadcrumbs. Place on a plate and chill until needed.

Just before serving, heat the oil for deep-frying. Deep-fry the parsnip and potato balls in batches until golden brown. Drain on kitchen paper and serve piping hot.

Clare Askaroff

Sweet Potato Bakes

675 g (1½ lb) sweet potatoes
salt and freshly ground black pepper
40-50 g (1½-2 oz) butter
grated rind of 1 orange, plus a little juice if necessary
seeds from 4 cardamom pods, freshly ground
15 ml (1 tbsp) light muscovado sugar

Peel the sweet potatoes and cut into cubes. Cook in boiling salted water for about 10 minutes until soft. Drain thoroughly.

Mash the potatoes with the butter, then stir in the orange rind (see note). Season liberally with salt and pepper. Divide the mixture between four buttered ramekins.

Mix the ground cardamom seeds with the brown sugar and sprinkle on top of each ramekin. Top with a small knob of butter. Pop under a preheated grill until the sugar has caramelised. Alternatively place in a preheated oven at 180°C (350°F) mark 4 for 10 minutes.

Clare Askaroff

Cook's Note

Use the orange-fleshed variety of sweet potato for this dish. If the mixture seems at all dry, stir in a little of the juice from the orange.

Sweet Potato Latkes

1 large sweet potato, about 225 g (8 oz)
2 large potatoes, each about 225 g (8 oz)
2 eggs, beaten
50 g (2 oz) plain flour, sifted
15 ml (1 tbsp) chopped onion
salt and freshly ground black pepper
50 ml (2 fl oz) oil

Peel all of the potatoes and immerse them in a bowl of cold water. Leave to soak for 1 hour. Drain and coarsely grate the potatoes. Add the eggs, flour and chopped onion. Mix thoroughly, seasoning with salt and pepper.

Heat the oil in a frying pan until it is quite hot. Place tablespoonfuls of the mixture in the pan, spacing them apart. Cook on one side for about 5 minutes until crisp and brown underneath, then turn and cook the other side for approximately 5 minutes until cooked through and brown and crispy on both sides. Serve piping hot.

Jill O'Brien

Sage Tagliatelle

310 g (10½ oz) Italian "00" flour
pinch of salt
3 eggs (size 2)
3 drops of olive oil
15 ml (1 tbsp) finely chopped sage

To Serve:
butter, to taste
sage leaves, to garnish

To make the pasta dough, put the flour, salt, eggs, olive oil and sage in a food processor and process for about 30 seconds or until the dough forms a ball. Flatten the ball slightly with your hands, wrap in cling film and leave to rest in the refrigerator for 30 minutes.

Cut off about one quarter of the dough and rewrap the remainder. Flatten the piece and shape into a rectangle. Pass it through a pasta machine on its widest setting. Fold the dough and pass through the machine repeatedly, narrowing the setting by one notch each time until it passes through the second to last notch. Repeat with the remaining dough, then fit the tagliatelle attachment. Pass the pasta sheets through to cut the tagliatelle. Lay on clean tea-towels and leave to dry slightly, for about 5 minutes, before cooking.

Cook the tagliatelle in a large pan of boiling salted water for about 2 minutes until al dente (tender but firm to the bite). Drain and toss with butter to taste. Serve garnished with sage leaves.

Holly Schade

Grilled Polenta

175 g (6 oz) polenta flour
salt
freshly grated Parmesan cheese

Bring 1.2 litres (2 pints) of salted water to the boil in a heavy-based saucepan. Add the polenta flour and stir vigorously for 5 minutes, to ensure that no lumps form.

Pour the polenta into a lightly buttered shallow baking tin, to a depth of about 2 cm (¾ inch). Allow to cool and solidify.

Using a 5-7.5 cm (2-3 inch) pastry cutter, cut out circles of polenta allowing 2-3 per person. Sprinkle with grated Parmesan cheese and flash under a preheated hot grill until the cheese has melted and the polenta is heated through. Serve immediately.

Andrea Ferrari

> "I went mad for the grilled polenta."
>
> **Robert Carrier**

Wild Rice with Lemon Grass

125 g (4 oz) wild rice
25 g (1 oz) brown rice
2 lemon grass stalks
50 g (2 oz) butter
finely pared rind of 1 lemon
salt and freshly ground black pepper

Bring a large pan of salted water to the boil and add the wild and brown rice. Halve one stalk of lemon grass lengthways, then add to the pan with the rice. Simmer for 40 minutes, or until the rice is tender. Drain well, discarding the lemon grass.

Meanwhile, discard any coarse outer leaves from the other lemon grass stalk and chop very finely. Melt the butter in a pan, add the rice, lemon grass and lemon rind, and mix well. Heat through and keep warm until ready to serve.

Elaine Bates

Fragrant Wild Rice Timbales

225 g (8 oz) easy-cook mixed long-grain and wild rice
salt
½ bunch of coriander

Bring a pan of salted water to the boil. Tie the coriander with string and add to the water. Bring to a rolling boil, then add the rice. Lower the heat and simmer gently for 15-18 minutes until al dente, cooked but still firm to the bite. Drain thoroughly, discarding the coriander.

Spoon the rice into 4 warmed dariole moulds, level the surface, then unmould onto warmed plates.

Gill Tunkle

DESSERTS

Lemon Tart

Pastry:
125 g (4 oz) plain flour
pinch of salt
grated rind of 1 lemon
25 g (1 oz) icing sugar
75 g (3 oz) butter, in pieces
1 egg yolk, mixed with 15 ml (1 tbsp) iced water

Filling:
6 eggs (size 2)
225 g (8 oz) caster sugar
125 g (4 oz) unsalted butter, in pieces
grated rind of 3 lemons
150 ml (¼ pint) freshly squeezed lemon juice

To Decorate:
lemon rind shreds, blanched (optional)
icing sugar, for dusting

To make the pastry, put the flour, salt, lemon rind, icing sugar and butter in a food processor and process, using the pulse button, just until the mixture resembles coarse breadcrumbs. With the motor running, add the egg yolk and water, processing briefly until the mixture just holds together, but does not quite form a ball. Pull the dough together with your hands and quickly form a ball.

Flatten the dough then roll out between 2 sheets of cling film and use to line a 23 cm (9 inch) loose-bottomed flan tin. Trim the edges and prick the base with a fork. Chill in the refrigerator for 30 minutes.

Line the pastry case with greaseproof paper and fill with baking beans or rice. Bake in a preheated oven at 200°C (400°F) mark 6 for 10 minutes. Remove the paper and beans, then return the pastry case to the oven for a further 10 minutes, to dry and cook the base. Cool on a wire rack. Lower the oven temperature to 190°C (375°F) mark 5.

To make the filling, place all the ingredients in a bowl over a pan of simmering water. Whisk until well blended and continue stirring until the mixture thickens slightly – just enough to coat the back of a wooden spoon. Stand the flan tin on a baking sheet. Pour the filling into the pastry case and bake in the oven for 25 minutes, or until set. Allow to cool slightly.

Serve warm or cold, cut into wedges, decorated with lemon rind shreds if liked, and dusted with icing sugar. Accompany with the Crème Fraîche Ice Cream.

Holly Schade

Crème Fraîche Ice Cream

225 g (8 oz) crème fraîche
125 ml (4 fl oz) milk
45 ml (3 tbsp) lemon juice
150 g (5 oz) caster sugar

Put all of the ingredients in a food processor and process briefly until evenly blended and smooth. Transfer to a bowl and chill until cold, then freeze in an ice-cream maker according to the manufacturer's instructions.

"...lovely, refreshing."

Jill Dando

If you do not have an ice-cream maker, freeze the ice cream in a shallow container, whisking 2-3 times during freezing to break down the ice crystals and ensure an even-textured result.

Serve the ice cream in scoops, with the lemon tart.

Holly Schade

Lemon Tart with Crème Fraîche Ice Cream

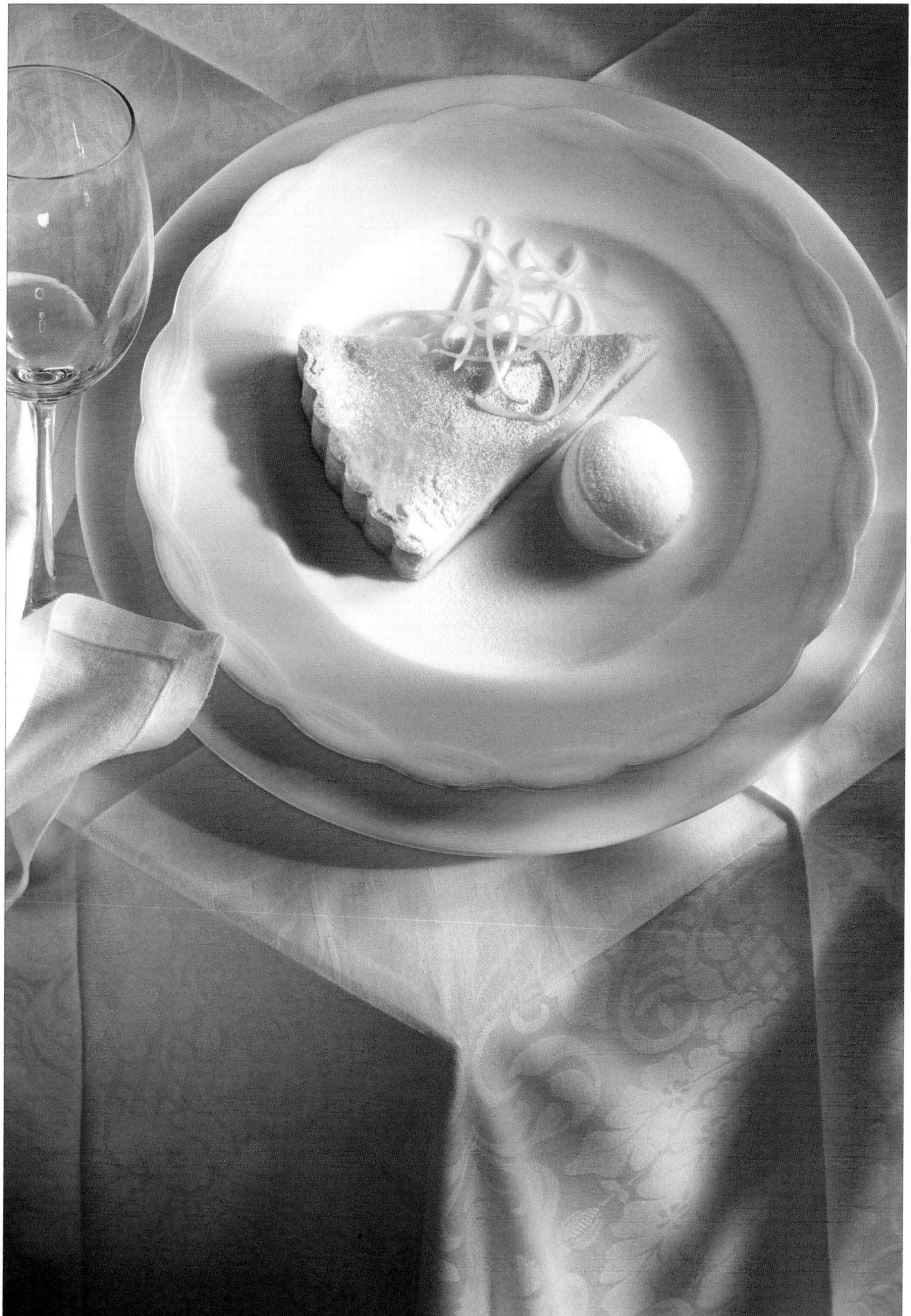

Bruléed Lime Curd Cream Tartlets

with Raspberry Coulis

Pastry:
250 g (9 oz) plain flour
pinch of salt
25 g (1 oz) ground almonds
15 ml (1 tbsp) icing sugar
150 g (5 oz) chilled unsalted butter, diced
1 egg yolk

Filling:
3 eggs (size 1), plus 3 egg yolks
scant 75 g (3 oz) vanilla caster sugar
finely grated rind and juice of 3 limes
15 g (½ oz) butter
185 ml (6 fl oz) double cream
225 g (8 oz) raspberries

Raspberry Coulis:
225 g (8 oz) raspberries
50 g (2 oz) sugar
squeeze of lemon juice (optional)

To Decorate:
icing sugar, for dusting
8 mint leaves
30 ml (2 tbsp) single cream

Mix the flour, salt, ground almonds and icing sugar together in a bowl. Rub in the butter until the mixture resembles breadcrumbs. Add the egg yolk and about 30 ml (2 tbsp) cold water, to form a smooth dough. Wrap in cling film and place in the freezer for 20-30 minutes to chill thoroughly until firm enough to handle.

Roll out the pastry thinly and use to line 4 individual loose-bottomed flan tins. Line with greaseproof paper and baking beans and bake blind in a preheated oven at 200°C (400°F) mark 6 for 10 minutes. Remove the paper and beans and return to the oven for 5 minutes or until the bases are cooked. Leave to cool in the tins, then turn out.

Meanwhile, make the filling. Whisk the eggs, extra yolks and sugar together in a bowl until thick and creamy. Add the lime rind and juice, and stand the bowl over a pan of simmering water for about 10 minutes, whisking occasionally. When the lime curd has thickened just enough for the whisk to leave a trail when lifted, remove the bowl from the heat. Stir in the butter and allow to cool.

For the raspberry coulis, put the raspberries in a shallow dish, sprinkle with the sugar and leave to macerate for about 1 hour. Press through a nylon sieve into a bowl to remove the pips. Add a squeeze of lemon juice to taste.

To finish the tartlets, whip the cream until thick and fold into the lime curd. Fill the tartlet cases with raspberries, reserving 4 for decoration. Cover with the lime curd and chill in the refrigerator for 30 minutes (if time permits).

Dust the tartlets with icing sugar. Protect the edges of the pastry with foil and place under a preheated high grill to caramelise the sugar; this will take about 10 seconds. Allow to cool.

Place each tartlet on a large serving plate and decorate with the reserved raspberries and mint leaves. Surround with the raspberry coulis, dot with the cream and feather with a skewer. Serve at once.

Gillian Humphrey

Note: This pastry is rich and a little difficult to roll out, so handle it as little as possible. The quantities below make twice as much pastry as you need; freeze the other half for another occasion.

Chocolate and Amaretto Cheese Tart

225 g (8 oz) chocolate digestive biscuits
50 g (2 oz) butter, melted
2 eggs
225 g (8 oz) cream cheese
25 g (1 oz) caster sugar
150 ml (¼ pint) double cream
125 g (4 oz) good quality plain chocolate
60 ml (4 tbsp) amaretto di Saronno liqueur
toasted flaked almonds, to decorate

"That was great – the mixture of cheese, it just kept it from being too sickly sweet."

Nicky Clarke

Grease 4 small clean baked bean tins, or similar ovenproof moulds. Finely crush the biscuits and mix with the melted butter. Spoon into the greased tins and press down firmly onto the bases, using the back of the spoon. Chill in the refrigerator while preparing the topping.

Place the eggs, cream cheese, sugar and cream in a food processor and process for 15 seconds.

Meanwhile, break the chocolate into pieces, place in a pyrex bowl and melt in the microwave on medium for 3 minutes. (Alternatively stand the bowl over a pan of simmering water until melted.) Let cool slightly, then add to the cream mixture, with the liqueur. Process for a further 10 seconds until evenly mixed.

Pour the mixture on top of the biscuit bases and bake in a preheated oven at 150°C (300°F) mark 2 for 15-25 minutes until just set. Remove from the oven and chill in the refrigerator for at least 1 hour.

Run a knife around the edge of each tart and carefully remove from their tins. Decorate with the toasted almonds and serve with single cream.

Keely Smith

COOK'S NOTE

When cooked, the tarts may have an uneven surface. Trim to level if necessary after turning out.

CHOCOLATE PECAN PIE

Pastry:

185 g (6½ oz) plain flour
2.5 ml (½ tsp) salt
5 ml (1 tsp) caster sugar
65 g (2½ oz) butter
25 g (1 oz) white vegetable shortening, in pieces
(2½-3 tbsp) iced water

Filling:

50 g (2 oz) plain chocolate, in pieces
50 g (2 oz) butter
4 eggs (size 1)
250 ml (8 fl oz) maple syrup
225 g (8 oz) caster sugar
5 ml (1 tsp) vanilla essence
350 g (12 oz) shelled pecan nuts, roughly chopped

To make the pastry, put the flour, salt, sugar, butter and vegetable shortening in a food processor. Process, using the pulse button, until the mixture begins to resemble breadcrumbs; do not over-mix. Transfer the mixture to a bowl and sprinkle over 40 ml (2½ tbsp) iced water. Toss with a fork, sprinkling in a little more iced water as necessary until the mixture begins to stick together. Working quickly, draw the dough together with your hands and form into a ball.

Roll out the pastry on a lightly floured surface and use to line a 23 cm (9 inch) fluted flan tin. Trim and crimp the edges. Chill in the refrigerator for 30 minutes.

Meanwhile, prepare the filling. Put the chocolate and butter in a bowl and melt together in the microwave on medium (or over a pan of simmering water). Stir until smooth, then set aside to cool.

Put the eggs, maple syrup, sugar and vanilla essence in a mixing bowl and beat until well combined. Stir in the chocolate mixture, then fold in the nuts. Pour into the chilled pastry case and bake in the middle of a preheated oven at 190°C (375°F) mark 5 for 50-60 minutes, or until a skewer inserted into the centre comes out only slightly fudgy. Serve warm, with the Vanilla Ice Cream.

Holly Schade

VANILLA ICE CREAM

300 ml (½ pint) double cream
200 ml (7 fl oz) semi-skimmed milk
1 vanilla pod
2.5 ml (½ tsp) vanilla essence
4 egg yolks (size 1)
125 g (4 oz) caster sugar

Pour the cream and milk into a saucepan. Scrape the seeds from the vanilla pod into the liquid and add the vanilla essence. Slowly bring the mixture just to the boil. Meanwhile, beat the egg yolks and sugar together in a bowl until well blended. Slowly add the hot liquid, stirring constantly.

Return to the pan and stir over a low heat until the custard is thick enough to lightly coat the back of the wooden spoon; do not boil or it will curdle. Strain into a clean bowl and leave to cool. Transfer to an ice-cream maker and churn, according to the manufacturer's instructions, until firm.

If you do not have an ice-cream maker, freeze the ice cream in a suitable container, whisking 2-3 times during freezing to break down the ice crystals and ensure a smooth-textured result.

Serve with the Pecan Pie.

Holly Schade

Pears in Pastry Lattice

with Lime Butterscotch Sauce

2 ripe, firm pears
225 g (8 oz) puff pastry
a little milk, to glaze

Sugar Syrup:
250 g (9 oz) caster sugar
25 ml (1 fl oz) lemon juice

Frangipane:
60 g (2¼ oz) unsalted butter, softened
60 g (2¼ oz) caster sugar
1 egg, beaten
60 g (2¼ oz) ground almonds
15 g (½ oz) plain flour

Sauce:
75 g (3 oz) caster sugar
50 ml (2 fl oz) liquid glucose
juice of 1 lime
250 ml (8 fl oz) double cream

To Decorate:
icing sugar, for dusting

To make the sugar syrup, put the sugar, lemon juice and 500 ml (16 fl oz) water in a saucepan and heat gently until the sugar is dissolved, then bring to the boil. Peel, halve and core the pears, then add to the syrup and poach for about 20 minutes until tender. Remove from the syrup and leave to cool on a plate.

To make the frangipane, put all the ingredients in a bowl and whisk together thoroughly using an electric whisk until smooth.

Roll out half of the puff pastry thinly on a lightly floured surface and cut 4 pear shapes, about 1 cm (½ inch) larger all round than the pears. Roll out the other half of the pastry, then roll with the lattice roller to make your pastry lattice.

Spread a small amount of frangipane on each pear-shaped piece of pastry, leaving a 1 cm (½ inch) border. Place a pear on top and brush the pastry edges with a little milk. Cut a piece of lattice pastry to fit over each pear and carefully position over the pears. Press the pastry edges together to seal and trim to neaten.

Place on a lightly greased baking tray and brush with milk to glaze. Cut 12 small leaves from the pastry trimmings, brush with milk and place on the baking tray. Cook in a preheated oven at 190°C (375°F) mark 5 for about 10 minutes until the pastry is crisp and golden brown.

To make the sauce, put the sugar and glucose in a saucepan with 25 ml (1 fl oz) water over a low heat until the sugar is dissolved. Add the lime juice and cream, bring to the boil and boil for 1 minute.

To serve, place a lattice pear on each warmed serving plate and decorate with the small pastry leaves. Dust with icing sugar and pour the sauce around each pear. Serve immediately.

Rachel Southall

> *"I can't imagine a better pudding than that... the sauce was immaculate."*
>
> Loyd

Cook's Note

To make the pastry lattice for this dessert you will need a lattice roller. This is a plastic or perspex cylinder with 'blades' set in it. As you roll the lattice roller over the pastry it cuts slits in the pastry. When the pastry is lifted from the work surface these slits open up to form the lattice. You can buy an inexpensive lattice roller from a kitchen shop or mail order cookware supplier.

Pears in Pastry Lattice with Lime Butterscotch Sauce

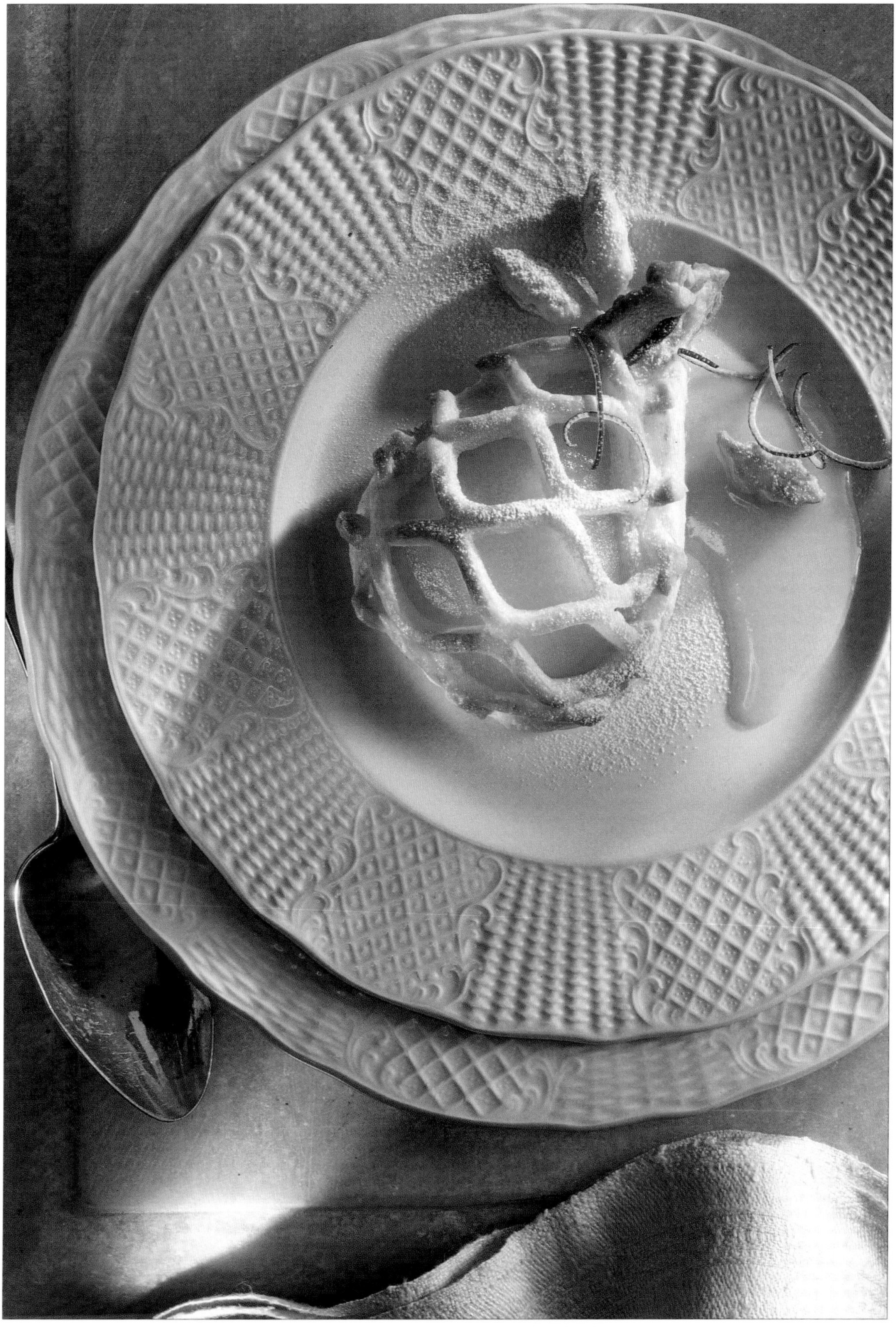

WALNUT PIE

WITH A PRUNE AND MARSALA SAUCE

Pastry:
250 g (9 oz) unbleached plain flour
25 g (1 oz) icing sugar
2.5 ml (½ tsp) salt
175 g (6 oz) cold unsalted butter, diced
1 (size 2) egg, plus 1 egg yolk

Filling:
150 g (5 oz) walnuts
2 (size 2) eggs
210 g (7½ oz) vanilla-flavoured caster sugar
1 egg yolk, mixed with a little milk

Prune and Marsala Sauce:
75 g (3 oz) Agen prunes, soaked overnight in 300 ml (½ pint) water
45 ml (3 tbsp) Marsala
15 ml (1 tbsp) double cream
a little sugar, to taste

To Decorate:
icing sugar, for dusting
12 walnut halves

Sift the flour, icing sugar and salt into a mixing bowl. Add the butter and rub in until the mixture resembles breadcrumbs. Lightly beat the eggs and add to the flour mixture. Mix to a smooth dough, using a round-bladed knife. Wrap in cling film and leave to rest in the refrigerator for at least 30 minutes.

To make the filling, put the walnuts in a food processor or blender and grind to a medium fineness. Put the eggs and sugar in a mixing bowl and stir with a balloon whisk for 2 minutes, without beating. Stir in the ground walnuts.

Set aside one third of the pastry for the lid. Roll out the larger piece on a lightly floured surface until big enough to line an oblong loose-bottomed tart tin, measuring 36 x 11 cm (14 x 4½ inches). Line the tin with the pastry and trim the edges. (Add the trimmings to the other portion of pastry.) Fill the pastry case with the walnut mixture.

Roll out the pastry to make a lid. Moisten the edges with a little of the egg mixture and carefully position the lid, pressing the edges together to seal. Trim off excess pastry. Make three slits in the lid and brush with the egg and milk. Bake in a preheated oven at 180°C (350°F) mark 4 for 35 minutes.

Meanwhile, make the sauce. Cook the prunes in the soaking water for 20 minutes or until soft. Allow to cool a little, then drain, reserving the liquor, and remove the stones. Press the flesh through a fine sieve with a wooden spoon. Put the prune pulp and Marsala in a blender and process until smooth adding enough prune juice to make a sauce the consistency of thin cream. Pour into a small bowl and stir in the cream. Adjust the sweetness if necessary, keeping the sauce slightly tart.

> *"The pudding was not too rich, and the pastry was just divine."*
>
> Rosemary Leach

Allow the tart to cool, then remove from the tin. Dust with icing sugar and cut into thick slices. To serve, pour a pool of sauce onto each serving plate. Place a slice of walnut pie in the centre and decorate with walnut halves.

Derek Morris

Orange Almond Tart

with Ginger and Honey Ice Cream

Pastry:

225 g (8 oz) plain flour
75 g (3 oz) icing sugar
125 g (4 oz) unsalted butter, diced
finely grated rind of 1 orange
1 egg, beaten

Tart Filling:

5 large firm oranges
15 ml (1 tbsp) Grand Marnier
30 ml (2 tbsp) icing sugar
125 g (4 oz) butter
75 g (3 oz) caster sugar
2 eggs (size 1)
150 g (5 oz) ground almonds
120 ml (4 fl oz) sieved orange marmalade

Ice Cream:

2 eggs, separated
25 g (1 oz) icing sugar
180 ml (6 fl oz) double cream
15 ml (1 tbsp) honey
2 pieces of preserved stem ginger in syrup, drained and sliced

Cook's Note

If you do not have an ice-cream machine, freeze the ice cream in a suitable container, whisking periodically during freezing to break down the ice crystals, for an even-textured result.

To make the pastry, sift the flour and icing sugar into a bowl and rub in the butter until the mixture resembles breadcrumbs. Add the orange rind and egg. Mix with a round-bladed knife, then lightly knead the dough until smooth. Wrap in cling film and leave to rest in the refrigerator for 30 minutes.

"The tart was good. The pastry was super."

Paul Reed

To make the ice cream, whisk the egg yolks and icing sugar together in a bowl until pale. In another bowl, whip the cream until thick and combine it with the honey; add to the yolk and sugar mixture. Whisk the egg whites until stiff, then fold into the mixture with the ginger. Transfer to an ice-cream maker and freeze until firm.

Roll out the pastry on a lightly floured surface to about a 3 mm (⅛ inch) thickness. Cut out 4 circles, large enough to line 4 individual flan tins, allowing some overhang. (Use a suitable plate or upturned bowl as a guide). Lightly grease and flour the flan tins, then fold the dough circles into them gently easing it into the corners and letting a little dough overhang. Line with greaseproof paper and fill with baking beans to ensure the sides are weighted as well as the base. Bake blind in a preheated oven at 180°C (350°F) mark 4 for 10 minutes. Remove the beans and paper and trim the edges of the pastry. Return to the oven for 10 minutes.

To prepare the tart filling, peel the oranges, removing all of the white pith. Cut the orange segments away from the membrane and place in a shallow dish. Squeeze any juice from the membranes over the segments and sprinkle with the Grand Marnier and icing sugar too. Cover and leave to macerate for 30 minutes.

Meanwhile, cream the butter and sugar together in a bowl, using an electric beater, until light and fluffy. Beat in the eggs, one at a time. Stir in the ground almonds and flour until evenly incorporated. Spread the almond mixture in the flan cases and bake in the oven for 20-25 minutes until golden. Allow to cool slightly.

Drain the orange segments, reserving 30 ml (2 tbsp) of the liquor. Place the marmalade and reserved liquor in a saucepan. Bring to the boil and reduce for 1-2 minutes. Brush this glaze onto the tarts, arrange the orange segments in circles on top and brush with more glaze.

Serve the tarts still slightly warm or cool, accompanied by the ginger and honey ice cream.

Michael Gray

Cranberry and Orange Charlotte

2 oranges
225 g (8 oz) cranberries
125 g (4 oz) sugar, or to taste
6 cardamom pods, seeds only – crushed
1 brioche loaf
125 g (4 oz) unsalted butter, melted

To Serve:
icing sugar, for dusting
a little fromage frais
finely pared orange rind, shredded (simmered in sugar syrup, if preferred)

Finely grate the rind from 1 orange, then squeeze the juice. Peel and segment the other orange, discarding all white pith.

Put the cranberries and sugar in a saucepan with 150 ml (¼ pint) water. Add the grated orange rind and crushed cardamom seeds. Heat gently until the sugar is dissolved, then simmer for 10 minutes. Taste for sweetness, adding a little more sugar if necessary. Transfer half of the mixture to a blender or food processor and work until smooth, then press through a sieve into a bowl. Stir in the orange juice to make a coulis; set aside.

Add the orange segments to the other half of the cranberry mixture.

To assemble the charlottes, you will need 4 individual round tins or individual pudding moulds, about 200 ml (7 fl oz) in capacity (see cook's note). Cut thin slices from the brioche loaf. From these, cut 8 circles to fit the base and top of the moulds. Dip 4 brioche circles into the melted butter and fit into the base of the tins. Cut thin strips of brioche to line the sides of the tin, dip in melted butter and position around the insides of the tins. Fill with the cranberry and orange segment mixture. Dip the remaining brioche circles in butter and position on top.

Place on a baking sheet and bake in a preheated oven at 200°C (400°F) mark 6 for 25 minutes or until crisp and well browned. Carefully remove the charlottes from the tins.

Transfer to individual plates and dust with icing sugar. Surround with the cranberry and orange coulis, dot with the fromage frais and feather with a wooden skewer. Decorate with orange rind shreds and serve immediately.

Mary Wilde

"Really Gorgeous."

Michael Ball

Cook's Note

I use cleaned small baked bean tins for these individual charlottes, but you can use any similar sized moulds.

Cranberry and Orange Charlotte

Raspberry Surprise

Whisked Sponge:
50 g (2 oz) plain flour
pinch of salt
2 eggs (size 2)
65 g (2½ oz) caster sugar

Topping:
225 g (8 oz) raspberries (fresh or frozen and defrosted)
300 ml (½ pint) soured cream
75 g (3 oz) caster sugar

To Decorate:
100 g (3½ oz) quality plain dark chocolate
300 ml (½ pint) double cream
5 ml (1 tsp) caster sugar

To make the whisked sponge, line two 15 cm (6 inch) round cake tins with non-stick baking parchment. Sift the flour and salt together; set aside. Put the eggs into a mixing bowl and gradually beat in the sugar. Place the bowl over a saucepan, one-third full of boiling water, making sure the bowl does not touch the water. Using an electric hand whisk, whisk the eggs and sugar together until the mixture is thick, light in colour and significantly increased in volume; this will take at least 5 minutes. Remove the bowl from the pan. Lightly fold the flour into the mixture, using a metal spoon.

Divide the mixture between the prepared cake tins. Bake in a preheated oven at 190°C (375°F) mark 5 for about 20 minutes, until well risen and golden brown. Turn out and cool on a wire rack. (You will only need to use one of the sponges for this dessert, so freeze the other one for another occasion.)

Line four individual 7.5-10 cm (3-4 inch) round tins with non-stick baking parchment. Slice the sponge horizontally into two layers, then cut into smaller pieces and use to cover the base of the tins. Scatter the raspberries over the sponge, reserving a few for decoration. Stir the soured cream and sugar together, then pour over the raspberries. Bake in a preheated oven at 180°C (350°F) mark 4 for 25 minutes until set. Allow to cool in the tins.

Meanwhile make the chocolate scrolls. Break the chocolate into pieces and place in a small bowl over a pan of hot water until melted. Stir until smooth, then pour onto a clean flat surface, preferably a marble slab, and allow to cool and set. Hold a long-bladed knife in both hands and push the blade away from you along the surface of the chocolate to shave off long scrolls.

To finish, carefully remove the desserts from their tins and place on individual serving plates. Whip the double cream with the 5 ml (1 tsp) caster sugar and spread over the top of the desserts. Decorate with the dark chocolate scrolls and reserved raspberries.

Alison Fiander

Cook's Note

If individual tins are not available, use a 20 cm (8 inch) loose-bottomed cake tin instead.

Bananas Baked en Papilotte

with Mango and Passion Fruit

1 ripe mango
8 passion fruit
juice of ½ orange
75 g (3 oz) caster sugar
4 bananas
juice of ¼ lemon
1 vanilla pod

Peel the mango and cut into fairly large chunks, discarding the stone. Put a quarter of the mango pieces in a food processor. Halve the passion fruit and scoop out the pulp and seeds into the processor. Add the orange juice and sugar. Process until the mango is puréed, then pass through a sieve to remove the passion fruit seeds.

> "It was a totally new experience to have all these fruits combined in their juices."
>
> Ken Russell

Cut 4 pieces of foil, about 60 x 30 cm (24 x 12 inches). Fold each one in half, to make 30 cm (12 inch) squares. Halve the bananas lengthwise and lay one piece on the lower half of each foil square. Sprinkle with a little lemon juice. Divide the mango chunks between the parcels.

Cut the vanilla pod into 4 pieces, then split open. Using a knife, scrape out the vanilla seeds and place on the banana. Include a piece of vanilla pod in each parcel. Spoon the mango and passion fruit purée over the banana and fold the top half of the foil over.

Starting at the top left corner begin neatly folding in the foil to seal the package. Continue until only the top right corner is left open, then blow into the package to inflate it before sealing.

Bake in a preheated oven at 190°C (375°F) mark 5 for 10 minutes. Let your guests slit open the parcels to reveal the contents! Serve with vanilla ice cream.

Suzanne Wynn

APPLE STREUSEL PIES

Pastry:
125 g (4 oz) plain flour
50 g (2 oz) unsalted butter
10 ml (2 tsp) icing sugar
1 egg yolk
15 ml (3 tsp) cold water (approximately)

Filling:
50 g (2 oz) plain flour
25 g (1 oz) unsalted butter
50 g (2 oz) caster sugar
225 g (8 oz) cooking apples
15 g (½ oz) sultanas
150 ml (¼ pint) double cream

Topping:
15 g (½ oz) caster sugar
2.5 ml (½ tsp) ground cinnamon
icing sugar, for dusting

To make the pastry, sift the flour into a bowl and rub in the butter until the mixture resembles fine breadcrumbs. Stir in the icing sugar. Add the egg yolk and sufficient cold water to mix to a soft dough. Wrap in cling film and chill in the refrigerator for 10-15 minutes.

Meanwhile, make the crumble for the filling. Sift the flour into a bowl and rub in the butter until it resembles fine breadcrumbs. Stir in the caster sugar.

Peel, core and thinly slice the apples. Roll out the pastry thinly and use to line four greased 10 cm (4 inch) loose-bottomed fluted flan tins. Sprinkle 10 ml (2 tsp) crumble mixture over the base of each pastry case. Divide the apples and sultanas between the pastry cases, arranging them neatly in layers. Pour on the cream. Sprinkle the remaining crumble mixture evenly over the fruit. (You may not need to use all of it.)

For the topping, mix the sugar and cinnamon together and sprinkle on top of the flans. Place on a baking sheet and bake in the centre of a preheated oven at 200°C (400°F) mark 6 for 20 minutes. Lower the setting to 190°C (375°F) mark 5 and cook for a further 10 minutes.

Leave to stand for a few minutes, then carefully remove from the tins and place on serving plates dusted with icing sugar. Accompany with the Pecan and Maple Ice Cream.

Clare Askaroff

PECAN AND MAPLE ICE CREAM

50 g (2 oz) pecan nuts
2 eggs, separated
30 ml (2 tbsp) caster sugar
150 ml (¼ pint) Jersey or double cream
30 ml (2 tbsp) maple syrup

Toast the pecan nuts under the grill, then chop (not too finely). Set aside a few chopped nuts for decoration.

In a large bowl, whisk the egg whites until very stiff. Whisk in the sugar 15 ml (1 tbsp) at a time. In another bowl, lightly whip the cream.

Add the cream, egg yolks, maple syrup and chopped nuts to the egg white mixture and carefully fold in.

Transfer the mixture to an ice-cream maker and churn for 15-20 minutes. Turn into a freezerproof container and place in the freezer until required. Unless serving within 2 hours, transfer the ice cream to the refrigerator 30 minutes before serving to soften slightly. Serve sprinkled with the reserved chopped nuts.

Clare Askaroff

PEARS IN SAUTERNES

WITH A GINGER AND CHOCOLATE SAUCE

4 ripe firm pears
250 ml (8 fl oz) Sauternes wine
25 g (1 oz) sugar
juice of ½ lemon

Sauce:
100 g (3½ oz) plain dark chocolate
30 g (1 oz) preserved stem ginger in syrup, drained

Peel the pears, leaving the stalks on. Carefully remove the cores from the base of the pears, using an apple corer or teaspoon.

Pour the Sauternes into a saucepan. Add 250 ml (8 fl oz) water, the sugar and lemon juice. Heat gently until the sugar has dissolved. Bring to the boil, then stand the pears in the liquid. Cover and simmer for 15-30 minutes depending on the ripeness of the pears, until they are translucent. To test the pears insert a fine skewer into the base of each one. Lift the pears out of the liquid and leave to cool; reserve the cooking liquid.

Meanwhile melt the chocolate in a heatproof bowl over a pan of simmering water. Finely chop the ginger and add to the melted chocolate. Stir in enough of the reserved liquid to give a smooth pouring consistency. Pour some of the sauce on to each serving plate and place a pear in the middle. Serve immediately.

Rachel Southall

ROASTED FIGS IN HONEY BUTTER AND ORANGE

8-12 fresh figs
50 g (2 oz) unsalted butter
30 ml (2 tbsp) honey
finely grated rind and juice of 1 orange

Orange Cream:
150 ml (¼ pint) double cream
juice of ½ orange

To Serve:
Orange Sablés (see right)

Peel the figs and cut each one vertically into quarters. Melt the butter and honey in an ovenproof dish, then stir in the orange juice. Place the figs in a single layer in the dish and sprinkle over the orange rind. Cook in a preheated oven at 190°C (375°F) mark 5 for 15 minutes, basting occasionally.

Meanwhile, to make the orange cream, lightly whip the cream with the orange juice.

Transfer the figs to warmed serving plates and spoon over some of the juices. Serve warm, with the orange cream and accompanied by the Orange Sablés.

Elaine Bates

ORANGE SABLÉS

100 g (3½ oz) butter
1 egg yolk
110 g (4½ oz) plain flour
50 g (2 oz) icing sugar
finely grated rind of 1 orange
10 ml (2 tsp) orange juice (approximately)

Place all the ingredients, except the orange juice, in a food processor and process quickly until smooth. Add enough of the orange juice to bind the dough. Wrap in cling film and chill in the freezer for 30 minutes.

Roll out the dough on a lightly floured surface to a 5 mm (¼ inch) thickness and cut into 5 cm (2 inch) rounds. Place on a lightly greased baking sheet and bake in a preheated oven at 190°C (375°F) for 6-8 minutes until light golden. Cool on a wire rack.

Elaine Bates

Roasted Figs in Honey Butter and Orange, with Orange Sablés

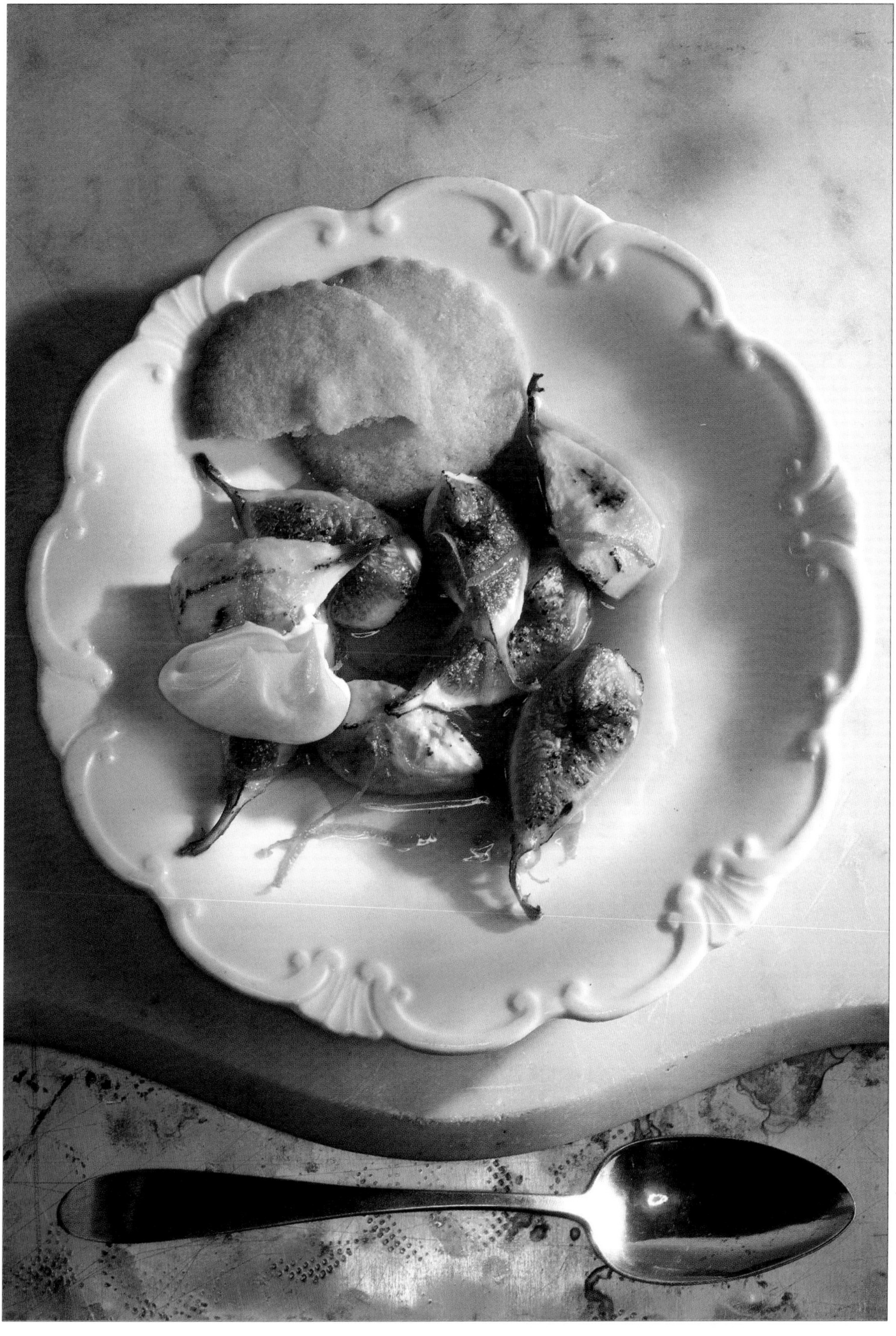

Chocolate Mille Feuille with Lemon Mousse

and a Caramel Orange Sauce

Chocolate Discs:
160 g (5½ oz) plain couverture chocolate

Mousse:
1 lemon
5 ml (1 tsp) powdered gelatine
2 eggs (size 4)
60 g (2 oz) vanilla caster sugar (see note)
120 ml (4 fl oz) double cream

Sauce:
2 oranges
175 g (6 oz) caster sugar
30 ml (2 tbsp) Grand Marnier or other orange liqueur

To Finish:
icing sugar, for dusting

Draw about 30 circles, 5 cm (2 inches) in diameter, on a sheet of non-stick baking parchment placed on a board or large baking sheet (ie 4 per person plus a few spares in case of breakages).

Melt the chocolate in a bowl over a pan of hot water. Spread the chocolate thinly to cover each circle evenly with the back of a teaspoon, using a circular motion. Leave in a cool place or refrigerate until set.

Using a zester, finely pare the rind from the lemon and one of the oranges. Blanch in boiling water, rinse, then simmer in water to cover for 20 minutes. Drain and allow to cool.

To prepare the mousse, squeeze the juice from the lemon into a small bowl and sprinkle on the gelatine. Leave to soften until spongy. Whisk the egg yolks and sugar in a large bowl until pale and creamy. In a separate bowl, whisk the egg whites until stiff but not dry. Lightly whip the cream in another bowl. Stand the gelatine bowl over a pan of simmering water until dissolved.

Stir the dissolved gelatine into the egg yolk mixture. Continue to stir until the mixture is cool and beginning to thicken; this only takes a few minutes. Fold in the cream, then fold in the whisked egg whites. Refrigerate until set.

To make the sauce, squeeze the juice from the oranges. Melt the sugar in a heavy-based saucepan over a low heat, then increase the heat to moderate and cook, without stirring, until caramelised. Carefully add the orange juice (protecting your hand with a cloth as it will spurt furiously). Heat, stirring until the caramel dissolves. Strain and return to the heat. Add the orange and lemon zest and simmer for 2-3 minutes. Allow to cool, then add the liqueur.

To assemble the dessert, sandwich 4 chocolate discs together with the lemon mousse on each serving plate. Dust the tops with icing sugar and pour a pool of sauce around the mille feuilles. Serve at once.

Ashley Wilson

Note: To make your own vanilla sugar, keep a vanilla pod in a jar of caster sugar. It will impart a delicate flavour.

Mango Brulée

1 ripe mango
600 ml (1 pint) double cream
3 drops of vanilla essence
2 eggs
2 egg yolks
30 ml (2 tbsp) caster sugar

Topping:
60 ml (4 tbsp) demerara sugar

Peel the mango and cut into slices, discarding the stone. Arrange the mango slices in the bases of 4 ramekins.

Pour the cream into a glass jug, add the vanilla essence and warm in the microwave. (Alternatively warm in a heavy-based pan over a low heat.) In a bowl, beat together the eggs, egg yolks and caster sugar. Pour on the warmed cream and blend well.

> *"I thought the crust was excellent..."*
>
> David Burke

Pour the mixture into the ramekins and place in a bain-marie (or a roasting tin containing enough water to come half-way up the sides of the ramekins). Bake in a preheated oven at 190°C (375°F) mark 5 for 30-40 minutes. Allow to cool.

When cool sprinkle each one with 15 ml (1 tbsp) demerara sugar and place under a hot grill for 2-3 minutes until caramelised. Leave to stand for 5 minutes before serving.

Robin Machin

Irish Goat's Milk Cheese Trinity

with Strawberry Coulis

600 ml (1 pint) fresh goat's milk
15 ml (1 tbsp) live yogurt culture (see note)
1 vanilla pod, split
50 g (2 oz) each of 3 different soft fruits (eg strawberries, raspberries, redcurrants), or unshelled nuts (eg hazelnuts)

Strawberry Coulis:
125 g (4 oz) strawberries

To Serve:
extra soft fruit
mint sprigs
icing sugar, for dusting

Put half of the goat's milk in a saucepan and bring to boiling point. Remove from the heat and allow to cool until lukewarm (ie blood temperature – 37°C [98.4°F]). Stir in the live yogurt culture and pour into a warmed vacuum flask. Set aside overnight.

The following day, put the remaining 300 ml (½ pint) milk in a heavy-based saucepan. Add the split vanilla pod and heat gently to boiling point. Add the yogurt, remove from the heat and stir once; soft curds will form.

Set a colander lined with muslin over a bowl. Pour in the milk curds. Allow to drain and cool for 10-15 minutes. Carefully gather up the muslin and squeeze out as much liquid whey as possible. Place a small flat plate on top of the muslin-wrapped cheese, then place a weight on top. Leave in the refrigerator for 1 hour.

Meanwhile make the strawberry coulis by pressing the strawberries through a fine nylon sieve into a bowl. Set aside.

Prepare the soft fruit and cut into small pieces, if necessary. Roast the nuts in their shells by placing in the microwave on high for 2 minutes. Shell and crush the nuts. (Alternatively, shell the nuts and toast under a preheated grill.)

Divide the cheese into three equal portions and mix each one with a chosen variety of soft fruit or roasted nuts.

Line 12 small moulds, about 25-50 ml (1-2 fl oz) capacity with muslin. Fill with the flavoured cheeses to make 4 moulds of each flavour. Cover with another piece of muslin and press down firmly. Chill in the refrigerator for about 1 hour. Remove the cheese moulds from the refrigerator 30 minutes before serving and allow to come to room temperature.

To serve, turn out three different fruit cheeses onto each individual serving plate. Spoon the strawberry coulis around the cheeses and decorate with extra soft fruit and mint sprigs. Dust with icing sugar just before serving.

Linda Doherty

"It was lovely... so clean, so tasty and uncomplicated."

Paul Reed

COOK'S NOTE

You will need to partially prepare this dessert the day before it is required, unless you buy the goat's yogurt rather than make it yourself.

Raspberry and Chianti Sorbet

225 g (8 oz) caster sugar
1 bottle of Chianti, or similar red wine
12 mint leaves
300 g (10 oz) frozen raspberries

Dissolve the sugar in the wine in a saucepan over a low heat. Increase the heat, add the mint leaves and boil for about 2 minutes. Remove from the heat, add the raspberries and leave to stand for 1 hour.

Discard the mint leaves, then purée the raspberries and wine syrup in a blender or food processor. Strain through a nylon sieve to remove pips.

Transfer the mixture to an ice-cream machine and churn until frozen, then transfer to the freezer (unless serving imediately). If you do not have an ice-cream maker, freeze the sorbet in a freezerproof container, whisking periodically during freezing to break down the ice crystals and ensure a smooth result.

To serve, scoop the sorbet into chilled serving dishes. Serve at once.

Alison Fiander

"Brilliant pudding."

Loyd

Ricotta Hearts with Pistachios and Kirsch

SERVED WITH RASPBERRY AND MANGO PURÉES

225 g (8 oz) ricotta cheese
60 ml (4 tbsp) icing sugar, sifted
1.25 ml (¼ tsp) vanilla extract
30 ml (2 tbsp) pistachio nuts, chopped
30 ml (2 tbsp) kirsch
150 ml (¼ pint) double cream
450 g (1 lb) raspberries, hulled
1 large ripe mango
4 mint sprigs, to decorate

"The pistachios inside were delicious."

Loyd

Line 4 heart-shaped moulds with dampened squares of muslin, which are large enough to overhang the sides.

Pass the ricotta cheese through a sieve into a bowl and beat until light and fluffy, then beat in 30 ml (2 tbsp) icing sugar and the vanilla extract. Fold in the pistachio nuts and kirsch, until evenly blended. Whip the double cream until thick, then fold into the cheese mixture.

Fill the lined moulds with the cheese mixture, piling it into a slight dome in the centre. Fold the muslin over the top to enclose and chill for at least 1 hour.

Set aside 2 large raspberries for decoration. Using the back of a ladle, press the remaining raspberries through a sieve into a bowl to remove the seeds. Stir in 15 ml (1 tbsp) icing sugar.

Peel, halve and stone the mango, then press the flesh through a sieve into a bowl. Add the remaining 15 ml (1 tbsp) icing sugar and stir well.

To serve, unmould each cheese dessert on to a flat dessert plate and carefully remove the muslin. Drizzle spoonfuls of raspberry purée around each cheese heart, followed by spoonfuls of mango purée. Using the tip of a knife, feather the fruit purées together decoratively. Top each cheese heart with a halved raspberry and a mint sprig to decorate. Serve immediately.

Tony Purwin

Ricotta Hearts with Pistachios and Kirsch

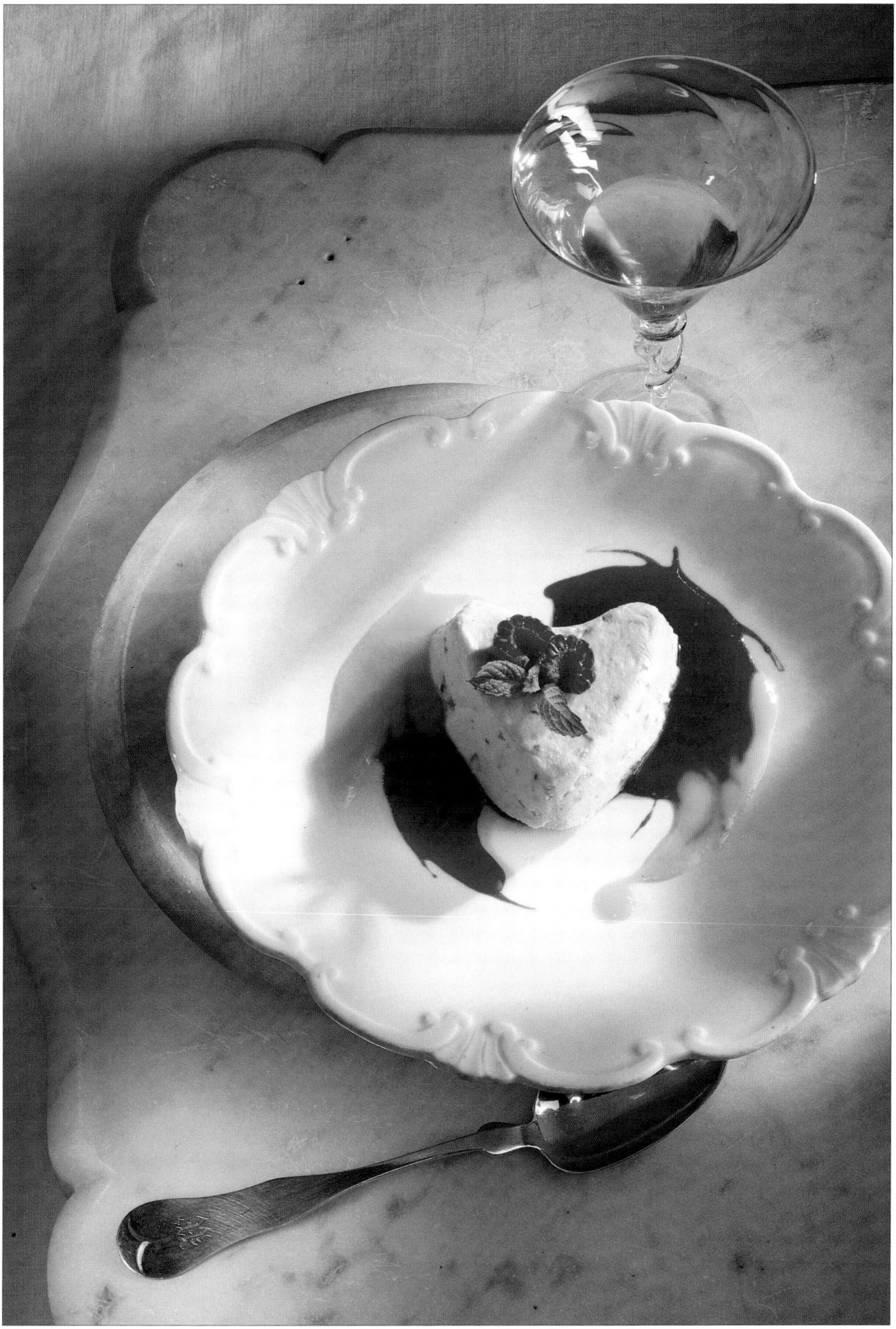

Pink Gin Syllabub with an Angostura Sauce

Syllabub:
5 ml (1 tsp) freshly ground mixed spice (cinnamon, juniper, allspice, nutmeg and clove)
105 ml (7 tbsp) gin
grated rind and juice of 1 lemon
15 ml (1 tbsp) angostura bitters
50 g (2 oz) caster sugar
1 drop of red food colouring
300 ml (½ pint) double cream

Angostura Sauce:
grated rind and juice of 1 lemon
150 g (5 oz) caster sugar
45 ml (3 tbsp) angostura bitters
45 ml (3 tbsp) water

Candied Lemon Zest:
finely pared rind of 1 lemon
25 g (1 oz) caster sugar
15 ml (1 tbsp) warm water
10 ml (2 tsp) grenadine

To Decorate:
mint sprigs

To make the syllabub, put the ground spice, gin, lemon rind and juice, angostura bitters and sugar in a bowl. Stir until the sugar is dissolved, then cover and leave to stand for 20 minutes. Strain into a mixing bowl and add the red colouring. Whisk, using an electric beater, then slowly add the cream in a steady stream, whisking constantly. As soon as the cream starts to thicken stop whisking, otherwise it will separate. Cover and chill in the refrigerator.

Meanwhile prepare the candied lemon zest. Cut the finely pared lemon rind into fine shreds, using a sharp knife. Blanch briefly in boiling water and drain. Dissolve the sugar in the water in a small pan over a low heat, then add the grenadine and bring to the boil. Add the lemon zest shreds and simmer for 10-15 minutes until candied. Remove the pink zests with a slotted spoon and spread out on a plate to cool.

To make the angostura sauce, put the lemon rind and juice in a saucepan with the sugar, water and angostura bitters. Place over a low heat until the sugar is dissolved, then bring to the boil and cook gently until you have a blush pink syrup with an aromatic lemon flavour. Strain and check the consistency: the sauce should just coat the back of a spoon; if too thick, add a drop or two of hot water.

To serve, pool a thin layer of the angostura sauce on each serving plate. Using two spoons dipped in hot water, quickly shape the syllabub into quenelles and arrange three on each plate, radiating from the centre. Decorate with the candied zests and mint sprigs. Serve immediately.

Roger Hemming

Hazelnut Torte with Mascarpone

and Bramble Coulis

Torte:
2 egg whites (size 3)
1.25 ml (¼ tsp) baking powder
125 g (4 oz) caster sugar
125 g (4 oz) hazelnuts, coarsely ground

Filling:
250 g (9 oz) mascarpone cheese
10 ml (2 tsp) icing sugar
22 ml (1½ tbsp) blackberry liqueur

Bramble Coulis:
175 g (6 oz) blackberries
40 g (1½ oz) icing sugar
7.5 ml (1½ tsp) lemon juice
7.5 ml (1½ tsp) blackberry liqueur

To Decorate:
50 g (2 oz) bitter chocolate, melted
few whole blackberries
mint sprigs

To make the torte, whisk the egg whites in a bowl until stiff. Whisk in the baking powder and half of the sugar, then carefully fold in the ground nuts and the rest of the sugar. Spoon onto baking sheets, lined with greaseproof paper or non-stick baking parchment, making two circles about 15 cm (6 inches) in diameter. Bake in a preheated oven at 180°C (350°F) mark 4 for about 30 minutes. Remove from the oven and allow to cool on the paper.

To make the bramble coulis, put the blackberries in a blender or food processor with the icing sugar and lemon juice and work to a purée. Pass through a sieve into a bowl to remove the pips, then add the liqueur and keep cool until required.

For the torte filling, mix the mascarpone with the icing sugar and liqueur. Invert one torte layer onto a serving plate and carefully spread with the filling. Place the other layer on top. Pipe fine lines of melted chocolate on top to decorate.

> *"I thought that meringue was just heaven... it was so beautiful and perfect."*

To serve, cut the torte into wedges and place on individual serving plates. Surround with the blackberry coulis and decorate with chocolate leaves if using, blackberries and mint sprigs.

Marion MacFarlane

COOK'S NOTE

Kirsch or crème de cassis can be used in place of the blackberry liqueur, but you may need to adjust the quantities according to taste.

VANILLA BAVAROIS

WITH ORANGE AND GRAND MARNIER SAUCE

Orange Jelly:
1 gelatine leaf
40 g (1½ oz) caster sugar
150 ml (¼ pint) fresh orange juice

Bavarois:
3 gelatine leaves
5 egg yolks
50 g (2 oz) caster sugar
250 ml (8 fl oz) milk
1 vanilla pod or vanilla extract
300 ml (½ pint) whipping cream

Sauce:
75 g (3 oz) caster sugar
275 ml (9 fl oz) fresh orange juice
finely pared zest of 1 orange, shredded
5 ml (1 tsp) arrowroot, mixed with a little water
30 ml (2 tbsp) Grand Marnier

To make the jelly, soak the gelatine leaf in cold water to cover. Meanwhile dissolve the sugar in the orange juice in a pan over a low heat. Bring to the boil, then remove from the heat. Squeeze excess water from the gelatine leaf, then add it to the pan and stir until dissolved. Pour the jelly into 4 dariole moulds to a depth of about 1 cm (½ inch). Place in the refrigerator until set.

To make the bavarois, soak the gelatine leaves in cold water to cover. Beat the egg yolks and sugar together in a bowl until thick and creamy. Put the milk and vanilla pod in a saucepan and bring to the boil. Remove from heat and discard vanilla pod. Add the milk to the egg and sugar mixture, stirring constantly, then return to the pan. Stir over a low heat until the custard thickens enough to coat the back of a spoon; do not boil. Squeeze excess water from the gelatine, then add to the warm custard off the heat, stirring to dissolve.

Pour the custard into a bowl set over ice and leave to cool, stirring occasionally, until it begins to set around the edge. Lightly whip the cream and fold into the mixture. Pour over the jelly to fill the dariole moulds. Refrigerate until set.

To make the sauce, place the sugar and orange juice in a pan with the orange zest strips and bring to the boil. Stir in the arrowroot and cook, stirring, for 1 minute to thicken to a syrupy consistency. Pour into a jug and allow to cool. Just before serving, stir in the Grand Marnier.

To serve, dip the moulds in warm water for a few seconds, then invert on to serving plates. Pour the sauce around and serve with Viennese Biscuits.

Michael Deacon

VIENNESE BISCUITS

125 g (4 oz) butter, well softened
25 g (1 oz) icing sugar, sifted
150 g (5 oz) plain flour, sifted
icing sugar, for dredging

Cream the butter and icing sugar together in a bowl until very soft and light. Stir in the flour. Put mixture into a piping bag fitted with a large star nozzle and pipe small rosettes onto a greased baking tray. Chill in refrigerator for 15 minutes, then bake in a preheated oven at 190°C (375°F) mark 5 for about 10 minutes until just beginning to turn golden brown. Cool on a wire rack. Dredge with icing sugar to serve.

Michael Deacon

Dark Chocolate Horns filled with a White Chocolate Mousse

Chocolate Horns:
225 g (8 oz) quality dark chocolate

White Chocolate Mousse:
50 g (2 oz) quality white chocolate
30 ml (2 tbsp) Browns liqueur Muscat
1 egg, separated
75 ml (2½ fl oz) double cream
2.5 ml (½ tsp) powdered gelatine
10 ml (2 tsp) milk

Apricot Sauce:
200 ml (7 oz) dried apricots
120 ml (4 fl oz) water
50 g (2 oz) caster sugar
15 ml (1 tbsp) lemon juice, or to taste
15 ml (1 tbsp) Browns liqueur Muscat

To Finish:
icing sugar, for dusting

To make the chocolate horns, carefully line 8 cream horn tins with non-stick baking parchment. Break the chocolate into pieces and place in a bowl standing over a pan of hot (recently boiled) water until melted. Stir until smooth. Using a clean pastry brush, apply an even coating of chocolate to the inside of each lined tin, making sure that there are no holes and that the chocolate reaches the top of the horn. Chill until set. Pipe any remaining chocolate into abstract shapes on a piece of non-stick baking parchment to use for decoration. Chill until set.

Gently remove the horns from the moulds, peel away the paper and leave in the refrigerator until needed.

To prepare the white chocolate mousse, break the chocolate into pieces and place in a heatproof bowl over a pan of hot (recently boiled) water. As the chocolate melts, incorporate the Muscat liqueur and 15 ml (1 tbsp) lukewarm water. Stir until smooth and evenly blended. Lightly beat the egg yolk and stir into the mixture.

Whip the double cream in a bowl until it just holds its shape. Carefully fold into the chocolate mixture. Soften the gelatine in the milk, then place the bowl over a pan of simmering water until the gelatine is dissolved. Stir into the chocolate mixture and chill the mixture until it begins to thicken.

Whisk the egg white until stiff, then fold gently into the chocolate mousse mixture. Leave until thickened to the consistency of whipped cream. Fill the chocolate horns with the mousse and chill for 1 hour before serving.

To make the apricot sauce, put the dried apricots in a saucepan with the water, sugar and lemon juice. Simmer for 20 minutes until the apricots begin to break up and form a syrup. Cool slightly, then purée in a food processor or blender. Pass through a sieve to ensure a smooth result. Add the muscat liqueur and adjust the flavour with more lemon juice if necessary. Chill in the refrigerator until required.

To serve, pool the apricot sauce on individual serving plates and arrange the chocolate horns on top. Decorate with the chocolate shapes and serve immediately, dusted with icing sugar.

Roger Hemming

Cook's Note

Avoid overhandling the chocolate horns as they are easily spoilt by fingerprints. Chocolate-dipped Cape gooseberries also make a pretty decoration.

Dark Chocolate Horns filled with a White Chocolate Mousse

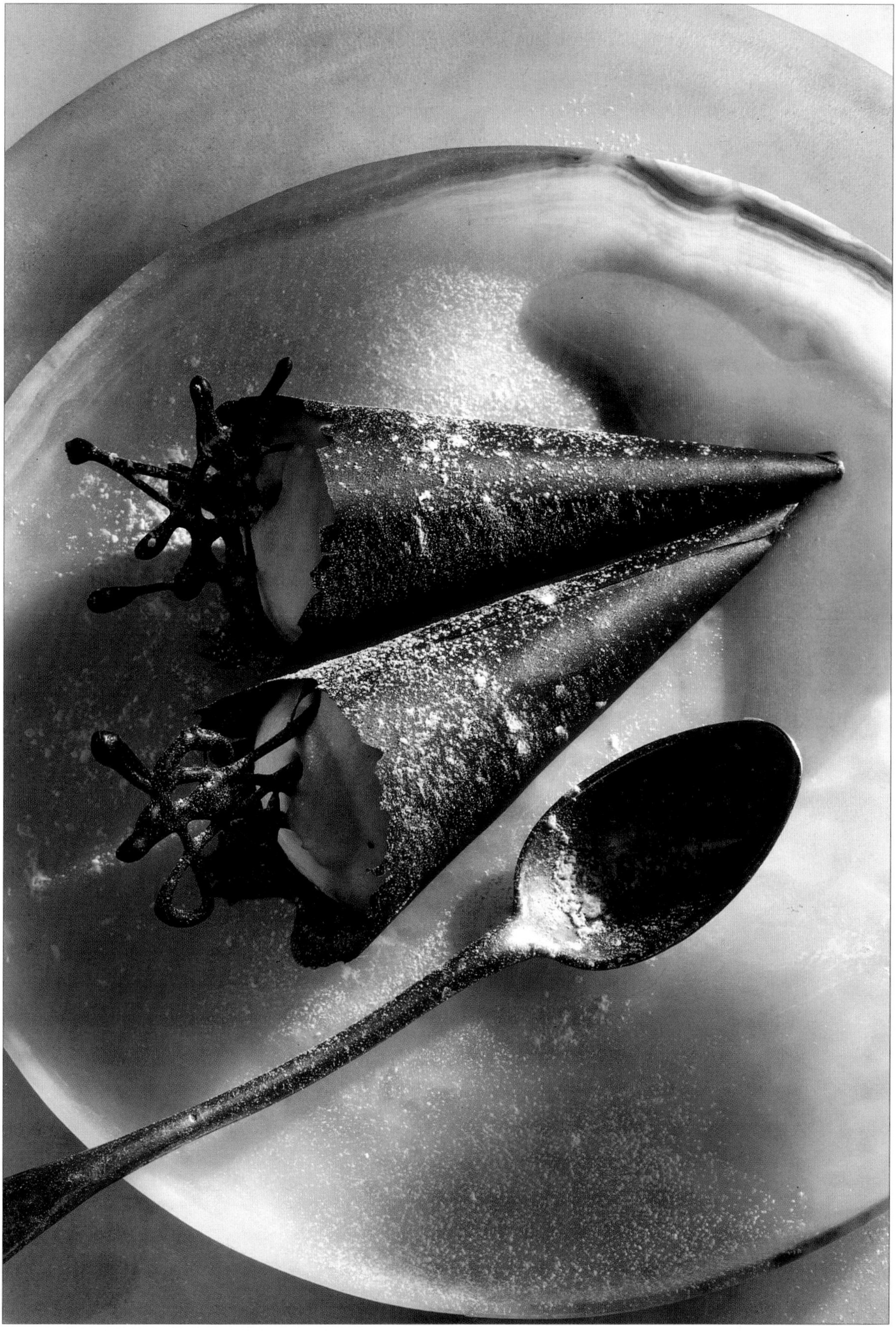

Cold Lemon Soufflé with a Lemon and Lime Sauce

Lemon Soufflé:
15 g ($\frac{1}{2}$ oz) sachet gelatine
finely grated rind and juice of 1$\frac{1}{2}$ lemons
2 eggs, separated
125 g (4 oz) caster sugar
150 ml ($\frac{1}{4}$ pint) double cream

Lemon and Lime Sauce:
125 g (4 oz) caster sugar
finely pared zest and juice of 1 lemon
finely pared zest and juice of 1 lime
5 ml (1 tsp) arrowroot

To Serve:
Brandy Snap Baskets (see right)

For the soufflé, sprinkle the gelatine over 30 ml (2 tbsp) cold water in a cup. Put the lemon rind and juice in a large bowl with the egg yolks and sugar. Stand the bowl over a saucepan of simmering water and whisk until the mixture turns pale and starts to thicken. Remove the bowl from the pan.

Stand the cup of gelatine in the saucepan of hot water until it has dissolved, then add to the egg yolk mixture, stirring well.

In a separate bowl, whip the cream until soft peaks form. In another bowl, whisk the egg whites until stiff. Allow the egg yolk mixture to cool, stirring occasionally, then fold in the cream, followed by the egg whites. Pour into individual moulds and chill in the refrigerator for at least 1$\frac{1}{2}$ hours.

Meanwhile, make the lemon and lime sauce. Put the sugar and 120 ml (4 fl oz) water in a small pan and heat gently, stirring to help dissolve the sugar. Add the lemon and lime zests and simmer gently for 15 minutes. Mix the arrowroot with the lemon juice and half of the lime juice. Add to the pan and stir until it returns to a simmer. Remove from the heat and leave to cool. Just before serving, stir in the rest of the lime juice.

To serve, position a brandy snap basket in the middle of each serving plate. Dip the soufflé moulds in a bowl of hot water for a few seconds, then carefully turn out into the brandy snap baskets. Pour the lemon and lime sauce around the baskets. Serve at once.

Kevin Sumner

Brandy Snap Baskets

50 g (2 oz) butter
50 g (2 oz) caster sugar
30 ml (2 tbsp) golden syrup
5 ml (1 tsp) brandy
5 ml (1 tsp) lemon juice
60 ml (4 tbsp) plain flour
5 ml (1 tsp) ground ginger

Melt the butter in a saucepan, add the sugar and syrup, and heat gently until dissolved. Remove from the heat and add all the other ingredients. Mix well. For each basket, spread 30 ml (2 tbsp) of the mixture into a round, about 12 cm (5 inches) in diameter on a baking sheet lined with non-stick baking parchment. (Shape and bake 2 baskets at a time.)

Cook in a preheated oven at 180°C (350°F) mark 4 for 6-8 minutes. Leave for 20 seconds, then remove the brandy snap using a palette knife and lay over an upturned ramekin. Shape to form a basket, then allow to cool.

Kevin Sumner

"The flavours were there, excellent."

Annie Wayte

St Clement's Mousse

with Caramel Oranges

Mousse:
1 sachet powdered gelatine
finely grated rind of 1 lemon
juice of 2 lemons
juice and finely grated rind of 1 orange
3 eggs, separated
125 g (4 oz) caster sugar
250 ml (8 fl oz) double cream, lightly whipped

Caramel Oranges:
2 large oranges
200 g (7 oz) sugar
30 ml (2 tbsp) Grand Marnier

Candied Peel:
finely pared rind of 1 lemon
finely pared rind of 2 oranges
15 ml (1 tbsp) sugar

To make the mousse, sprinkle the gelatine over the lemon and orange juices in a small bowl and leave to soften. In a large bowl, whisk the egg yolks, sugar and grated lemon and orange rinds together until thick and pale. Stand the gelatine bowl in a pan of hot water until the gelatine dissolves, then strain onto the egg yolks. Stir until the mixture starts to set, then fold in the whipped cream. Whisk the egg whites until stiff but not dry, then fold into the mousse. Divide the mixture between 4 individual moulds and leave in the refrigerator for at least 1 hour to set.

> *"A brilliant dessert."*
>
> Carl Davis

To prepare the caramel oranges, finely pare the rind from the oranges; reserve for the candied peel. Peel all the pith from the oranges, then cut crosswise into thin slices; halve each slice. Put the sugar in a heavy-based pan with 120 ml (4 fl oz) water and dissolve over a low heat, then slowly bring to the boil. (Remove any sugar crystals from the sides of the pan with a dampened pastry brush.) Boil until the syrup caramelises to a rich brown colour. Take the pan off the heat.

Meanwhile, mix the Grand Marnier with 90 ml (3 fl oz) cold water. As soon as the syrup caramelises, take off the heat and add the diluted Grand Marnier, protecting your hand with a cloth because it will splutter furiously. Reheat, stirring constantly until the caramel dissolves, then remove from the heat and dip the base of the pan into cold water to stop further cooking. Once the caramel is cool, pour it over the orange slices and chill in the refrigerator for at least 1 hour.

To prepare the candied peel, cut the reserved lemon and orange rind into julienne strips. Blanch in boiling water for 2 minutes, then drain. Dissolve the sugar in 30 ml (2 tbsp) water in a small heavy-based pan over a low heat. Bring to the boil and add the citrus rind strips. Leave to simmer until all of the water has evaporated. Transfer the candied peel to a large plate and leave to cool.

To serve, dip the moulds into hot water for a few seconds, then turn out the mousses onto 4 large serving plates. Surround with the caramel orange slices and decorate with candied peel strips.

Judi Geisler

Iced Passion Fruit Soufflé

in a Caramel Cage

Soufflé:
2 eggs (size 3), separated
75 g (3 oz) icing sugar
90 ml (3 fl oz) passion fruit juice (see cook's note)
250 ml (8 fl oz) double cream

Caramel Cages:
250 g (9 oz) caster sugar
50 ml (2 fl oz) liquid glucose
a little vegetable oil

To Decorate:
12 small strawberries
½ passion fruit

Strawberry Coulis:
125 g (4 oz) fresh strawberries
icing sugar, to taste

Cook's Note

For the required quantity of juice you will need 8-10 ripe passion fruit. Halve the passion fruit, scoop out the seeds and pulp into a sieve over a bowl to strain the juice.

Whisk the egg yolks and half of the icing sugar together in a bowl, using an electric whisk if possible, until very pale and foamy. Add the passion fruit juice. In a separate bowl, whisk the egg whites until stiff, then whisk in the rest of the icing sugar. Whip the cream in another bowl until thick. Fold the passion fruit mixture into the whipped cream, then carefully fold in the whisked egg white mixture.

Divide the mixture between 4 individual 150 ml (¼ pint) freezerproof moulds. Cover with cling film and freeze until firm.

For the caramel, dissolve the sugar in 90 ml (6 tbsp) water in a heavy-based pan over a low heat, then bring to the boil. Add the liquid glucose and cook until the syrup turns a pale caramel colour, ie until it registers 165°C (330°F) on a sugar thermometer. Take off the heat and leave to rest for 2 minutes.

Meanwhile with your hand, spread the tiniest amount of oil over the back of a ladle. Dip a spoon into the caramel, let the excess run off then trickle the thread to and fro over the ladle to create a basket. Repeat this procedure if necessary, then gently twist the cage free. Repeat to make a further 3 cages and place into an airtight container. Do not leave them in a humid atmosphere, otherwise they will go sticky and collapse.

Dip the 12 strawberries for the decoration into the remaining caramel. If the caramel is too thick at this stage, gently reheat. Place the strawberries on non-stick baking parchment and keep in an airtight container.

To make the strawberry coulis, purée the strawberries in a blender or food processor, adding icing sugar to taste. Pass through a sieve into a bowl, cover and chill in the refrigerator until required.

About 30 minutes before serving, turn out the soufflés onto individual serving plates and place in the refrigerator to soften slightly while still retaining their shape.

To serve, spoon the passion fruit pulp on top of the soufflés and cover each soufflé with a caramel cage. Place a spoonful of strawberry coulis to one side of the plate and top with 3 caramel strawberries. Serve immediately.

Gill Tunkle

"The passion fruit soufflé was incredible... wonderful, the texture... it was perfect."

Loyd

Iced Passion Fruit Soufflé in a Caramel Cage

Bramble Mousse

with Bramble Sauce

675 g ($1\frac{1}{2}$ lb) wild blackberries
1 sachet powdered gelatine
150 ml ($\frac{1}{4}$ pint) whipping cream
50 g (2 oz) icing sugar, sifted
2 egg whites (size 1)

Sauce:
120 ml (8 tbsp) reserved blackberry purée (see recipe)
25 g (1 oz) icing sugar, sifted

To Decorate:
borage or other edible flowers
mint leaves

Set aside a few blackberries for decoration. Put the rest into a blender or food processor and work until smooth. Set aside about 120 ml (8 tbsp) blackberry purée for the sauce.

Sprinkle the gelatine over 45 ml (3 tbsp) cold water in a small bowl and leave to soak for 2-3 minutes. Stand the bowl over a pan of simmering water until dissolved.

Lightly whip the cream until soft peaks form. Stir the icing sugar into the blackberry purée with the dissolved gelatine, then fold in the cream. Whisk the egg whites until stiff and gently fold in the blackberry mousse mixture.

Divide the mousse between four 150 ml ($\frac{1}{4}$ pint) ramekins or other individual moulds. Chill the mousses in the refrigerator for at least 1 hour until set.

"I thought the texture of that mousse was sensational."

Brian Turner

To serve, turn each mousse out on to a dessert plate. For the bramble sauce, stir the icing sugar into the reserved blackberry purée and spoon around the mousse. Decorate with borage or other edible flowers, mint leaves and the reserved blackberries. Serve accompanied by the Almond Biscuits.

Ann Neale

Almond Biscuits

50 g (2 oz) butter
25 g (1 oz) caster sugar
50 g (2 oz) plain flour, sifted
50 g (2 oz) ground almonds
5 drops of almond essence
icing sugar, for dusting

Cream the butter and sugar together in a bowl until smooth. Add the flour, ground almonds and almond essence. Mix together, using a round-bladed knife, until evenly incorporated. Knead lightly.

Roll out the dough on a lightly floured surface to a 5 mm ($\frac{1}{4}$ inch) thickness. Cut into shapes, using a pastry cutter and transfer to a baking sheet lined with non-stick baking parchment. Prick all over with a fork. Bake in a preheated oven at 180°C (350°F) mark 4 for 10-12 minutes until golden brown but not firm.

Leave to cool on the paper for 1 minute to firm up slightly, then carefully lift the biscuits on to a wire rack. Leave to cool, then dust with icing sugar. Serve with the bramble mousse.

Ann Neale

Melt-in-the-Mouth Meringue

5 egg whites
225 g (8 oz) caster sugar
5 ml (1 tsp) wine vinegar
5 ml (1 tsp) vanilla extract
10-15 ml (2-3 tsp) cornflour

To Assemble:
200 ml (7 fl oz) crème fraîche (not low-fat)
15 ml (1 tbsp) toasted flaked almonds
vanilla icing sugar (see cook's note), for dusting

Caramel:
60 ml (4 tbsp) caster sugar

To Serve:
Red Berry Compote (see right)
4 mint sprigs

Cook's Note

To make vanilla icing sugar, bury a vanilla pod in a jar of icing sugar and leave for a few days to infuse. As you use it, top up the jar with more icing sugar.

Line a 33 x 23 cm (13 x 9 inch) Swiss roll tin with non-stick baking parchment.

Whisk the egg whites in a bowl until very stiff. Whisk in the caster sugar 15 ml (1 tbsp) at a time, then whisk in the vinegar, vanilla extract and cornflour.

Spread the meringue evenly in the Swiss roll tin. Bake in a preheated oven at 180°C (350°F) mark 4 for 10 minutes. Leave in the tin to cool.

When cold, cut the meringue into eight 6 cm (2½ inch) squares. Grease a sheet of foil or a very clean baking sheet with oil. Place 4 meringue squares on the foil and top with the crème fraîche. Place another square of meringue on top at an angle. Sprinkle with a few toasted flaked almonds and dust with vanilla icing sugar.

> *"A fabulous pudding... it was delicious."*
>
> Loyd

Just before serving make the caramel. Dissolve the sugar in 120 ml (8 tbsp) water in a heavy-based pan over a low heat. Increase the heat and cook, without stirring, to a golden brown caramel. Drizzle the caramel over the top of the meringues, allowing it to run down the sides.

Dust each serving plate with vanilla icing sugar and carefully position a meringue on the plate. Place a generous spoonful of fruit compote alongside and decorate with mint. Serve immediately.

Clare Askaroff

Red Berry Compote

450 g (1 lb) mixed soft fruits, (eg raspberries, redcurrants, blackcurrants, strawberries, stoned cherries, blackberries)
15 ml (1 tbsp) concentrated blackcurrant Ribena
125 g (4 oz) caster sugar
15 ml (1 tbsp) potato flour (approximately)
icing sugar, for dusting

Put the fruit in a heavy-based pan and heat very gently for about 1 minute until the juices start to run. Drain the fruit very carefully so as not to damage it; transfer to a bowl and set aside. Measure the strained juice together with the Ribena. Add the caster sugar.

Return the juice to the pan and thicken with the potato flour: use 5 ml (1 tsp) flour per 100 ml (3½ fl oz) juice. Mix the flour with 15 ml (1 tbsp) water, stir into the juice and cook, stirring, for 1-2 minutes. Cool slightly, then pour over the fruit. Sift a little icing sugar over the surface to prevent a skin forming, then cover and chill in the refrigerator until needed. Serve with the Melt-in-the-Mouth Meringue.

Clare Askaroff

Tropical Fruit and Vanilla Ice

with Peaches, Mango and Paw Paw

125 g (4 oz) sugar
juice and finely pared rind of 1 lime
2 paw paws
4 peaches
2 mangoes
15 ml (1 tbsp) vanilla extract
400 ml (14 fl oz) crème fraîche
peach liqueur or cointreau, to taste

To Serve:
diced paw paw
mango and/or peach slices
few redcurrants

First prepare the sugar syrup. In a heavy-based pan over a low heat, dissolve the sugar in 300 ml (½ pint) water, with the lime juice and rind added. Increase the heat and boil steadily for 5 minutes. Allow to cool, then strain and measure 60 ml (2 fl oz) for the ice cream,

Halve and peel the paw paws, then scoop out the seeds. Peel, halve and stone the peaches. Peel the mangoes and cut the flesh away from the stone. Cut all the fruit into large chunks.

Put the fruit, cooled syrup and vanilla extract in a blender or food processor and work to a smooth cream. Add the crème fraîche and peach liqueur to taste.

Put the mixture in an ice-cream maker and churn for 25 minutes. Transfer to a freezer container and freeze (unless eating straight away). If you do not have an ice-cream maker, freeze in a suitable container, whisking 2-3 times during freezing to break down the ice crystals and ensure a smooth textured result.

Ten minutes before serving, transfer the ice cream to the refrigerator to soften. Scoop into serving dishes and add the diced paw paw, mango and/or peach slices, and redcurrants. Spoon a little of the sugar syrup over the fruit to serve.

Katina Beale

Individual Chocolate and Rum Bombe

served with Rum and Praline Cream

Praline:
50 g (2 oz) unblanched almonds
50 g (2 oz) caster sugar

Chocolate Bombes:
250 g (9 oz) plain chocolate
50 g (2 oz) unsalted butter
60-90 ml (4-6 tbsp) rum, to taste
200 ml (7 fl oz) double cream, lightly whipped

Rum and Praline Cream:
300 ml (½ pint) double cream
25 g (1 oz) praline (see method)
15 ml (1 tbsp) rum, or to taste

To Decorate:
chocolate leaves or curls

Place four 150 ml (¼ pint) individual moulds in the refrigerator to chill thoroughly.

To make the praline, place the almonds and sugar in a heavy-based pan over a low heat until the sugar melts and turns a nut-brown colour. Immediately remove from the heat and pour into an oiled shallow baking tin. Leave to cool until set hard. When set hard, remove from the dish and grind to a powder in a food processor or blender.

For the chocolate bombes, break up the chocolate and put it into a pan with 90 ml (3 fl oz) water. Place over a gentle heat until melted to the consistency of a thick cream. Remove the pan from the heat. Cream the butter in a bowl, then add the melted chocolate and rum to taste. Gradually beat in three quarters of the praline, then fold in the cream. Divide the mixture between the chilled moulds and leave in the refrigerator for approximately 2 hours until set.

For the rum and praline cream, whip the cream very lightly, adding the praline and rum.

To serve, dip the moulds quickly into hot water and invert on to individual serving plates to release the bombes. Spoon the praline cream around each bombe. Decorate with chocolate leaves or curls and serve immediately.

Jill O'Brien

> *"A chocolate euphoria – gorgeous and beautifully presented."*
>
> Cherie Lunghi

Tropical Fruit and Vanilla Ice with Peaches, Mango and Paw Paw

Peppered Pineapple Flambéed in Kirsch

served with
a Pineapple Sorbet

Pineapple Sorbet:
1 large or 2 medium pineapples, enough for 675 g (1½ lb) peeled and cored weight
275 ml (9 fl oz) stock syrup (see right)
juice of ½ lemon

Pineapple Flambé:
1 medium pineapple
freshly ground black pepper
25 g (1 oz) unsalted butter
50 ml (2 fl oz) kirsch

To Decorate:
16 angelica diamonds
Spun Sugar (optional – see right)

To make the sorbet, top and tail the pineapple, then peel away the skin, removing the brown 'eyes'. Quarter, core and cut up into chunks. Put in a food processor with the stock syrup and lemon juice. Process until smooth and creamy, then pass through a nylon sieve into a bowl. Transfer to an ice-cream machine and churn according to the manufacturer's instructions for about 25 minutes until firm.

Transfer to a plastic freezerproof container, cover and place in the freezer until ready to serve. If you do not have an ice-cream maker, freeze the sorbet in a suitable container, whisking several times during freezing to break down the ice crystals and ensure an even-textured result.

"The sorbet combined with the pineapple... it was very, very good."

Willi Elsener

For the pineapple flambé, put 4 large serving plates in the freezer to chill. Top and tail the pineapple, then peel away the skin, making sure you remove the brown 'eyes'. Cut into slices, about 1 cm (½ inch) thick. Cut out the central core from each slice, then sprinkle with a little black pepper. Heat the butter in a frying pan and, when hot, add the pineapple slices to heat through and colour slightly. Pour over the kirsch and immediately set alight. Once the flames have died down, the dish can be assembled.

To serve, place a pineapple slice in the centre of each large chilled serving plate and spoon a little of the pan juices into the hollow. Place 4 scoops or quenelles of sorbet around the plate. Position angelica diamonds in between. For an elegant presentation, top the pineapple slices with spun sugar to resemble angel's hair.

Gill Tunkle

Stock Syrup: Put 100 g (3½ oz) granulated sugar and 250 ml (8 fl oz) water in a heavy-based saucepan and dissolve over a low heat. Bring to the boil and boil steadily for 2 minutes. Cool and use as required.

Spun Sugar: Dissolve 250 g (9 oz) caster sugar in 90 ml (6 tbsp) water in a heavy-based pan over a low heat, then bring to the boil. Add 50 ml (2 fl oz) liquid glucose and cook the syrup to a pale caramel; ie until it registers 165°C (330°F) on a sugar thermometer. Take off the heat and leave to rest for 2 minutes. Hold 2 forks back to back, dip into the syrup, then quickly trickle the threads to and fro over a sheet of non-stick baking parchment to form spun sugar, or angel's hair. Use within 1 hour or keep in an airtight container with a drying agent. Do not leave in a humid atmosphere.

Cappuccino Ice Cream

with Dark Chocolate Sauce

40 g (1½ oz) caster sugar
2 egg yolks
150 ml (¼ pint) cold strong black coffee
150 ml (¼ pint) double cream
150 ml (¼ pint) milk

Dark Chocolate Sauce:
50 g (2 oz) plain chocolate, in pieces
45 ml (3 tbsp) milk

"I very much liked the cappuccino ice cream."

Loyd

Dissolve the sugar in 30 ml (2 tbsp) water in a pan over a low heat, then increase the heat and boil for 2-3 minutes. Allow the syrup to cool slightly. Whisk the egg yolks in a bowl until light in colour, then pour in the syrup in a steady stream, whisking continuously.

In a large bowl, whisk together the coffee, cream and milk until light and frothy. Gradually add this to the whisked egg mixture, whisking thoroughly.

Transfer the mixture to an ice-cream maker and churn for 15-20 minutes until thick and well chilled, but not frozen solid. Transfer to 4 chilled serving dishes and freeze until solid.

If you don't have an ice-cream maker, transfer the mixture to a shallow freezerproof container and freeze for 2-3 hours until mushy. Turn into a bowl and whisk with a fork to break up the ice crystals. Refreeze until half-frozen, then whisk once more. Freeze in the serving dishes.

Meanwhile make the chocolate sauce. Melt the chocolate in a heatproof bowl set over a pan of hot water or in the microwave on low. Whisk the milk into the melted chocolate until smooth. Leave to cool for about 15 minutes.

To serve, transfer the ice cream to the refrigerator about 15 minutes before serving to soften slightly. Pour on the chocolate sauce and serve with Langue de Chat Biscuits.

Kerry Church

Langue de Chat Biscuits

25 g (1 oz) butter
40 g (1½ oz) vanilla sugar
½ egg, size 3, beaten
25 g (1 oz) plain flour, sifted

Cream the butter and sugar together in a bowl until soft and light. Beat in the egg a little at a time, then fold in the flour.

Transfer the mixture to a piping bag fitted with a 1 cm (½ inch) plain nozzle. Pipe 7.5 cm (3 inch) lengths on a baking sheet lined with non-stick baking parchment, spacing them well apart.

Cook in a preheated oven at 220°C (425°F) mark 7 for 6-7 minutes until pale and golden. Leave on the baking sheet for 1 minute then, using a spatula, transfer the biscuits to a wire rack to cool completely.

Kerry Church

Cook's Note

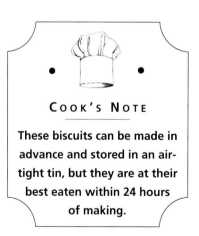

These biscuits can be made in advance and stored in an airtight tin, but they are at their best eaten within 24 hours of making.

Lime Sherbet with Hot Cherries

Lime Sherbet:
3 limes
7.5 ml (1½ tsp) lemon juice
85 g (3 oz) caster sugar
20 ml (4 tsp) golden syrup
280 ml (½ pint) milk
140 ml (¼ pint) single cream

Hot Cherries:
680 g (1 lb 8 oz) jar pitted morello cherries in syrup
100 g (3½ oz) sugar
5 ml (1 tsp) lemon juice
30 ml (2 tbsp) kirsch

To Serve:
Pepper Tuile Baskets (see right)
lemon balm or mint sprigs, to decorate

"I think the pudding was just, just right."

Loyd

Drain the cherries. Purée 225 g (8 oz) of them and pass through a sieve into a small saucepan. Add the sugar, 15 ml (1 tbsp) water and the lemon juice. Bring to the boil, reduce the heat and cook until reduced to approximately 150 ml (¼ pint). Add the rest of the cherries and the kirsch and heat through.

To make the lime sherbet, squeeze the juice from the limes and pour it into a shallow freezerproof dish. Add the lemon juice. Place in the freezer for about 30 minutes until frozen to a slushy consistency.

Meanwhile, pare the zest from two of the limes in fine shreds and put it in a saucepan. Cover with cold water, bring to the boil and drain. Cover the zest with fresh cold water, bring to the boil and simmer for 20 minutes, then drain.

Melt the syrup in a little of the milk. Combine all the ingredients and churn in an ice-cream maker for about 20 minutes. Transfer to the freezer, removing the sherbet 5 minutes before serving. Serve the sherbet in the Pepper Tuile Baskets, decorated with mint sprigs and accompanied by the hot cherries.

Ashley Wilson

Pepper Tuile Baskets

1 egg white (size 3)
50 g (2 oz) caster sugar
pinch of salt
30 g (1 oz) plain flour
30 g (1 oz) unsalted butter, melted
freshly ground black pepper

In a bowl, whisk the egg white with the sugar, salt and 10 ml (2 tsp) water until well blended. Stir in the flour and melted butter until smooth. Season generously with black pepper to taste (I use about 5 or 6 turns of the pepper mill).

Spread the batter thinly to form 5 circles, each about 12 cm (5 inches) in diameter on a baking tray lined with non-stick baking parchment. (I always make an extra basket in case of a breakage when shaping the biscuits.) Bake in a preheated oven at 200°C (400°F) mark 6 for 5 to 6 minutes until the edges are golden.

As soon as the tuiles are removed from the oven, lift from the baking sheet, using a fish slice, and mould each one over an upturned greased teacup to form a basket. If the tuiles become too cool to mould easily, return them to the oven for about 30 seconds to soften. When cool and firm, carefully remove the tuile baskets from the teacups.

Ashley Wilson

Lime Sherbet with Hot Cherries and Pepper Tuile Baskets

Chocolate Gelato

with Bitter Orange Sauce, in Chocolate Cups

Ice Cream:
225 g (8 oz) sugar
500 ml (16 fl oz) milk
125 g (4 oz) cocoa powder, sifted
100 g (3½ oz) plain dark chocolate
4 large egg yolks

Chocolate Cups:
175 g (6 oz) dark chocolate, in pieces

Orange Sauce:
30 ml (2 tbsp) caster sugar
30 ml (2 tbsp) finely pared orange zest, shredded
250 ml (8 fl oz) freshly squeezed orange juice
125 g (4 oz) orange marmalade
15 ml (1 tbsp) Grand Marnier or other orange liqueur

Cook's Note

You only need 4 chocolate cups, but make a few extra to allow for breakages.

To make the ice cream, melt 50 g (2 oz) of the sugar in a large heavy-based saucepan over a low heat, without stirring. Increase the heat to moderate and cook, stirring with a fork, until it forms a deep golden brown caramel. Remove from the heat and briefly dip the base of the pan into a bowl of iced water to stop further cooking; the caramel will harden at this stage. Leave to cool for 5 minutes, then add the milk and return to the heat, whisking until the caramel has melted. Whisk in the cocoa until well combined; keep warm.

"The chocolate ice cream was very good."

Raymond Blanc

Meanwhile, melt the chocolate in a heatproof bowl over a pan of simmering water or in the microwave on medium.

In another bowl, beat the egg yolks and remaining 175 g (6 oz) sugar, together until thick and pale. Gradually whisk in the caramel mixture, then the melted chocolate until evenly combined. Transfer to a clean saucepan and cook gently until the custard thickens slightly, just enough to lightly coat the back of a wooden spoon. Pour into a bowl set over another bowl of iced water to cool. Freeze in an ice-cream maker. (If you don't have an ice-cream machine, freeze in a suitable container, whisking 2-3 times during freezing.)

To prepare the chocolate cups, melt the chocolate in a heatproof bowl over a pan of simmering water or in the microwave on medium. Stir until smooth, then allow to cool until it begins to thicken again. Take a teaspoonful of the melted chocolate and drizzle around the top inside edge of a paper muffin case, allowing it to drip down the sides and line the base. Spread the chocolate to coat the sides and base of the paper case evenly, adding a little more if necessary. Do not use too much chocolate, only 5-10 ml (1-2 tsp) per paper cup. Repeat to make 6 or 8 cups (see cook's note). As the chocolate cools, it may drip down the sides to the base; if so spread it back up the sides, otherwise the base of the cups will be too thick. Chill until firm.

To make the sauce, melt the sugar in a medium heavy-based pan over a low heat, without stirring. Increase the heat to moderate and cook, stirring with a fork, until it forms a golden caramel. Remove from the heat and allow to cool.

While the caramel is cooking, blanch the orange zest in a small pan of boiling water for 15 seconds; drain.

Add the orange zest and juice to the caramel. Cook over a moderate heat, stirring until the caramel is melted. Whisk in the marmalade until evenly combined. Stir in the Grand Marnier and remove from the heat. Allow to cool.

Fill 4 chocolate cups with the ice cream and freeze until the ice cream is firm. Peel away the paper cases and place the cups on individual serving plates. Surround with the sauce and serve at once.

Holly Schade

INDEX

Page numbers in italic refer to the illustrations